With love to
Ira and Ali
M Shahijahan
6/22/'03

# Income, Debt and the Quest for Rich America

## The Economic Tale of Small and Mid-Sized U.S. Cities

# Income, Debt and the Quest for Rich America

*The Economic Tale of Small and Mid-Sized U.S. Cities*

**Mirza Shahjahan**
**Professor of Economics**
**University of Arkansas Pine Bluff**

*Writers' Inc. International*
Beltsville, MD

**Income, Debt and the Quest for Rich America**
The Economic Tale of Small and Mid-Sized U.S. Cities

---



---

**Library of Congress Cataloging-in-Publication Data**

Shahjahan, Mirza, 1932-
Income, debt and the quest for rich America : the economic tale of small and mid-sized U.S. cities / Mirza Shahjahan.
p. cm.
Includes index.
ISBN 0-9627854-5-8
1. Consumer credit--United States. 2. Income distribution--United States. 3. Debt--United States. 4.Family–Economic aspects–United States. I. Title.

HG3756.U54 S5 1999
332.7'43'097309049–dc21

99-059720

---

**Cover:** KUFIC GRAPHICS, INC

THIS BOOK IS DEDICATED TO

**Perveen, Zoheb, Zain
Sonia and Noman**

# TABLE OF CONTENTS

Preface xi
Methodology . . . . . . . . . . xiii
Objectives . . . . . . . . . . xiii

Acknowledgments xv

CHAPTER ONE
**THE ECONOMIC SAGA OF JAY** 1
Jay's Agonizing Debt-Burden . . . . . . . . . . 5
Attributes of Jay and his Class . . . . . . . . . . 8
The Magnanimity of Jay's Group . . . . . . . . . . 9

CHAPTER TWO
**CHARACTERISTICS OF HOUSEHOLD INCOME** 13
The Trend of Average Household Income . . . . . . . . . . 15
Income Groups and Frequencies . . . . . . . . . . 17
Increases or Decreases in Group Income Levels . . . . . . . . . . 28
Household Income Below Poverty Level . . . . . . . . . . 29
Per Capita Income of Households below Poverty Level . . . . 30
Income Groups and Frequencies . . . . . . . . . . 30
The Disparity in Income and the Trend of GNP . . . . . . . . . . 31
The Trend of Average Household Income and GNP . . . . . . . 33
Typical Levels of Compensation
in Small and Mid-sized Cities . . . . . . . . . . 34

CHAPTER THREE:
**HOUSEHOLD DEBT** 37
Average Size of the Debt . . . . . . . . . . 37
The Average Size of Household Debt . . . . . . . . . . 38

CHAPTER FOUR:
**THE BURDEN OF HOUSEHOLD DEBT** 69
Introduction . . . . . . . . . . 69
The Trend of Overall Interest Payments: Sample Averages . . 72
Sample Average Size of Interest Paid (Item Wise) . . . . . . . . . 73
Average Size of Interest Paid by Indebted Household . . . . . . 75
Interest Payments by Different Income Groups . . . . . . . . . . . 77
Interest Paid on Home Loan and Car Loan Together . . . . . . . 96
Interest Paid on Household Debt and Other Debt . . . . . . . . . . 98
Interest Paid as Percent of Income . . . . . . . . . . . . . . . . . . . . . 98
Percentage of Households Paying Interest . . . . . . . . . . . . . . . 99

CHAPTER FIVE:
**INTEREST PAYMENTS & SIMPLE REGRESSION** 103
Models of Interest Payments on
Home, Car and Credit Card Loans . . . . . . . . . . . . . . 104
Models on Total Interest Paid . . . . . . . . . . . . . . . . . . . . . . . . 107
Models on Prime Rates and Regional Rates . . . . . . . . . . . . . 110

CHAPTER SIX:
**THE REAL BURDEN OF DEBT** 117
FIELD REPORTS . . . . . . . . . . . . . . . . . . . . . . . . . . . . . . . . 118

CHAPTER SEVEN:
**INTEREST EARNED** 127
The Trend of Average Size of
Interest Earned by Households . . . . . . . . . . . . . . . . 129
Interest Earned by Different Income Groups . . . . . . . . . . . . 130
Interest Earned as % of Income . . . . . . . . . . . . . . . . . . . . . . 137
Interest Earned and Paid by Interest Paying Households . . . 138
Average Debt, Interest Paid and
Interest Earned Relationship . . . . . . . . . . . . . . . . . . 139

CHAPTER EIGHT
**TRACING THE CAUSES OF BURDENSOME DEBT** 141
A. PRIME RATE OF NEW YORK BANKS . . . . . . . . . . . 141
Adverse Affects of the Recession of 1980 . . . . . . . 142
The Birth of the Prime Rate . . . . . . . . . . . . . . . . . . 143

Determinants of the Prime Rates of New York Banks .................. 147
Dual Allegiance of Commercial Banks .......... 148
The Future of Prime Rate .................... 149
B. FEDERAL RESERVE BANK AND DISCOUNT RATE .......................................... 151
Economic Episodes of the Early Seventies Collapse of the Gold Standard .......... 155
C. REGIONAL RATES ............................ 165
Discount Rate, Prime Rate and Regional Rate .... 166
The Average Regional Rate .................. 168
Arkansas Consumer Rate ..................... 170
Michigan Consumer Rate ..................... 171
Mortgage Rate ............................. 172
Civilian Unemployment and Bank Rate ......... 173
D. RAY, CREDIT BUREAUS & CREDIT INSTITUTIONS .................... 177
The Uses of the Credit Report ................. 179
Credit Reports and Credit Outcasts ............. 181
The Vicious Cycle of Credit Reporting .......... 184
Pawnshops and Small Loan Companies ......... 185
Debt Associated Other Costs .................. 186
E. BALLET OF BILLS ........................... 187
Additional Work Hours Forced on Households ... 189

CHAPTER NINE
**DEBT SETTLEMENT BOARD AND NEW BANKS** 191
The Rationale for Debt Settlement Board ............. 191
Composition of the Debt Settlement Board ............ 193
The Rationale for a New Bank ...................... 193
Functions, Objectives and Philosophy of the New Banks: .. 195

CHAPTER TEN
**SUMMARY OF FINDINGS & RECOMMENDATIONS** 199
The Trend of Average Household Income ............. 199
Household Income Below Poverty Level .............. 203
Per Capita Income of Households Below Poverty Level ... 203
The Trend of Average Size of Household Debt .......... 204

Sample Average Size of Debt . . . . . . . . . . . . . . . . . . . . . . . . 204
Frequencies and Debt Average . . . . . . . . . . . . . . . . . . . . . . . 205
Average Size of Debt and Frequencies of
Indebted Households . . . . . . . . . . . . . . . . . . . . . . . . 205
Household Debt and Other Debts . . . . . . . . . . . . . . . . . . . . . 206
Per Capita Debt . . . . . . . . . . . . . . . . . . . . . . . . . . . . . . . . . . 206
Interest Paid by Different Groups . . . . . . . . . . . . . . . . . . . . . 207
The Trend of Interest Paid . . . . . . . . . . . . . . . . . . . . . . . . . . 208
The Average Amount of Interest Paid by Indebted Households . . . . . . . . . . . . . . . . . . . . . . . . . . . . . . . . . . . . . . . . 208
Interest Earned by Different Income Groups . . . . . . . . . . . . 211
Regression Summary . . . . . . . . . . . . . . . . . . . . . . . . . . . . . 214

CHAPTER ELEVEN
**CONCLUSION:**
**AUTHOR'S COMMENTS AND RECOMMENDATIONS** 221

INDEX 237

# Preface

We often hear about the frightening size of the federal debt and its "crowding-out" effects in the economy. There is much noise about "corporate borrowing," "takeovers," "restructuring," "downsizing," "mergers," and "bankruptcies." It has also been observed that the heavy indebtedness of households accounted for the slow recovery from the 90's recession. However, we seldom hear about the size, trend, and burden of household leverage and how it affects households economically, emotionally and socially in small and mid-sized cities in the U.S. In this study, we estimate the size and trend of household debts, unfold the untold tale of the economic woes of indebted households and focus on the causes that make debts so burdensome and unbearable to low and middle-income households in these cities.

Most household debts originate in the process of acquiring of tangible assets such as homes, cars, furniture, and other goods and services. Some households buy financial assets such as bonds, equity, and deposits with borrowed money, but the number of lower and middle class households owning credit market instruments in these cities are few. Homes, land, vehicles, televisions, and appliances do not constitute quick-income generating portfolios; they are illiquid in nature and are not easily liquefiable to service debts or to overcome the emergencies that often overwhelm the average household in these cities.

As the cost of credit is an important element in assessing the burden of debt, we have developed simple models to estimate the amount of interest paid by households for consumer durables purchased on credit. In this cross-section study, we have estimated the correlation between household income and the amount of interest paid on home, car, personal, business, and credit card loans. In doing this, we determined how much is spent to finance interest payments on household debts for each one dollar increase in income. Later, we included in our model another variable, "interest earned," to find the difference it makes in the amount of interest paid out.

We also discuss the policies of the Federal Reserve Bank and those of the New York banks because their rates play important roles in initiating and influencing changes in other money market rates. The change in the discount rate affects the prime rate of New York banks which, in turn, influences regional rates. In reality, an upward change in the discount rate tends to widen the existing gap between the discount rate and the prime rate of New York banks and the gap between the prime rate of New York banks and the regional rates. We have estimated the average size of the gap between these different rates for a period of more than two decades. A larger gap between the discount rate of the Federal Reserve Bank and other rates generally implies a higher cost of credit for households.

We have analyzed both the monetary and the real burden of debt, examined the deficiencies in the distribution system, the concentration of wealth, the disparity in income and the strength of the U.S. economy. Some harmful "traditions" have been at work as invisible determinants in the pricing of goods and services. Also, the "tradition" of some big banks in New York of pronouncing unasked for interest rates causes a higher cost of credit at the regional level. We challenge the usefulness of these "traditions" in this book.

For a better understanding of the economic character of our population, we have divided the households in our study into different income groups. Averages for each group's "income," "interest paid," "interest earned," and the "sizes of the debt," have been estimated. Group averages have then been compared with sample averages to find the difference between the sample mean and the group mean. The GNP of the U.S. economy far exceeds the eight trillion dollar mark – making the U.S. the richest economy in the world. But the economic woes of millions of households – a significant number of whom are living below the poverty level – speak of the glaring disparity of income that exists among households in this economy. We discuss this issue both in Chapter two and in the concluding part of the book.

Regarding our data and estimates, the 1985 and 1988 data have been used as base points of reference. In describing "trends" we have used the data for 1990-1993 throughout this book. Since 1985, when we began collecting data, the average increase in the income level of households in small and mid-sized cities in the U.S. has been insignificant. In fact, many households have been experiencing a stagnant economy for quite sometime. The economic characteristics of these households have not changed very much over the last decade. In view of this fact, our estimates can be assumed to represent closely what is occurring economically to these households in 1999. We hope the "data," "trend analysis," "estimates," and socio-economic issues identified at the local and national levels will inspire further research as a follow-up to this work. The author will feel rewarded when this happens for he has himself ventured into this research project with that particular end in view.

## Methodology

In collecting data, we depended on information submitted by households. Because of limited resources and other problems associated with the collection of data, we were required to have different sample sizes in different years. A random sampling was used in selecting our primary data. Our sample sizes for the years '85, '88, '90, '91, '92, '93 were 174, 216, 380, 361, 361, 359, households respectively. Publications from the Federal Reserve Bank, the U.S. Government, the International Monetary Fund, the *Statistical Abstract of the U.S.A.*, *The Dallas Morning News*, and other periodicals were used for facts and secondary data.

## Objectives

Finally, the purpose of this book is twofold: 1) To identify current problems of household debts and the disparity of income as it exists in the American society, and 2) to provide reference materials for future researchers. Our conclusion recommends that: 1) more responsibility be assumed by the federal government in reducing the current income gap and in preventing the gap from widening in the future; 2) new financial institutions with a broader philosophy of operation be brought into existence to cater to the needs of large segments of households in American society; 3) Debt Settlement Boards be brought into existence to provide succor to the suffering millions who are struggling to survive their burdensome debt; 4) the present credit reporting process be modified or replaced by one that more readily reflect the current ability of the account holder to repay debt or to qualify for further loans (rather than focusing, as now, on the past negatives of the account holder); and (5) since raising the discount rate based solely on an anticipated inflation is harmful for most Americans, specially low-income households, it should be avoided.

We strongly believe that our findings will provide new information to policy makers, academics, students, and the general public in identifying the problems that low and middle-income households encounter in everyday life in the small and mid-sized cities of the U.S.

# Acknowledgments

It is almost a miracle that we were able to publish this book. We started this work a decade ago, collecting, organizing, processing, and analyzing the data until now. Unforeseen circumstances interrupted our gathering of data for the years '86, '87, and '89. From the very outset, we encountered every conceivable obstacle in carrying out our study. The computer that we were initially working with was so old that we could not store our data on disks, and until recently we had to ship our data outside Arkansas to run some statistical programs. It was not easy to administer questionnaires, collect data, locate the facts and episodes which illustrate the economic woes of indebted households.

The lack of funds was of course a pertinent obstacle in conducting research of this kind. On the other hand, I was fortunate to have moral support, help, and encouragement from my colleagues and students. More than a dozen students made commendable contributions in administering questionnaires, gathering, and processing the data. I want to thank Mr. Joseph Steele and Mrs. Diana Elders who were the first two students to come forward to help me in organizing and processing the data. Then came Shannon, Rosalind McBride, Kimberley McBride, Chanda Johnson, J. Millard, Duncan, and Arnette Pierce. Theopolis Carpenter volunteered to check, process and organize the data and worked long hours with me.

I would like to mention the name of Dr. Lawrence A. Davis, Jr., our popular chancellor. When he was the dean several years ago, he mentioned in his annual report that I was writing a book. He will be glad to see that the book is now published. Our vice chancellor, Dr. Mary Benjamin who always encourages the faculty to make intellectual contributions, will be happy to see that this book is printed. The present Dean of the School of Business and Management at the University of Arkansas at Pine Bluff, Dr. Andrew Honeycutt, will be delighted to see that the book is out. He always inspires all faculty members to engage in research and publications. Dr. John Fluker, the former Dean, has always encouraged me to complete my work. From among colleagues and friends, Dr. Lorenz and Dr. P. Syril ran some programs for my data. Dr. P. Syril was a consultant and advisor who worked with devotion and sincerity that are only expected of a close friend or a coauthor of a book. Dr. Lorenz, another dear friend of mine with all the patience in the world, read my manuscript, checked all the tables in the book, and made some invaluable suggestions and corrections. I am immensely indebted to him. Another generous colleague, Phillip McBee, was kind enough to sacrifice his convenience by giving me his own computer, which expedited my work considerably. I also appreciate the various suggestions made by Dr. Sivramakrishnan, Dr. Satish Vadlamani and Mr. George Weaver.

Finally, I would like to thank my wife who put up with my staying at the office long hours on weekdays, weekends, and on holidays. She has been a constant source of encouragement and inspiration to me in writing this book and she was also the first person to correct the manuscript. Finally, in keeping with tradition, the author accepts the responsibility for any errors and omissions in the book.

# CHAPTER ONE

## THE ECONOMIC SAGA OF JAY

Often Jay wakes up from his nightmares frightened and shaken. His wife anxiously inquires if he is all right. With a sigh of relief, Jay replies that he was only dreaming — he dreamt that his creditors forcibly entered his home threatening to force him to vacate his house, surrender his car, his wife's wedding ring, their furniture, and all their other belongings. Often he experiences these bad dreams, and often his wife shakes Jay vigorously to wake him up from his nightmares. Jay has been living in the same small city since his birth. His father moved here from New York State during the Great Depression of 1929.

Small and mid-sized cities are a refuge for a large segment of the American population and differ in their economic character from the sprawling big cities such as New York, Chicago and Los Angeles. Our interest lies in the economies of the low and middle-income household in these cities. In general, the income levels and expenditure patterns of households in these cities are very similar.

Jay's economic status is typical of a large section of households in the small and medium sized cities of the U.S. We will now take a brief sojourn into Jay's life to gather information about the state of his household economy, which, in fact, reflects the economy of millions of households of this nation. Jay's dreadful dream was very closely related to his economic woes and was the result of his mind being preoccupied with worries and anxieties stemming from unpaid bills and debts. He bought a home, a car, furniture, and other necessities of life on credit. His wife has been in the hospital several times in connection with the births of their children. He himself and his children have visited physicians a number of times and received their services on credit. A hot summer and a severe winter left him a large outstanding bill with the utility company. The replacement of old appliances, carpets, as well as household repair work was also done on credit. Occasionally, Jay needed counsel from an attorney who agreed to be paid at a later date.

Unfortunately, Jay's income does not permit him to pay for these goods and services with cash so he obtains them on credit. On the list of his creditors are banks, credit card issuers, physicians, hospitals, lawyers, stores, plumbers, utility companies, finance companies, loan sharks, friends, and relatives. In the real world, he is surrounded by these creditors and swamped in bills that give him relentless worries and with no escape route. On any payday, the amount of his bills far exceeds his take-home pay. This situation has forced him to develop various strategies in the matters of bill payments. Some bills are deferred until next month's payday or until some borrowed funds are available. As the awaited payday arrives, the deferred bills are paid first, but the bills that were paid on previous paydays are now deferred until the next payday. This is how Jay is struggling to keep his creditors satisfied, but in the process, most of his accounts acquire "late payment" or "past due" status in the eyes of his creditors and the credit bureau.

Jay's ritual of paying bills has the following pattern: On the receipt of his paycheck he hurries to a local drug store that collects telephone bills to restore his telephone line, which was disconnected and drives to a bank to make a house payment and cringes as the loan officer charges penalties on his past due account. He then drives to the water supply company, picks up a round metal token, runs upstairs to get the payment date extended, and then races to the hospital to make a partial payment to halt the handing over of his account to a collection agent.

From there, Jay goes to the electricity company and waits in line to meet officers to arrange a payment schedule to cover the current bill plus the past due amount which accrued last year when the summer and winter were severe, resulting in much higher energy bills. After having paid these priority items, he breathes a sigh of relief thinking that at least the supply of water and electricity is assured for the time being. Now, he feels, it is time to relax. He goes to McDonald's, indulges in a sip of inexpensive coffee and plans his next move to keep the rest of his creditors at bay. As he is leaving the restaurant, he can see a man at the corner staring at him. He is a pawnshop owner who has been looking for Jay to collect storage fees for his pawned articles.

The story behind the pawned articles is as follows: Jay's name appeared in the local newspaper along with the names of several hundred defaulters who failed to pay property taxes on time. This had happened several times in the past. Each time he saw his name among defaulters, Jay felt embarrassed and promised himself to prevent it from happening again.

Despite his determination, Jay continued to fail to save the required funds to pay his property taxes on time. The last time this happened, he was forced to pawn his ancestors' guns and his wife's jewelry to pay the property tax. To date, he has not been able to recover these pawned articles.

Jay is in a hurry. From a distance he uses sign language to communicate to the pawnshop owner that he will soon take care of the storage fees, then runs to another bank to make payments on his personal and business loans. As Jay's mind is preoccupied with the thought of paying his creditors and hurrying to reach another bank, his car runs through a yellow light at an intersection near downtown. A police officer from a nearby police car pounces on him, and fines Jay $85. Jay tries to explain that it was unintended, and that knowingly he would not break any law. The officer turns a deaf ear to his appeal and dismisses him by saying that he can appear in court if he wishes to contest the ticket.

At heart, Jay always considers himself a law-abiding citizen, but in the eyes of the officers he is proven to be a lawbreaker. To his creditors, he appears to be a bad guy, although he is always concerned with paying his obligations on time and in their entirety. The frequent loss of his job, low income, sickness, and family emergencies accounted for his defaulting in payments. Creditors and society at large misread him. They down grade Jay's integrity as a person for no fault of his own: he is not what he has been proven to be by man-made laws. This thought hurts him.

Finally Jay reaches the bank just before 2 o'clock when the bank generally closes. The bank officer is not particularly happy to see him because his account is past due. Jay attempts to explain the problems he is facing due to the loss of his wife's job and emergencies that have engulfed his family. This does not mean anything to the bank officer. He, however, accepts Jay's partial payment.

The next morning, as Jay is about to leave for his workplace, his wife rushes to him and breaks the bad news that the heater has stopped functioning. He calls the repair people and finds out that he has to change the unit. This will cost several hundred dollars - another unanticipated addition to his already unmanageable monthly payments. "I cannot bear any more!" Jay shouts to himself and runs for the office.

After his return from the office, he opens some envelopes containing credit card bills, looks at them, gets mad, and starts murmuring, at times screaming: "This balance never goes down. It is taking forever to reduce it by even a few dollars although I have been paying for so many months." His wife notices his anger and asks if something is wrong. He replies that he is angry because his balance on the credit cards never goes down. Taking a closer look at the bills he discovers, to his dismay, that the finance charges on those bills is 22% and a late fee of $15 has also been regularly added. No wonder his minimum monthly payments made no dent in reducing his balance. He consoles himself by imagining that when his income increases he will pay more than the minimum payments and settle his debts once and for all, even though with his present level of income, a decade may elapse before Jay's dream of settling his credit card balances can become a reality.

Jay now, drives to the insurance agent to plead for an extension of time for the full payment, and makes only partial payments on his home and car insurance. After paying the insurance bills, Jay feels completely drained of all his energies. As he is driving back home, he realizes that his payments exceeded the balance he has in the bank. The thought of insufficient funds, the return of checks, and penalties for inadequate funds almost stops his heart beat momentarily.

As Jay reaches home, his wife notices the mark of anguish in the face of her husband and asks if there was anything wrong with him. Jay tells her about the insufficient funds in his account and the prospect of facing penalties for the returned checks. His wife comes to his rescue by offering a small amount of money she earned after a month of baby sitting for a neighbor. Making the deposit Jay concludes his monthly payment obligations to his creditors and feels relieved that at least, for the time being, there will be no telephone calls or certified letters from his creditors asking him for immediate payment.

The next day with a feeling of relief and some peace of mind, Jay is on his way to work. As he is driving his car, he suddenly hears an unusual noise coming from his muffler. "There must be some hole in it," Jay shouts to himself. His heart sinks as he contemplates his own helplessness in controlling problems that entail the opening of yet another new account, a new bill, and a new creditor. This time he decides not to fix it, to put up with the noise until a compelling situation develops with the total breakdown of the muffler.

Having been raised amidst wants, Jay knows the art of making compromises. But, compromises and a long, drawn–out struggle to make a reasonably decent living have taken their toll on Jay's health and mind. These days he suffers from constant headaches and he needs a thorough medical check up, including a costly MRI test, but he has avoided these tests up to now fearing that it would add more bills to the existing ones which are, by themselves, overwhelming him. The other compromises he makes are: not sending his children to better schools; not being able to take his family on a vacation in years; inability to buy nice clothes and gifts for his wife and children on anniversaries and at Christmas; and postponing the surgery that his wife needs badly. These compromises Jay feels, have deprived him of the joys of life and at times put his family's health and lives at risk.

As he is driving back home, he is planning to get another part-time or weekend job to supplement his inadequate income so that he can overcome his bill payment problems. Often this aspiration of Jay, and for a thousand others like Jay, remains just wishful thinking in the small and mid-sized cities of the U.S. where employment opportunities are limited.

## JAY'S AGONIZING DEBT-BURDEN

Jay's crippling debt-burden, and his inability to pay his creditors on time has given rise to an outstanding economic issue which has remained unrecognized by contemporary economists and policy makers alike. The tale of Jay's woes, pains, sufferings, and sacrifices arising from debt burden do not figure in most economic literature. There are data on the number of households living below the poverty level or per capita income, on interest payments and rates on their loans and the like, but behind the economic data are human beings with flesh, blood, emotions, and feelings. Unfortunately, dry data and economic models fail to represent accurately the feelings of helplessness and deprivation arising out of economic hardship, and the callous attitude of society.

We will now continue walking with Jay to identify how grievously household leverage afflicts human emotions and the economy of a household. We have noticed that Jay is hopelessly in debt and his mind is constantly tormented with fears of what would happen to him if he loses his job again, fails to support his family, or meet the demands of his creditors. These agonizing thoughts constantly crowd his mind. No wonder he has frequent nightmares and is haunted in dreams by his creditors. At times, he wishes he were like his prosperous, fortunate neighbor who has a carefree mind and enjoys his work, family, and life itself.

Agonies, worries, and anxieties arising out of his inadequate income, his inability to pay for the necessities of life, and his constant fear of encountering his creditors have simply rendered him incapable of doing his best in the workplace, giving proper attention to his family, or enjoying life as his counterpart, the fortunate neighbor does. His low income, mounting bills, and never-ending debt problem make him appear depressed while he is with friends, morbid while with his family, and a loner in the midst of a crowd. At times he is overcome by a strange feeling of abandonment by the society in which he lives. This plunges him into an overwhelming sense of depression

Jay's melancholy demeanor reflects his precarious economic status. He and his class send misleading signals to the rest of the community. To a casual onlooker Jay, with his home, car, and other belongings, gives the appearance of a regular, normal guy: nothing about him seems to be out of the ordinary. To those who are aware of his agonies, he appears to be drowning in an ocean of troubles. To Jay himself, everything is falling apart. The procurement of the things he needs to lead a decent life has given him more pain, suffering, and sacrifice than comfort and happiness.

At the root of his problem is his woefully inadequate income which compels him to acquire the necessities of life on credit. Engulfed in leverage, defaulting in payments. Jay is now emotionally disturbed by the thought that he must now service the debt for many years to come, thus sacrificing the most productive part of his life, his youth, in serving his creditors. Jay's story is a poignant narrative which exemplifies an indebted household's ceaseless struggle to pacify its creditors. In acquiring the bare essentials of life, Jay has become heavily laden with debt — so much so that he is on the verge of losing his sanity.

As Jay's budgetary constraints fail to keep his creditors satisfied, credit institutions are unwilling to accommodate his needs, creating an agonizing tale that has remained mostly untold. Jay's helpless status arising out of indebtedness and the current credit culture forces him into an alien world where "kindness," "sympathy," and "leniency" are unknown. His journey through this harsh, unkind world takes him through a series of heart-rending experiences with no known outlet.

We are about to unfold Jay's sad and depressing experience in coping with his creditors. He desperately attempts to find a better paying job or an additional source of income. As this is not easily available, friends, relatives and others initially try to help him out. But soon, these sources dry up. Then begins the disinvestment of some household assets: home, land, appliances, jewelry and other personal belongings are sold to meet the bare necessities of life.

His agony and tension escalate as he starts getting certified letters from his aggressive creditors and their attorneys threatening to sue him. His unwarranted morning wake up call is often from his creditors. As late fees and penalties keep on increasing and interest is being compounded, the size of the debt begins swelling.

In order to cope with the situation, he manipulates his last resort by taking the maximum allowable exemptions in paying federal taxes. By deferring tax payments, Jay has added one more difficult creditor to his already crowded list. Initially, this gives him an increase in income, but the temporary relief derived from tax exemptions soon proves to be an illusory and costly mistake.

In reality, the exemptions result in accumulation of outstanding tax balances that increase his existing liabilities. Jay's attempt to gain a respite from his debt burden through tax exemptions only accomplishes the weaving of an inescapable debt net around him which contributes to his eventual economic collapse.

By now, he is bound by agreements with his creditors and committed to slavish services for his creditors for a considerable period of time – long enough to be crushed under the burden of debt service. Jay's economic woes are multiplied because the law allows some creditors to collect compound interest and penalties at a rate of ½ of 1% of the outstanding balance per month.

Per month compound interest together with penalties becomes extraordinarily punitive in its nature. For example, an outstanding balance of $6000 may accrue more than $3000 in interest payments and penalties over a little more than 3 years. Besides, some creditors garnish the salary of the debtor to collect their debts by forcible payroll deductions. This reduces the take home pay of the debtor to a ridiculously small amount. At the top of all this, the certified letters from creditors' attorneys and collection agencies deepen the anger and anguish of the debtor. Over the years, the collection agents have developed extremely unkind methods of frightening and forcing people like Jay to meet their demands at any cost.

Under these stressful circumstances, Jay sinks into an ocean of depression, becomes desperate, and borrows further, if possible, from loan sharks to meet his most pressing needs, such as the demand of collection agents – often paying more than 300% in interest charges – hurting himself further. For the alcoholic, drug addict, and AIDS victim there are agencies which provide emergency shelters, but there exists no 911 call or other arrangement to provide relief to the indebted householder who has been overwhelmed by debts through no fault of his own and has been rendered the helpless prey of his creditors' abuses. He has fallen from society's grace to be pushed around by his creditors.

Society and the government have been callous to Jay's hardships and have failed this able and willing indebted household by not providing him with an adequate income to meet his credit needs. On the contrary, laws have been enacted to punish him heavily for his so-called failures to meet the demands of his creditors. Under the financial strain, to retain his dignity Jay would not mind working seven days a week, day or night, to meet the need of his creditors. But Jay's "no fault" reason for his low income or defaulting payments has no appeal to society, government, or his creditors. His cries for help go unheard.

This helpless and hopeless situation leads the debtor into a state of depression. He starts abusing himself by drinking, hurts his family by mistreating them, and in extreme cases kills himself. The economic status of Jay, with this debt burden, has been reduced to nothing. Unnoticed and untold, the economic saga of Jay and his class continues without any relief in sight. Jay's day breaks with the concern of working for his employer, procuring the essentials of life for his family and engaging his mind to devise ways to pay his bills to survive the onslaught of his creditors. He makes compromises with his wants, sacrifices basic comforts of life and fails to provide the simple joys which Jay's family deserves as their natural right and which should be assured to them by the society in which they live.

### Attributes of Jay and His Class

How can we recognize Jay's fellow sufferers in the community? In their physical features, they are no different from other Americans, but close observation reveals some distinct characteristics. They look generally subdued and distracted as if their minds are somewhere else, busy exploring the ways of getting funds to meet their obligations to their creditors. Their eyes and minds are in two different places. This can be discovered by noticing their being unmindful during the course of conversation with them. They are not very vocal about their problems. They can be seen running to various sections of the office of the utility company for extending payment dates or the restoration of water, gas, and telephone connections that have been disconnected. One can see them crowding the discount centers, McDonald's, Burger King, Kentucky Fried Chicken, and other cheap fast food places. They also can be located at used car lots or at unemployment offices waiting hours and hours to collect their meager unemployment benefits.

The mailboxes of these households contain mostly bills, certified letters from their creditors threatening to sue them, and "shut-off" and "cut off" notices. A great part of their life, energy, money, and time is devoted to negotiating with creditors and those who serve "shut-off" notices while attempting to cling to their aspirations and efforts for a better economic status. At times these households attempt to grab a little joy of life by taking the family out to a local fair or rodeo or for a dinner to McDonald's, Burger King or, Kentucky Fried Chicken after attending church. The simple happiness and wholesome joy of family outings are the only meager outlets of relief in their life.

As soon as people like Jay who aspire to acquire a higher education enter college, they start experiencing the realities of life. In order to support themselves, they work part-time or full-time in fast food restaurants, convenience stores, manufacturing plants, delivery services, department stores, or other places. Some work on night shifts. The inability of parents to support these young people forces them to be on their own. Some of them may eventually obtain a degree, but not without paying a price. The financial inadequacies of student life and the struggle to stay in school at the undergraduate level make them lose interest in pursuing higher studies after their graduation from college.

The other price paid for working while studying is the sacrifice of better grades, which were within their reach but could not be achieved because their jobs made a heavy demand on their time. These same financial constraints do not allow many high school and college graduates to pursue higher studies for better degrees and internships. They remain unprepared and under qualified for high-paying jobs or the better opportunities of life. Jay's group enter the real world at a disadvantage: their parents' financial constraints stood in the way of their (Jay's group) being adequately prepared for a better opportunity of life.

## The Magnanimity of Jay's Group

The households in this study are made up of hard-working people who are always willing to work and have proved to be one of the most productive elements in society. Collectively they contribute significantly to the growth of the wealth in this country, but the share they receive constitutes a very insignificant part of the vast wealth they help create. Even with their meager share in the national wealth they become the source of income to their next door neighbors, the doctors, lawyers, plumbers, utility companies and others from whom they buy their goods and services.

Despite their disappointment and grievances about their economic status, they have continued to help build America. One can smell the sweat and toil of these groups in the roads, coast-to-coast highways, factories, schools, hospitals, ports, railways, offices, homes, and all the other physical structures in this country. They continue working in the sun, rain, and snow, day and night to build America.

Many of these workers live in squalor, sometimes with no heat and air conditioning, but nothing has daunted their spirit to work for the country. They are frustrated and bitter because of their poor economic status, however, they are not rebellious and do not seek desperate, radical alternatives to the present U.S. economic order. Their lack of opportunities for a better life, the frequent loss of jobs, the problems of debt burden, the threats of creditors, the inability to meet the necessities of life, and the unkind attitude of society have not diminished the zeal and will of these households to build America, nor have their unshrinkable faith in the American political and economic institutions diminished. They are ever poised to contribute to building the giant U.S. economy, which in fact is being built and carried on the sore, bent backs and debt-burdened shoulders of the low and middle-income households in America.

The unnoticed and unheralded heroes of America live in these cities. Their patriotism, faith in the American system and, above all, their patience and magnanimity have prevented social and political unrest and upheavals which would otherwise have destabilized society and interrupted the progress of the country. We should be grateful to these people and reciprocate by alleviating their economic woes.

The households in our study include an extraordinary group of people in American society who start their working lives at a disadvantage. The low income of their parents did not permit them to prepare for better opportunities in life. They are in a vicious cycle of poverty but they are not without dreams. They dream of climbing higher in life, of reaching far beyond the debt-ridden horizon to a place where agonies, anxieties, and hardships resulting from low income cannot reach them. In their flights of dreaming, they are not aspiring for a luxurious or indolent lifestyle. All they want is a reasonable income that would be adequate to provide shelter, food, clothes, education for their children, health care for the family, and which would enable them to meet their obligations to their creditors.

Unfortunately society has left Jay and his group alone to overcome their economic woes. Jay knows that his economic hardship stems from his inadequate income. His wage, as a component of the nation's wealth, is pitifully small. Often Jay fantasizes climbing out of the abyss of his debt-bill-crisis and being at par with his prosperous fellow citizens. But, unless society institutes a fair, just, and equitable distribution system, Jay and his kind have no chance of being redeemed or salvaged. Unfortunately for them, this rightly deserved but very modest goal is hard to attain under the present callousness of society. This should lead to soul searching for all of us.

Why are the low or middle-income householders not earning enough to meet their needs? Why are their outstanding debts inflicting such grievous burdens on them? Why is it taking so long for society to discover the plight of these households trapped in debt, poverty, stagnation, and a depressed household economy? We attempt in this book to identify the magnitude of these problems which have remained unnoticed for decades, and to shed some light on the causes which account for these problems in the midst of the affluent U.S. economy.

# CHAPTER TWO
## CHARACTERISTICS OF HOUSEHOLD INCOME

The U.S. economy is one of the largest and richest in the world. However, the startling fact is that poverty, pure and simple, engulfs 36.5 million of our population, causing a large number of poverty-stricken households to live in squalor, struggling for the basic comforts of life. Another outstanding feature of this economy is that there exists a world of difference in income level among households, different professions, and regions. Against this background of the U.S. economy, we will be analyzing the economies of low-income households living in the small and mid-sized cities of the U.S. Household income is an important variable in this study and has assumed a pivotal role as nearly all other variables affecting the study have been expressed in terms of income.

In order to explain the economic characteristics of these households, we have estimated the mean income of our samples, the average income of each income group, the variations in the level of income within each group and the percentages of sampled households belonging to each group. The characteristics and the averages of this group, as we show, demonstrate these households' deviation from the overall mean income and may be used as points of reference by future researchers.

The income data demonstrates the current economic status of the households surveyed asp well as the trend of changes in their income that have occurred over the last decade. The economic well being of a household is closely associated with the income of the family, so we have determined the correlation between household income and the other important variables in our study. Our estimates and findings represent the economic status of millions of Americans living in mid-sized cities of the United States, highlighting those who are living at the poverty level.

Finally, our analysis focuses on how flawed distribution principles contribute to increasing disparity in income and to the concentration of wealth in the hands of a few. In formulating equations and drawing graphs, household income functioned as an explanatory variable.

The Trend of Average Household Income
$35,000
$30,000
$25,000
$20,000
$15,000
$10,000
$5,000
$0
1985
1988
1990
1991
1992
1993
Average Income of Households

**Figure 1**

**The Trend of Average Household Income[1] (Nominal)**

| | 1985 | 1988 | 1990 | 1991 | 1992 | 1993 |
|---|---|---|---|---|---|---|
| **Average Household Income** | **$26,019** | **$25,323** | **$30,082** | **$29,107** | **$28,342** | **$30,532** |
| **Average Income of group for the 1990-1993 period was** | | | | | | **$29,516** |

During the 1990-1993 period, the average income of households varied from a low of $28,342 in 1992 to a high of $30,532 in 1993, yielding an average income of $29,516 and an average decrease in income of $150 per year per household. The household incomes in 1985 and 1988 were $26,019 and $25,323 respectively. These households were worse off in 1988 than they were in 1985 when we started collecting data by an amount of $696. The graph also indicates that there has been no significant change in the income levels of households since 1990.

Our survey covers almost a decade. We were interested in finding whether any appreciable improvements had occurred in the economic status of households living in small and mid-sized cities in the U.S. As the overall average does not represent faithfully the economic status of low and middle-income households, we divided our population into different income groups and estimated the changes that had occurred in each income level over the decade. The estimated positive and negative changes in the income levels of households for all six years of the survey indicate whether they were better or worse off than they were in the mid 80's. The tables below show the changes that occurred in the nominal income of the different income groups for the 1990-1993 period.

---

[1]In determining the average for the 1990-1993 period, we added the data for 1990, 1991, 1992, and 1993 and divided by four. We have followed this principle throughout the book. All estimates of averages are nominal in this book.

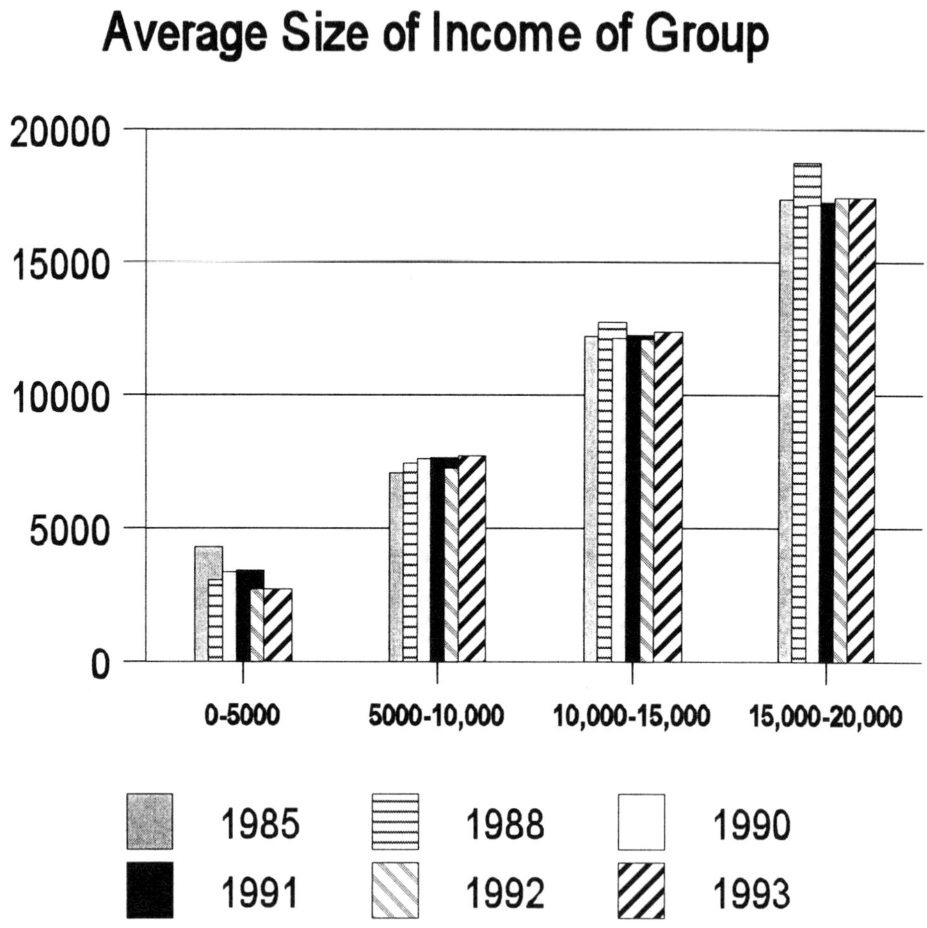
Average Size of Income of Group
20000
15000
10000
5000
0
0-5000
5000-10,000
10,000-15,000
15,000-20,000
1985
1988
1990
1991
1992
1993

Figure 2

INCOME GROUPS AND FREQUENCIES[1]

$0 - $5, 000

| | 1985 | 1988 | 1990 | 1991 | 1992 | 1993 |
|---|---|---|---|---|---|---|
| Average Size of Group Income | $4,300 | $3,052 | $3,343 | $3,424 | $2,710 | $2,723 |
| Frequency of Group as % of Entire Sample | 1% | 1% | 2% | 6% | 6% | 7% |
| Average size of income for the 1990-1993 period was | | | | | | $3,050 |
| Average change in income (1990-1993) | | | | | | ($207) |
| Per capita[2] change in income (1990-1993) | | | | | | ($83) |

For this group, the average income of households varied from $2,723 in 1993 to $3,343 in 1990, yielding an average of $3,050 and an average decrease of $207 per year per household for the 1990-1993 period. The per capita decrease in income stood at $83 for the same period. Two to seven percent of the surveyed households belonged to this group. In the early years of the survey, 1985 and 1988, only 1% of households were in this group, implying that the number of households that fell below poverty level has increased over the years.

$5,000 - $10, 000

| | 1985 | 1988 | 1990 | 1991 | 1992 | 1993 |
|---|---|---|---|---|---|---|
| Average Size of Group Income | $7,079 | $7,461 | $7,602 | $7,665 | $7,247 | $7,706 |
| Frequency of Group as % of Entire Sample | 12% | 10% | 12% | 11% | 10% | 9% |
| Average size of income for the 1990-1993 period was | | | | | | $7,555 |
| Average change in income (1990-1993) | | | | | | $35 |
| Per capita change in income (1990-1993) | | | | | | $14 |

[1]In determining the average rate of increase or decrease for the 1990-1993 period we took the average of net changes in income for this period and divided by three.

[2]Per capita change is determined by dividing the average change in income by 2.5, which represents the average number of persons per household.

For this group, the average income of households varied from $7,602 in 1990 to $7,706 in 1993, yielding an average of $7,555 and an average increase of $35 per year, per household for the 1990-1993 period. The per capita increase in income for the same period amounted to $14. Nine to twelve percent of the surveyed households belonged to this group. The average income for this group in 1985 and 1988 were $7,079 and $7,461 respectively, and percentages of households in this group were 12% and 11% respectively. There was a small increase in the income level of this group for the 1990-1993 period.

**$10,000 - $15, 000**

| | 1985 | 1988 | 1990 | 1991 | 1992 | 1993 |
|---|---|---|---|---|---|---|
| Average Size of Income of Group | $12,231 | $12,767 | $12,152 | $12,232 | $12,113 | $12,390 |
| Frequency of Group as % of Entire Sample | 11% | 17% | 11% | 14% | 11% | 12% |
| Average size of income for the 1990-1993 period was | | | | | | $12,222 |
| Average change in income (1990-1993) | | | | | | $79 |
| Per capita change in income (1990-1993) | | | | | | $32 |

The average income of this group varied from $12,152 in 1990 to $12,390 in 1993, yielding an average income of $12,222 and an average increase of $79 per year, per household for the 1990-1993 period. The per capita increase in income was $32 for the same period. Eleven to fourteen percent of the surveyed households belonged to this group.

The average income levels in 1985 and 1988 of this group were $12,231 and $12,767, respectively, and the percentages of surveyed households were 11% and 17% respectively. A small increase in the income level of this group was noticeable for 1990-1993 period, although the increase was significant during 1985-1988 period. The average income of the group, however, declined to $12,152 in 1990 from $12,767 in 1988. The percentages of households that belonged to this group have remained between 11% and 14% over the last decade.

$15,000 - $20, 000

| | 1985 | 1988 | 1990 | 1991 | 1992 | 1993 |
|---|---|---|---|---|---|---|
| Average Size of Group Income | $17,381 | $18,756 | $17,190 | $17,285 | $17,446 | $17,464 |
| Frequency of Group as % of Entire Sample | 13% | 12% | 13% | 12% | 13% | 12% |
| Average size of income for the 1990-1993 period was | | | | | | $17,346 |
| Average change in income (1990-1993) | | | | | | $91 |
| Per capita change in income (1990-1993) | | | | | | $36 |

The average income level of this group varied from $17,190 in 1990 to $17,464 in 1993, yielding an average income of $17,346 and an average increase of $91 per year, per household for the 1990-1993 period. This gives a per capita, per year increase of $36 for the same period. Between 12% and 13% of the sampled households belonged to this income group.

In 1985 and 1988, the average incomes for the group were $17,381 and $18,756 and the percentages of households in this group were 13% and 12%, respectively. It is interesting to note that this group contains a large number of households for all six years of the survey. Unfortunately, there has been no remarkable change in the income level of this group.

$20,000 - $25, 000

| | 1985 | 1988 | 1990 | 1991 | 1992 | 1993 |
|---|---|---|---|---|---|---|
| Average Size of Income of Group | $22,164 | $23,301 | $21,927 | $22,270 | $22,732 | $22,793 |
| Frequency of Group as % of Entire Sample | 12% | 10% | 10% | 8% | 9% | 8% |
| Average size of income for the 1990-1993 period was | | | | | | $22,431 |
| Average change in income (1990-1993) | | | | | | $289 |
| Per capita change in income (1990-1993) | | | | | | $116 |

The average household income of this group varied from $21,927 in 1990 to $22,793 in 1993, yielding an average income of $22,431 and an average increase of $289 per year, per household for the 1990-1993 period. This gives a per capita increase in income of $116. This increase in income was significant, although the income increase in 1993 was small.

Between 8% and 10% of households surveyed belonged to this income group. In the earlier surveys (1985 and 1988), 10% to 12% of households belonged to this group, and the average income varied from $22,164 in 1985 to $23,301 in 1988.

$25,000 - $30, 000

| | 1985 | 1988 | 1990 | 1991 | 1992 | 1993 |
|---|---|---|---|---|---|---|
| Average Size of Group Income | $27,522 | $27,892 | $26,951 | $28,080 | $27,273 | $27,475 |
| Frequency of Group as % of Entire Sample | 15% | 13% | 6% | 4% | 7% | 7% |
| Average size of income for the 1990-1993 period was | | | | | | $27,445 |
| Average change in income (1990-1993) | | | | | | $175 |
| Per capita change in income (1990-1993) | | | | | | $70 |

The average income of these households varied from $26,951 in 1990 to $27,475 in 1993, giving an average income of $27,445 and an average increase of $175 per year, per household for the 1990-1993 period. Per capita income for this group increased by $70. From 4% to 7% of the households surveyed belonged to this income group.

It was encouraging to note that some positive changes in the income of this group occurred for the 1990-1993 period. In 1985 and 1988, 15% and 13% of households belonged to this group, and the average incomes of this group were $27,522 and $27,892 respectively.

$30,000 - $35, 000

| | 1985 | 1988 | 1990 | 1991 | 1992 | 1993 |
|---|---|---|---|---|---|---|
| Average Size of Income of Group | $32,617 | $31,706 | $32,752 | $32,511 | $32,326 | $32,680 |
| Frequency of Group as % of Entire Sample | 14% | 9% | 8% | 7% | 8% | 6% |
| The average size of income for the 1990-1993 period was | | | | | | $32,567 |
| Average change in income (1990-1993) | | | | | | ($24) |
| Per capita change in income (1990-1993) | | | | | | ($10) |

The average income of this group varied from $32,752 in 1990 to $32,326 in 1992, yielding an average of $32,567 and an average decrease of $24 per year, per household for the 1990-1993 period. Per capita income during the same period decreased by $10. Between 6% and 8% of the surveyed households belonged to this group. In 1985 and 1988, 14% and 9% of households were in this group, and the averages of household income of the group were $32,617 and $31,706, respectively. A small negative change in the income level of this group was noticed. In fact, this group has been facing declining income since 1990, with the exception in 1993, when a small increase in income occurred.

**$35,000 - $40, 000**

| | 1985 | 1988 | 1990 | 1991 | 1992 | 1993 |
|---|---|---|---|---|---|---|
| **Average Size of Group Income** | **$38,617** | **$39,048** | **$37,604** | **$37,397** | **$37,200** | **$37,052** |
| **Frequency of Group as % of Entire Sample** | 6% | 11% | 5% | 6% | 4% | 8% |
| **Average size of income for the 1990-1993 period was** | | | | | | **$37,313** |
| **Average change in income (1990-1993)** | | | | | | **($184)** |
| **Per capita change in income (1990-1993)** | | | | | | **($74)** |

The average household income of this group varied from $37,604 in 1990 to $37,052 in 1993, reflecting an average of $37,313 and an average decrease of $184 per year, per household for the 1990-1993 period. This implies a per capita decrease of $74 for the same period. Between 6% and 8% of households belonged to this group. In 1985 and 1988, 6% and 11% of households were in this group, and their average incomes were $38,617 and $39,048 respectively. An increase in income of this group was noticeable in 1988, but households have experienced declining income since 1991.

**$40,000 - $45,000**

| | 1985 | 1988 | 1990 | 1991 | 1992 | 1993 |
|---|---|---|---|---|---|---|
| **Average Size of Group Income** | **$42,843** | **$42,474** | **$43,006** | **$42,282** | **$42,317** | **$42,214** |
| **Frequency of roup as % of Entire Sample** | 8% | 7% | 7% | 7% | 7% | 7% |
| **Average size of income for the 1990-1993 period was** | | | | | | **$42,455** |
| **Average change in income (1990-1993)** | | | | | | **($264)** |
| **Per capita change in income (1990-1993)** | | | | | | **($106)** |

The average income level of this group varied from $42,214 in 1993 to $43,006 in 1990, giving an average income of $42,455 and an average decrease of $264 per household, per year for the 1990-1993 survey period. Per capita income during the period decreased by $106. In fact, the average income decreased in 1991, 1992, and 1993 from the income level of 1990. Seven percent of the surveyed households belonged to this income group.

Interestingly, the percentages of households that belonged to the group remained the same for the last four years of the survey. In 1985 and 1988, the average incomes of this group were $42,843 and $42,474. The percentages of households of this group were 8% and 7% respectively. It is obvious that there has been a considerable decrease in the income level of this group, and households in the group experienced a declining standard of living during this period.

**$45,000 - $50,000**

| | 1985 | 1988 | 1990 | 1991 | 1992 | 1993 |
|---|---|---|---|---|---|---|
| Average Size of Group Income | $47,994 | $46,586 | $47,071 | $47,697 | $47,993 | $47,660 |
| Frequency of Group as % of Entire Sample | 5% | 7% | 6% | 7% | 6% | 4% |
| Average size of income for the 1990-1993 period was | | | | | | $47,605 |
| Average change in income (1990-1993) | | | | | | $196 |
| Per capita change in income (1990-1993) | | | | | | $78 |

The average household income of this group varied from $47,071 in 1990 to $47,660 in 1993 yielding an average of $47,605 and an average increase of $196 per year, per household for the 1990-1993 period. The per capita income during the same period increased by $78. The average incomes for this group in 1985 and 1988 were $47,994 and $46,526, and percentages of households for this group were 5% and 7%, respectively. A noticeable increase in the income of this group occurred during the survey's last three years.

$50,000 - $55,000

| | 1985 | 1988 | 1990 | 1991 | 1992 | 1993 |
|---|---|---|---|---|---|---|
| Average Size of Group Income | $51,847 | $52,671 | $52,682 | $52,159 | $52,343 | $52,802 |
| Frequency of Group as % of Entire Sample | 1% | 2% | 4% | 4% | 3% | 4% |
| Average size of income for the 1990-1993 period was | | | | | | $52,497 |
| Average change in income (1990-1993) | | | | | | $40 |
| Per capita change in income (1990-1993) | | | | | | $16 |

The average income of this group varied from $52,682 in 1990 to $52,802 in 1993, yielding an average income of $52,497 and an average increase of $40 per year, per household for the 1990-1993 period. The per capita income during the period increased by $16. From 3% to 4% of surveyed households belonged to this group. One to two percent of households were in this income group in 1985 and 1988, and the average incomes of this group were $51,847 and $52,671 respectively for those two years. A small increase in income of this group was noticeable for the 1990-1993 period.

$55,000 - $60,000

| | 1985 | 1988 | 1990 | 1991 | 1992 | 1993 |
|---|---|---|---|---|---|---|
| Average Size of Group Income | $56,898 | $55,676 | $57,758 | $57,142 | $57,491 | $57,463 |
| Frequency of Group as % of Entire Sample | 2% | 2% | 5% | 5% | 3% | 4% |
| The average income for the 1990-1993 period was | | | | | | $57,464 |
| Average change in income (1990-1993) | | | | | | ($98) |
| Per capita change in income (1990-1993) | | | | | | ($39) |

The average household income of this group varied from $57,463 in 1993 to $57,578 in 1990, yielding an average income of $57,464 and an average decrease of $98 per household, per year for the 1990-1993 period. The per capita income during the same period decreased by $39. 3% to 5% of households belonged to this income level. The average incomes for this group in 1985 and 1988 were $56,898 and $55,676, and percentages of households were 1% and 2% respectively. On average, the income of this group declined for the 1990-1993 period.

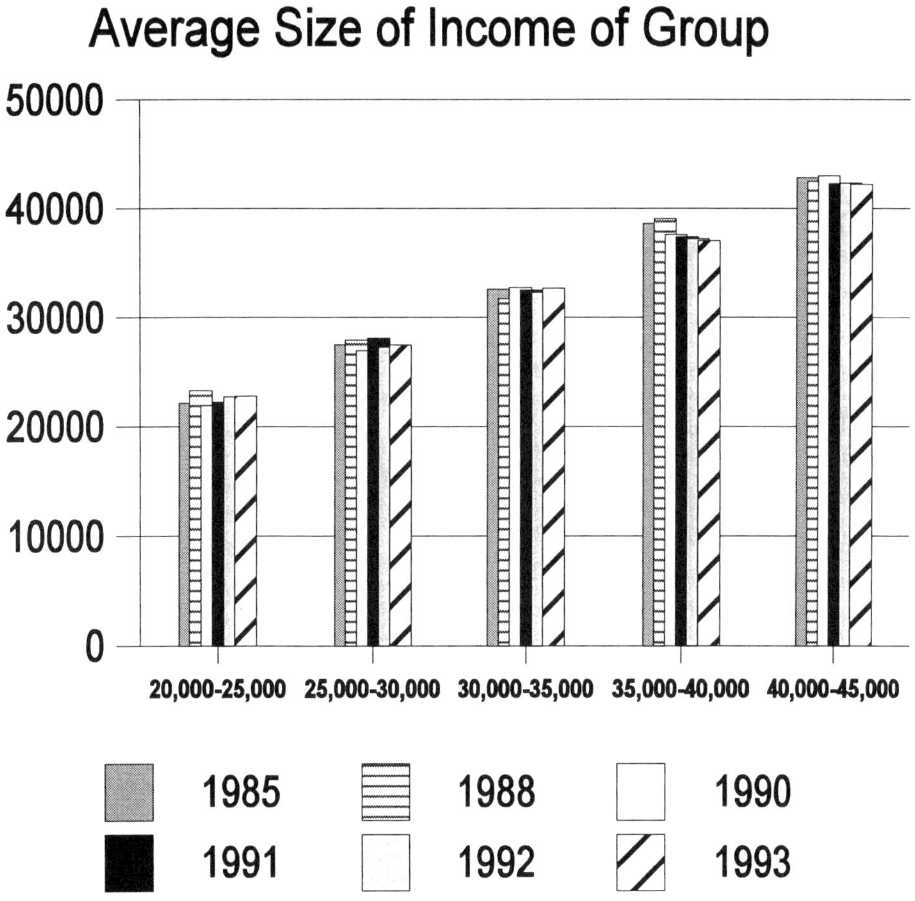
Average Size of Income of Group
50000
40000
30000
20000
10000
0
20,000-25,000
25,000-30,000
30,000-35,000
35,000-40,000
40,000-45,000
1985
1988
1990
1991
1992
1993

Figure 3

**$60,000 and Over**

| | 1985 | 1988 | 1990 | 1991 | 1992 | 1993 |
|---|---|---|---|---|---|---|
| **Average Size of Group Income** | **$60,176** | **$65,711** | **$71,310** | **$67,811** | **$70,126** | **$71,435** |
| **Frequency of Group as % of Entire Sample** | **1%** | **2%** | **8%** | **8%** | **8%** | **11%** |
| **Average size of income for the 1990-1993 period was** | | | | | | **$70,171** |
| **Average change in income (1990-1993)** | | | | | | **($42)** |
| **Per capita change in income (1990-1993)** | | | | | | **($17)** |

The average income level of this group varied from $71,310 in 1990 to $71,435 in 1993, yielding an average of $70,171 and an average decrease of $42 per year, per household for the 1990-1993 survey period. The per capita income during the same period decreased by $17. The number of households in this group varied from 8% to 11% of all households.

The average income for the 1985 and 1988-period were $60,176 and $65,711 and percentage of households in this group were 1% and 2% respectively. The summary of the changes that occurred to the different income groups during the survey period is given below.

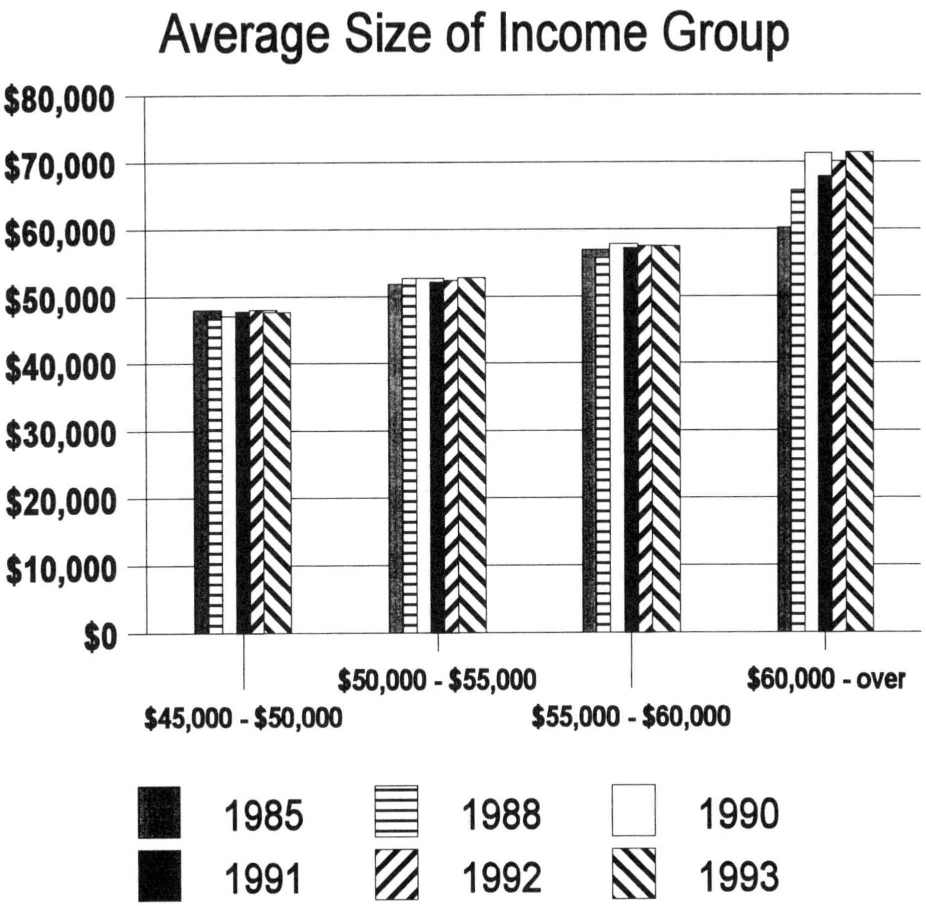
Average Size of Income Group
$80,000
$70,000
$60,000
$50,000
$40,000
$30,000
$20,000
$10,000
$0
$45,000 - $50,000
$50,000 - $55,000
$55,000 - $60,000
$60,000 - over
1985
1988
1990
1991
1992
1993

Figure 4

INCREASES OR DECREASES IN GROUP INCOME LEVELS

| **Income Groups Having Positive Changes (increases) in Income for 1990-1993** | **Average Positive Change (increases) in Income for 1990-1993** | **Per Capita Positive Change (increase) in Income for 1990-1993** |
|---|---|---|
| $5,000-$10,000 | $35 | $14 |
| $10,000-$15,000 | $79 | $32 |
| $15,000-$20,000 | $91 | $36 |
| $20,000-$25,000 | $289 | $116 |
| $25,000-$30,000 | $175 | $70 |
| $45,000-$50,000 | $196 | $78 |
| $50,000-$55,000 | $40 | $16 |
| **Income Groups Having Negative Changes (decreases) in Income for 1990-1993** | **Average Negative Change (decreases) in Income for 1990-1993** | **Per Capita Negative Change (decrease) in Income for 1990-1993** |
| $0-$5000 | ($207) | ($83) |
| $30000-$35000 | ($24) | ($10) |
| $35000-$40000 | ($184) | ($74) |
| $40000-$45000 | ($264) | ($106) |
| $55000-$60000 | ($98) | ($39) |
| $60000-over | ($42) | ($17) |

Of the 13 different income groups, seven groups: 5,000-10,000, 10,000-15,000, 15,000-20,000, 20,000-25,000, 25,000-30,000, 45,000-50,000, and 50,000-55,000 showed positive changes in their income level. The average changes per household varied by $35, $79, $91, $289, $175, $196, and $40, respectively, for those groups.

The per capita changes for those groups were $14, $32, $36, $116, $70, $78, and $16, respectively. We observed negative changes for six groups: less than 5,000, 30,000-35,000, 35,000-40,000, 40,000-45,000, 55,000-60,000, 60,000 and over income levels. The average per household negative changes for those groups were $207, $24, $184, $264, $98, and

$42 respectively. The per capita negative changes for those groups were $83, $10, $74, $106, $39, and $17 respectively.

From the analysis of the changes in the income level of the groups, we can claim that, except for a rare few, most households have been experiencing either very small increases in income or a total stagnancy in their economy. In other words we may conclude that most households in mid-sized cities have received very little or no significant benefit from the tremendous growth in the wealth that has taken place in the U.S. economy over the last several decades. In fact per household income in the survey area equals half of average per household Gross National Product — implying that the gap in the income level between households in mid-sized cities and those in big cities has been widening unchecked. We will explain this point later in this chapter under the section "The Disparity of Income and the Trend of the GNP." We need to take appropriate measures to reduce this trend of widening of disparity of income so that it does not become a major political issue in the near future.

HOUSEHOLD INCOME BELOW POVERTY LEVEL

| Income | 1985 | 1988 | 1990 | 1991 | 1992 | 1993 |
|---|---|---|---|---|---|---|
| **$0-5,000** | $4,300 (1%) | $3,052 (1%) | $3,343 (2%) | $3,424 (6%) | $2,710 (6%) | $2,723 (7%) |
| **$5,000-10,000** | $7,079 (12%) | $7,461 (11%) | $7,602 (13%) | $7,665 (11%) | $7,247 (10%) | $7,706 (9%) |
| **$10,000-15,000** | $12,231 (11%) | $12,787 (18%) | $12,152 (11%) | $12,232 (14%) | $12,113 (11%) | $12,390 (12%) |

**PER CAPITA INCOME[1] OF HOUSEHOLDS BELOW POVERTY LEVEL**

| Income (in Thousands) | 1985 | 1988 | 1990 | 1991 | 1992 | 1993 |
|---|---|---|---|---|---|---|
| **$0 - 5000** | $1,720 | $1,221 | $1,337 | $1,370 | $1,084 | $1,089 |
| **$5,000 - 10,000** | $2,832 | $2,984 | $3,041 | $3,066 | $2,899 | $3,082 |
| **$10,000 - 15,000** | $4,892 | $5,115 | $4,861 | $4,893 | $4,845 | $4,956 |
| Percentage of households in our survey living below poverty level | | | | | | 25% to 30% |
| Average income of households living below poverty level varied from | | | | | | $2,710 to $12,787 |
| Per capita income of households living below poverty level varied from | | | | | | $1,084 to $5,115 |
| Percent of households in our survey that earn less than $15,000 per year | | | | | | 24% to 30% |
| Percent of households in our survey that earn less than $10,000 per year | | | | | | 13% to 17% |

**INCOME GROUPS AND FREQUENCIES**
(under poverty level)[2]

| Group | Average Income | 1985 f/N | 1988 f/N | 1990 f/N | 1991 f/N | 1992 f/N | 1993 f/N |
|---|---|---|---|---|---|---|---|
| I[3] | $0-4999 | 1% | 1% | 2% | 6% | 6% | 7% |
| II[4] | $5,000-9,999 | 12% | 11% | 13% | 11% | 10% | 9% |
| III[5] | $10,000-14999 | 11% | 18% | 11% | 14% | 11% | 2% |

---

[1]Per capita income is estimated by dividing average household income by 2.5, which represents the average number of persons per household.

[2]Assuming a city with a population of 100,000.

[3]1,000 to 7,000 households earn between $2710 and $4300 per year. The per capita income of this group is between $1,084 and $1,720.

[4]9,000 to 13,000 households earn between $7,079 and $7,706 per year. The per capita income of this group is between $2,832 and $3,082.

[5]11,000 to 18,000 households earn between $12,113 and $12,787 per year. The per capita income of this group is between $4,845 and $5,115.

In all six years, 13% to 17% of households reported yearly income below $10,000. Additionally, 24% to 31% of households surveyed reported to have had income that was below $15,000, and 49% to 54% of households, almost half of all households in these cities, earn less than $25,000. The per capita income of households living below the poverty level is less than $5,115 (in our survey per capita income varied between $1,084 and $5,115). In a nutshell, it can be claimed that 25% to 30% of all households in small and mid-sized cities are living below the poverty level.

## THE DISPARITY IN INCOME AND THE TREND OF GNP

After ascertaining the extent of poverty prevailing in the mid-sized cities both in terms of average and per capital income, we examined the link between poverty and the distribution system of the economy in the context of growth of wealth trends in this country and the way wealth trickles down to the grass-roots level. Often it is the case that an unfair distribution system gives rise to gross inequality of income and results in the increase of poverty-stricken households in a society. Below we analyze the distribution system in the U.S. to shed some light on the trend of increasing disparity of income in the U.S. economy.

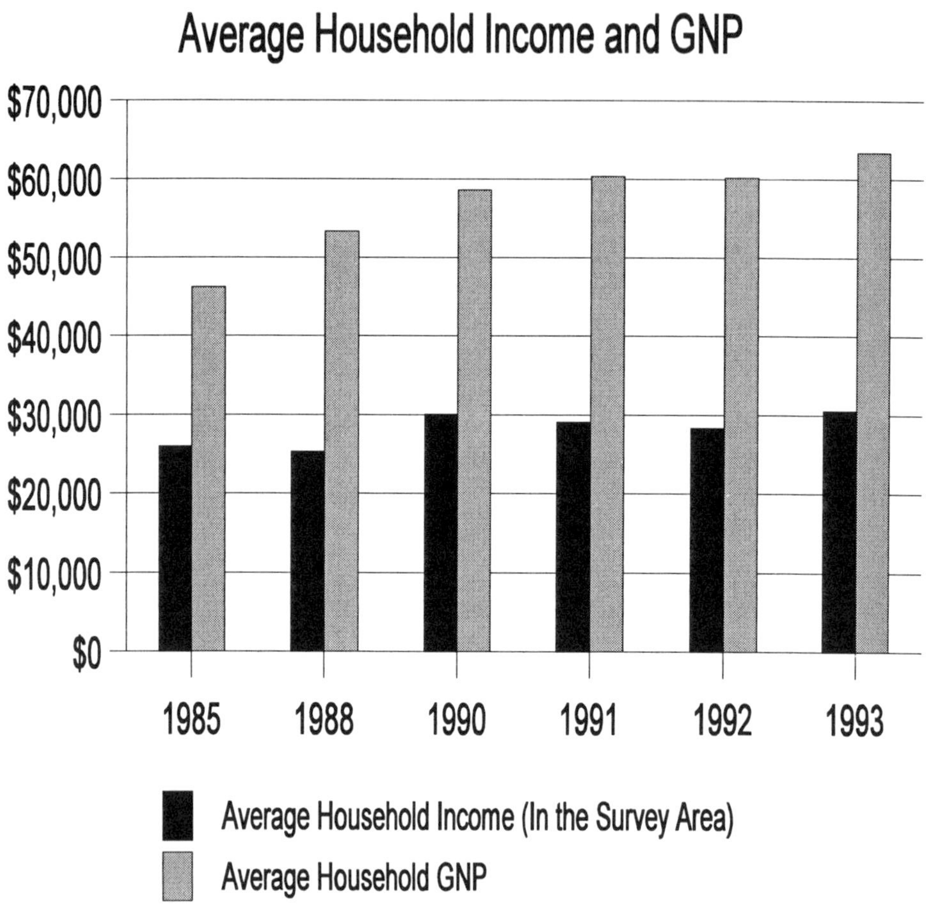
Average Household Income and GNP
$70,000
$60,000
$50,000
$40,000
$30,000
$20,000
$10,000
$0
1985
1988
1990
1991
1992
1993
Average Household Income (In the Survey Area)
Average Household GNP

Figure 5

The Trend of Average Household Income and GNP
Average Income of Household ( in survey area)

| | 1985 | 1988 | 1990 | 1991 | 1992 | 1993 |
|---|---|---|---|---|---|---|
| Average Income of Household (as estimated in survey area) | $26,019 | $25,332 | $30,082 | $29,107 | $28,342 | $30,532 |
| Average Household GNP[1] | $46,260 | $53,350 | $58,570 | $60,391 | $60,258 | $63,438 |

| | |
|---|---|
| The average Household Income for 1990-1993 was (as estimated in the survey area) | $29,516 |
| The average change in per Household Income for 1990-1993 was (as estimated in the survey area) | $150 |
| The average household GNP for 1990-1993 was (nationally) | $60,665 |
| The average change in per household GNP for 1990-1993 was (nationally) | $1,623 |

Our findings show that the average household income in the survey area increased from $26,109 in 1985 to $30,532 in 1993. On the average, the per year increase in household income was $150 for the 1990-1993 period. During the same period the average household GNP (at the national level) rose from $46,260 in 1985 to $63,438 in 1993.

The average increase in GNP per U.S. household for 1990-1993 amounted to $1,623 per year, yielding a ratio between the change in per household GNP and the change in per household income in our survey of 10.7, implying that the per household GNP increased more than ten times the average household income in mid-sized cities of the U.S. during the survey period. This establishes the fact that the share in the national wealth commanded by households living in the mid-sized cities of the U.S. has been decreasing at an alarmingly increasing rate and the income gap among households living in small cities with that of big cities is widening rapidly.

This also demonstrates that some households are commanding a vastly larger share of the national wealth while most households in small and mid-sized cities do not. One can conclude that the present distribution system

[1]The average household GNP is found by dividing GNP for the year by the number of households in the country.

of national wealth is far from fair and is at the root of the widening inequality of income among different sections of the society and different regions. Society has allowed this imbalance in the distribution process over the last several decades because of their unawareness of the disparity issue and of the causes which account for it. A prolonged refusal to act to reduce the gross inequality of income among different professions and regions may give rise to a social unrest which is highly undesirable.

**Typical Levels of Compensation in Small and Mid-sized Cities**

| Professionals | Wages Per Annum |
|---|---|
| Minimum Wage Worker | 11,000 |
| Bank Counter Clerk | 12,000 |
| Secretary I | 13,000 |
| Food Processing Worker | 14,000 |
| Secretary II | 15,000 |
| Laborer | 17,000 |
| Correction Officer | 19,000 |
| Instructor (College) | 28,000 |
| Non-skilled earners (Paper mills) | 25,000 |
| Patrolman | 28,000 |
| Assistant Professor | 29,000 |
| Associate Professor | 33.000 |
| Accountant | 37,000 |
| Director of Finance | 55,000 |
| Lawyer, CPA | 80,000 |
| President (College) | 100,000 to over 250,000[1] |
| President or Executive of a company | |
| Bank Presidents | |
| Physicians | |

The table shows that the presidents and the chief executives of companies, physicians, and lawyers are enjoying salaries that far exceed the average earnings of the majority of the labor force. We accept the fact that talented, inventive, innovative, enterprising, and gifted workers deserve much better and larger compensation for their work than their counterparts,

[1]These salaries could not be confirmed.

the average wage earners, earn. What concerns us most is the degree of difference in the income levels and the current trend of increase in the disparity of income among different professions and regions. Some of the underlying causes for this wage differential can be described as follows.

The GNP growth trend has been outstanding – from less than 1,600 billion in 1975 to more than 6,343.3 billion dollars in 1993.[1] This speaks of the unparallel prosperity that this country has achieved. It also suggests that there has been a tremendous surge in the production of goods such as homes, cars, furniture, appliances and other durable goods that households need. To keep a family afloat, expenses have to be incurred not only for food, clothing, and shelter, but also for health, medicine, insurance, education, attorney's fees, repairs and emergency services. All these have resulted in a tremendous rise in household expenses during the last decade.

To stay in the course of mainstream living[2], households in small cities have had to work more hours. Either two jobs – one full-time and one part-time – are needed, or the wife has to be drafted for work, even when she may be ill or needed to take care of small children. In view of the rise in prices of essential goods and services (homes, cars, etc.), households in smaller cities are facing declining real wages.

In these cities large numbers of householders work as unskilled workers in fast food services such as McDonald's, KFC, Hardees, or in paper mills, food processing plants, department stores and other businesses to supplement their incomes. These jobs are insecure with few fringe or pension benefits. Their agonizing debt/bill problems (as discussed in Jay's life) and their struggles for survival lead us to be concerned with the deplorably low wages that are paid to the majority of the working population.

As we stated earlier, the distribution system determines the amount of command households have on goods and services or material well-being. Our estimate shows that there has been a tiny increase in household income among low-income households over the last eight years of our survey. Most households in the cities we studied are suffering from a stagnant economy. The distribution principle followed by a country profoundly effects the material destiny of its people and directly determines the rates of compensation that an individual receives in exchange for the services he renders or goods he produces.

---

[1]The GNP increase exceeds six trillion dollars.

[2]This refers to a decent living.

Briefly speaking, in a market economy such as the U.S. economy, we claim that the price of goods and services is determined by market forces. But we tend to lose sight of pertinent variables such as time honored customs, "tradition," "convention," and the "greed elements" that invariably enter into determining the price of goods and services. For example, in a society where the teaching profession is held in great esteem, a teacher may end up getting much better wages than other workers do.

On the other hand in a society that, by tradition, values sports and the legal and medical professions more than other professions, athletes, lawyers and physicians are paid much higher wages than other workers. A "going along with the status quo attitude" also influences the distribution system in a society. In some societies no one raises an eyebrow or feels concerned if an athlete is paid $50 million in five or six years, or an entertainer receives $50,000 per week or a company president receives several million dollars a year even though a secretary or an unskilled worker may be receiving between $10,000 and $13,000 a year. This world of difference in earnings and benefits among different professions for many societies may be in keeping with their "tradition," but it may not be in keeping with just or fair principles of distribution.

Inherent in such traditions and customs lies the callous attitude of a society that helps preserve gross income differentials among different professions and regions at a socially unacceptable level. Our concern is not for the equality of compensation among different professions, but for an acceptable reduction in the current level of disparity. More precisely, our concern is to upgrade the income of the low and middle-income households in the U.S. economy.

Along with market forces, the "convention" element accounts for higher prices for some goods and services, but the "convention" or "tradition" element itself is often born out of historical or social episodes. The tradition of posting the prime rate of the New York banks was the creation of several big banks in New York to preserve their own self interest. But this "tradition" has been costing American households and businesses billions of dollars each year. The insignificant increase in household income in the survey area when compared against a vast increase in national income disturbs and depresses a rational mind.

# CHAPTER THREE
## HOUSEHOLD DEBT

### AVERAGE SIZE OF THE DEBT

Of the many problems with which low-income householders wrestle in their everyday lives, the most worrisome and devastating is household debt. It is a double-edged sword. While debt is unavoidable, inadequate income renders householders unable to service the debt efficiently. This makes debtors psychologically depressed and prone to constant anxiety and restlessness. The concern of householders regarding their inability to keep creditors satisfied involves constant anguish, unease, and the absence of peace of mind.

We do not often hear about the size of the debt that households bear at any point in time, although most households in small and mid-sized cities in the U.S. are in perpetual debt. The necessities of life, such as home, car, food, clothing, and medicine, cannot be met with the current level of income of these households. They supplement their income by borrowing or by buying goods and services on credit.

For the head of a household, finding a means of making payments to creditors is just as important as providing the necessities of life to their families. As debt problems weigh so heavily on the minds of the householders, we are attempting here to give an in-depth analysis of these problems and to venture into estimating the trend and the size of household leverage.

We have estimated the size of home, car, personal, business, and credit car loans as well as the overall size of household debt. We have also determined how these loans average out for different income groups. Often, an indebted household is not aware of the magnitude of the debt that it has incurred or the full nature of the debt burden with which it is encumbered.

To make this point, the size of each household's debt has been related to its income to determine how large the household debt is relative to income. We have also compared the average size of the debt of different income groups with each group's mean income to determine which groups bear regressive debt burdens.

**The Average Size of Household Debt (Sample Average)**

| | 1985 | 1988 | 1990 | 1991 | 1992 | 1993 |
|---|---|---|---|---|---|---|
| **The Sample Average[1] Size of Debt** | $16,300 | $14,050 | $15,430 | $15,280 | $11,340 | $12,210 |
| **The Average size of Debt of Indebted Household** | $16,780 | $22,820 | $33,320 | $31,880 | $31,180 | $33,590 |
| **Sample average of last four years' household debt was (1990-1993)** | | | | | | $13,565 |
| **Per year average decrease in debt for 1990-1993 was (sample average)** | | | | | | ($1,073) |
| **Average size of indebted households debt for the period 1990-1993** | | | | | | $32,493 |
| **Per year per household average increase in indebted households' debt** | | | | | | $90 |

In determining the trends and central tendencies of our estimates we have used the data of the 1990-93 period and for the purposes of knowing what these averages were a decade ago – in the mid and late eighties – we refer to our estimates of 1985 and 1988. This is a strategy we have followed throughout the book. The data shows that the sample average size of household debt varied between $11,340 and $15,430 for the 1990-1993 period, yielding an average of $13,565, indicating a trend of decrease in the average size of household debt for this period of $1,073 per household.

The sample average of household debt for the years of 1985 and 1988 varied between $14,050 and $16,300. The data for indebted households however gives a different picture. During the 1990-1993 period, the average size of the debt for the indebted household varied between $31,180 and $33,590, yielding an average size of the debt of $32,493, showing an increase in the size of the debt of $90 per year per household. The average of indebted households for the years of 1985 and 1988 varied between $16,780 and $22,820 respectively.

---

[1]The "sample average" implies the average of all households in the sample including those who have not contracted any loans at all.

The outstanding fact in the trend of the household debt appears to be the rapid increase in the size of the debt of the indebted household – reaching twice the size of the sample average of the 1990-93 period. This was an increase of more than 100% in the size of the indebted households' debt from what it was in the beginning of the survey.

In summary, we found that the sample average size of household debt was approximately $13,500, and that of the indebted household's average debt was in the proximity of $32,500. We should bear in mind that in determining sample averages, we took all households in the sample into account, including those who did not incur any debt at all.

The sample averages are of course useful for macro analysis and the policy making process. They do not, however, reflect the true position of households relative to their debts. The averages of indebted households, on the other hand, do reflect the realities of their situation in relationship to debt. Because of this, we focused more on the analysis of the data that were directly associated with debt than the data that represented the sample averages. After having determined the overall average size of household debt, we estimated the average size of debt in several other subsidiary categories.

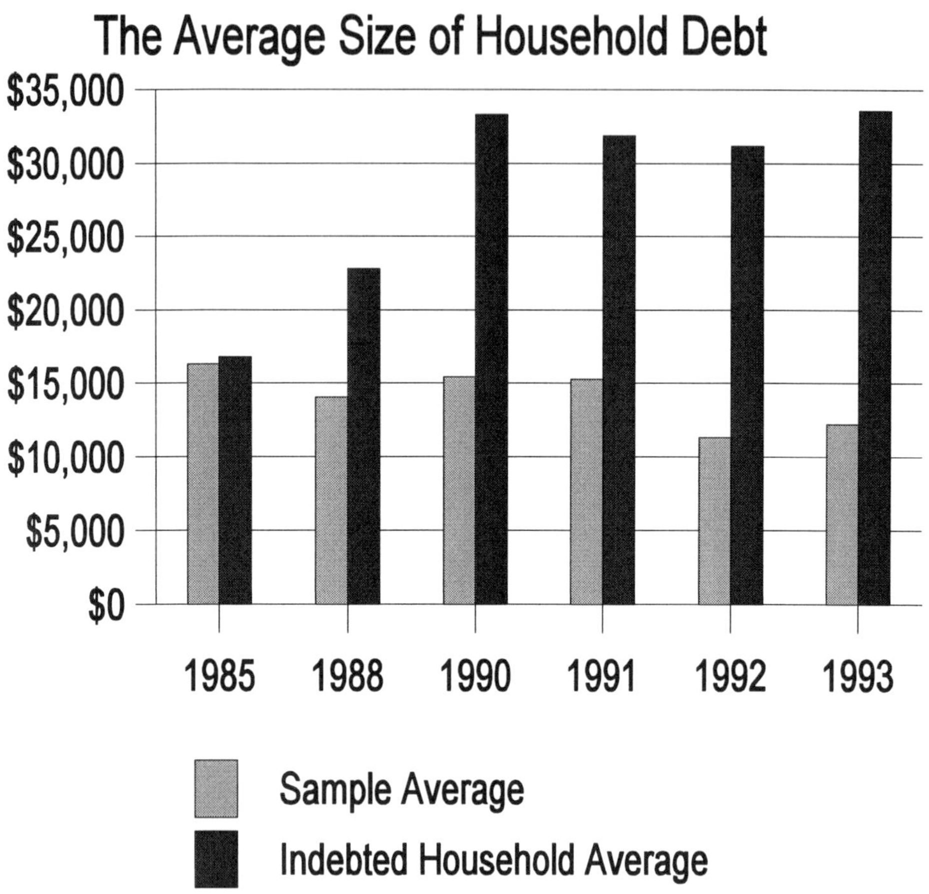
The Average Size of Household Debt
$35,000
$30,000
$25,000
$20,000
$15,000
$10,000
$5,000
$0
1985
1988
1990
1991
1992
1993
Sample Average
Indebted Household Average

**Figure 6**

**Sample Average Size of Debt**[1]
(item wise per household)

| Average Size Of Debt For All Sampled Households | 1985 | 1988 | 1990 | 1991 | 1992 | 1993 |
|---|---|---|---|---|---|---|
| Average Household Income | $26,019 | $25,323 | $30,082 | $29,107 | $28,342 | $30,532 |
| Home Loan | $10,703 | $8,446 | $10,533 | $9,598 | $7,693 | $8,861 |
| Car Loan | $1,366 | $641 | $2,165 | $3,630 | $2,170 | $2,800 |
| Personal and Business Loans | $3,352 | $4,403 | $420 | $736 | *$1,420 | *$1,530 |
| Credit Card Loan | $490 | $312 | $2,310 | $1,310 | $1,450 | $1,560 |

**Estimated Figures based on data collected*

| | |
|---|---|
| **Sample average size of home loan for 1990-1993 period:** | $9,171 |
| **Sample average size of car loan for 1990-1993 period:** | $2,691 |
| **Sample average size of personal and business loan for 1990-1993 period:** | $1,027 |
| **Sample average size of credit card loan for 1990-1993 period was:** | $1,658 |
| **Sample average size of household income for 1990-1993 period was:** | $29,516 |

[1]The over all sample average size of debt is determined by dividing household debt by the number of households in the sample, including those who have not incurred any debt at all.

The data shows that the sample averages for home loans varied from $7,693 to $10,533, yielding an average of $9,171 which constituted 31% of the average household income[1]. The average car loan varied from $2,165 to $3,630 giving an average of $2,691 which equaled 9.1% of the average household income. Personal and business loans varied from $420 to $1,530 yielding an average of $1,027,or 3.5% of the average household income. The average credit card loan varied from $1,310 to $2,310 giving an average of $1,658 which equaled 5.6% of the average household income.

**Frequencies of Indebted Households**

| | 1985 | 1988 | 1990 | 1991 | 1992 | 1993 |
|---|---|---|---|---|---|---|
| Averages of Indebted Households' Debt | $16,780 | $22,820 | $33,320 | $31,880 | $31,180 | $33,590 |
| Frequencies of Indebted Households | 97% | 62% | 46% | 48% | 33% | 32% |

In our first four years of study (1985, 1988, 1990, 1991), 48% to 97% of all households were in debt. In the early period of the survey, 1985, 97% of households were in debt. At that time, most households maintained records of interest payments on all items because these payments were deductible under the tax code. In 1985 and 1988, 97% and 62% of households reported to have had debts for one reason or another. Frequencies for 1992-1993 have been under-reported because households did not keep accurate records of nondeductible interest-bearing loans due to changes in the tax code.

---

[1] "Average income" here represents the average of four years income (1990-1993 period.)

**Average Size of Debt and Frequencies[1]**
**Of Indebted Households** (Item wise)

| Average Size Of Debt For Indebted Households | 1985 | 1988 | 1990 | 1991 | 1992 | 1993 |
|---|---|---|---|---|---|---|
| Home Loan | $16,628 (64%) | $21,719 (39%) | $27,227 (39%) | $27,281 (35%) | $23,942 (32%) | $26,731 (33%) |
| Car Loan | $4,850 (28%) | $6,929 (9%) | $16,132 (13%) | $15,789 (23%) | $11,260 (8%) | $10,000 (15%) |
| Personal and Business Loans | $6,553 (51%) | $9,233 (48%) | $11,394 | $8,855 | $8,500 | $9,160 |
| Credit Car Loan | $844 (84%) | $1,684 (19%) | $7,430 (31%) | $5,140 (25%) | $4,400 (13%) | $4,220 (20%) |

*Numbers in ( ) Denote Frequencies*

| | |
|---|---|
| Average size of home loan for the 1990-1993 period: | $26,295 |
| Average size of car loans for the 1990-1993 period: | $13,295 |
| Average size of personal & business loan for 1990-1993 period: | $9,477 |
| Average size of credit card loan for the 1990-1993 period: | $5,298 |

Data shows that the average size of home loans varied between $23,942 and $27,281, yielding an average $26,295 during the last four years of the survey (1990-1993). Except in 1992, the average size of home loans in recent years has been hovering around $27,000 while in the earlier years of our survey, in 1985 and 1988, it was $16,628 and $21,719 respectively.

The average size of car loans varied between $10,000 and $16,132 yielding an average of $13,295 during the same period, although it was only $4,850 in 1985 and $6,929 in 1988, indicating the beginning of a faster rate of increase in the size of car loans. The average size of personal and business loans increased from $8,500 to $11,394 for the same period, yielding an average of $9,477. The size of credit card loans varied between $4,220 and $7,430, an average of $5,298 for the 1990-1993 period. The averages were only $844 and $1,684 in 1985 and 1988, indicating a sixfold

[1]Since the early nineties many households have neglected keeping records of interest payments on items that are no longer deductible for tax purposes.

increase in the size of credit card loans since we started collecting data in 1985.

The frequencies for home loans surpassed the frequencies of other loans. In 1985, 64% of households incurred home loans, but for the other years of the survey, the frequencies varied from 32% to 39%. The percentages of households that borrowed on credit cards (during 1985, 1988, 1990 and 1991) varied between 19% and 84%. In 1985, 28% of the households reported to have had outstanding balances on car loans.

**Household Debt and Other Debts**[1]

| | 1985 | 1988 | 1990 | 1991 | 1992 | 1993 |
|---|---|---|---|---|---|---|
| Average Per Household Debt | $16,780 | $22,820 | $33,320 | $31,880 | $31,180 | $33,590 |
| Average Per Household Corporate Debt | $19,570 | $28,597 | $34,654 | $38,866 | $42,516 | $45,183 |
| Average Per Household Federal Debt | $21,048 | $28,736 | $33,369 | $38,160 | $41,870 | $45,183 |
| Average Per Household GNP | $46,260 | $52,568 | $58,576 | $59,510 | $63,031 | $65,916 |
| Average Per Household State Debt | $2,443 | $3,044 | $3,436 | $3,815 | $4,185 | $4,518 |
| Average size of per household debt for 1990-1993 (in survey area) | | | | | | $32,493 |
| Average size of per household corporate debt for 1990-1993 period | | | | | | $40,305 |
| Average size of per household federal debt for the 1990-1993 period | | | | | | $39,646 |
| Average size of per household GNP for the 1990-1993 period | | | | | | $61,758 |
| Average size of per household state debt for the 1990-1993 period | | | | | | $3,989 |

Out of curiosity, we compare below the trend of per household and per capita debt with that of other important debts such as federal, corporate and state debts. Average per household debt varied between $31,180 and

[1] All averages have been calculated by taking into account the amounts of debt outstanding and the numbers of households.

$33,590 during 1990-1993, yielding an average increase of $90 per year. The average per household corporate debt varied between $34,654 and $45,183 during the same period, yielding an average rate of increase of $3,510 per year. The average per household federal debt varied between $33,369 and $45,183, yielding an average increase of $3,938 per year during the same period.

It is quite interesting to note that the per household corporate and federal debts are growing at a pace akin to each other. The average per household state debt was the smallest of all other debts in size and varied between $3,436 and $4,518 during 1990-1993 period, yielding an average increase of $361 per year. On the other hand, the average per household GNP grew from $58,576 to $65,196 for this period, yielding an average increase of $2,447 per year per household. The average per household increase or decrease of all these debts is as follows:

**Average per Household per Year Increase in Debt**[1]

| | |
|---|---|
| **Average increase of per household GNP per year for 1990-1993 period (in survey area)** | **$2,447** |
| **Average increase of per household corporate debt per year for 1990-1993** | **$3,510** |
| **Average increase of per household federal debt per year for 1990-1993** | **$3,938** |
| **Average increase of per household state debt per year for 1990-1993** | **$361** |
| **Average increase of per household debt per year for 1990-1993 (in survey area)** | **$90** |

The data shows that all outstanding debts have been increasing, and the rates of increases in the federal debt and that of corporate debt were in close proximity to each other. These debt-sizes are more meaningful when expressed in terms of average household income. The table below shows the sizes of debts as percentages of average household GNP.

[1]The net increase or decrease of household debt for the 1990-1993 period has been divided by three to arrive at per household per year average increase or decrease in household debt for that period.

**Debt as Percent of Average Household GNP[1]**

| | 1985 | 1988 | 1990 | 1991 | 1992 | 1993 |
|---|---|---|---|---|---|---|
| The Average Household Debt (survey area) | 63% | 55% | 52% | 53% | 40% | 40% |
| The Average Household Corporate Debt | 42% | 57% | 59% | 65% | 67% | 69% |
| The Average Household Federal Debt | 45% | 54% | 57% | 64% | 66% | 69% |
| The Average Household State Debt | 5% | 6% | 6% | 6% | 7% | 7% |

The above data shows that our estimate of household debt equaled 37% to 57% of average per household GNP during our survey period. The per household corporate debt equals 42% to 69% and the per household federal debt equals to 45% to 69% of the average per household GNP for the same period.

It is interesting to observe that both the per household corporate and the per household federal debts are growing in a remarkably similar fashion. The per household state debt equals 5% to 7% of the average per household GNP for the 1985-1993 period.

### The Per Household[2] Averages of Important Debts

The average size (per household) of important outstanding debts for the year 1993 (the last year of our survey):

| Per Household Debt (survey area) | | Per Household Corporate Debt | | Per Household Federal Debt | | Per Household State Debt | | Total |
|---|---|---|---|---|---|---|---|---|
| $12,210 | + | $45,183 | + | $45,183 | + | $4,518 | = | $107,094 |

The average household debt, the average household federal debt, the average corporate debt, and the average household state debts (for the year 1993) have been added to gauge the immensity of debt-size that has engulfed the nation. The total of these debts amounts to $107,094 per household. The debt is intimidating in its size and raises a serious question:

---

[1]These percentages have been estimated by dividing per household debt by per household GNP for the respective years.

[2]Outstanding total debts have been divided by the total number of households to determine per household debt.

Is the economy heading for bankruptcy? The answer is "No," but excessive national debt under certain circumstances and government policy may pose a threat and a real problem for the low-income households. Visible debts directly affect the debtor who contracts the debt and accepts responsibility for servicing and paying the debt. Invisible debts are debts that have not been contracted by households, but they could be forced to bear a part or the entire responsibility for servicing or paying the debts. This happens when the contractor of the debt is a government and fails to service or repay the debt. This possibility is inherent in the character of public debt.

To explain this point further, all debts have their own attributes. Corporate debts are generally serviced and paid off from the earnings of assets acquired by borrowed funds. As such, corporate debt does not pose a threat to be a burden in any form for households. The payment of state debts is generally secured by bonds, but state or local government debts carry some risk if the issuers fail to service the debt or repay principal amounts.

The federal debt in the U. S. on the other hand, has some peculiar characteristics: The government is prohibited by the constitution from printing dollar bills to cover deficits or pay its debt. The sale or disinvestment of government assets is not always encouraged. Furthermore, the attainment of a sufficiently large and continuous surplus in the federal budget to repay the debt under present budgetary conditions is questionable. The track record of the last two decades of huge budget deficits in the U.S. government attests to this fact.

The alternative left to settle the federal debt is for the government to tax its citizens. This will force the indebted households to participate in the program of repayment of the federal debt. If this happens, the average household debt will be much greater in size than our estimates suggest. We feel strongly that without bringing significant changes in the economic status of households, any attempt to make them pay for government debts in any form would enhance the size of household debts considerably and multiply their economic woes, giving rise to political and social unrest in the country.

**Per Capita Debt**[1]

| | 1985 | 1988 | 1990 | 1991 | 1992 | 1993 |
|---|---|---|---|---|---|---|
| Per Capita | $6,780 | $9,128 | $13,328 | $12,752 | $11,536 | $12,668 |
| Per Capita Federal Debt | $7,635 | $10,617 | $12,518 | $14,271 | $15,780 | $16,879 |
| Per Capita Corporate Debt | $7,100 | $10,565 | $13,000 | $14,535 | $16,023 | $16,879 |
| Per Capita State Debt | $886 | $1,125 | $1,289 | $1,427 | $1,577 | $1,688 |
| Per Capita Household Income | $16,779 | $19,422 | $21,974 | $22,256 | $23,755 | $24,625 |
| Per Capita Interest Paid | $748 | $869 | $1,065 | $1,132 | $1,152 | $1,135 |
| Average per capita household debt for 1990-1993 (in survey area) | | | | | | $12,571 |
| Average per capita federal debt for the 1990-1993 period: | | | | | | $14,862 |
| Average per capita corporate debt for the 1990-1993 period: | | | | | | $15,109 |
| Average per capita state debt for the 1990-1993 period: | | | | | | $ 1,495 |
| Average per capita GNP for the 1990-1993 period: | | | | | | $23,153 |

The per capita federal and corporate debts interestingly enough, appear to have been growing at a pace akin to each other. The per capita household debt was almost at par with the federal per capita debt in 1990, but since then its pace of growth has fallen behind federal per capita debt by 20% to 28% for the 1990-1993 period. In recent times, the federal per capita debt far out paced the growth of the per capita household debt.

[1] Per capita debt at the national level is determined by dividing outstanding debts by total population. For the sake of simplicity, in determining per capita household debt in this survey area, we divided per household debt by 2.5 which is assumed to be the average number of persons living in a household.

## GROUP ANALYSIS[1]

### The Average Size of Home Loans and Income Groups (Income Group)

As home loans in terms of size and importance dominate over other loans, we intend to describe some of the important characteristics of home loans. In highlighting these characteristics, we determined the averages for different income groups, the percentages of households which incurred home loans in the various income groups as well as in the sample. Finally, we have compared the average size of loan for each group with the average size of income of the group to determine the ratio between debt and income.

**$10,000 - $15,000**

| | 1985 | 1988 | 1990 | 1991 | 1992 | 1993 |
|---|---|---|---|---|---|---|
| Average Size of Home Loan | $18,570 | $9,260 | $12,330 | $13,960 | $25,940 | $15,750 |
| Percentages of Indebted Households in this group | 53% | 14% | 9% | 6% | 2% | 7% |
| Indebted Households as % of All Households in this Sample | 6% | 2% | 1% | 1% | 0% | 1% |
| Average Income | $12,231 | $12,787 | $12,152 | $12,232 | $12,413 | $12,390 |
| Average size of home loans of this income group for 1990-1993 period | | | | | | $16,995 |
| Average per year increase in size of home loans for this group during 1990-1993 period | | | | | | $1,140 |
| Average household income for 1990-1993 period | | | | | | $17,323 |

The average size of home loans varied from a low of $13,960 to a high of $25,940, yielding an average of $16,995. This average constitutes 98%

[1]Note to Readers: All group analyses is meant for future researchers. The size of debt, level of income, and interest payments in the future for different income groups can be compared with our findings to determine what changes have occurred to them. The pattern of analysis has a repetitive format and may not be interesting to general readers, but researchers may find our estimates as valuable reference materials. General readers may find a summary of all group analysis in Chapter Ten.

of average household income.[1] The number of households reported to have had home loans in this group varied from 2% to 9%, representing 1% of all households in our sample.

The average per household increase in the size of home loans for this group during the years 1990-1993 was $1,140. The average size of home loans in 1985 and 1988 were $18,570 and $9,260 respectively. The percentages of households that had these loans for these years were 53% and 14% for the group representing 6% and 2% of all households in the sample.

**$15,000 - $20,000**

| | 1985 | 1988 | 1990 | 1991 | 1992 | 1993 |
|---|---|---|---|---|---|---|
| Average Size of Home Loan | $13,510 | $21,380 | $16,790 | $33,303 | $19,431 | $25,018 |
| Percentages of Indebted Households in this group | 82% | 27% | 22% | 26% | 27% | 14% |
| Indebted Households as % of All Households in this Sample | 1% | 3% | 3% | 3% | 3% | 2% |
| Average Income | $17,361 | $18,756 | $17,190 | $17,285 | $17,446 | $17,464 |
| Average size of home loans of this income group for 1990-1993 period | | | | | | $23,567 |
| Average per year increase in size of a home loan for this group during 1990-1993 | | | | | | $2,743 |
| Average household income for 1990-1993 period | | | | | | $17,346 |

The average size of home loans varied from a low of $19,430 to a high of $33,030, yielding an average of $23,567 for the 1990-1993 period. This average constitutes 136% of average household income. The number of households having had home loans in this group varied from 14% to 27%, representing 2% to 3% of all households in our sample.

The average per household increase in the size of home loans for this group during the years 1990-1993 was $2,743. The average size of home loans in 1985 and 1988 were $13,510 and $21,380 respectively. The percentages of households with these loans were 27% and 82% for the group representing 1% and 3% of all households in the sample.

---

[1]Here the average household income represent the average of the last four years (1990 - 1993).

$20,000 - $25,000

| | 1985 | 1988 | 1990 | 1991 | 1992 | 1993 |
|---|---|---|---|---|---|---|
| Average Size of Home Loan | $14,140 | $27,350 | $20,500 | $17,440 | $13,026 | $19,961 |
| Percentage of Indebted Households in this group | 48% | 36% | 31% | 25% | 21% | 29% |
| Indebted Households as % of All Households in Sample | 6% | 4% | 3% | 2% | 2% | 2% |
| Average Income | $22,164 | $23,301 | $21,927 | $22,270 | $22,732 | $22,793 |
| Average size of home loans of this income group for 1990-1993 period | | | | | | $17,732 |
| Average per year decrease in size of a home loan for this group during 1990-1993 | | | | | | ($180) |
| Average household income for 1990-1993 period | | | | | | $22,431 |

The average size of home loans varied from a low of $13,026 to a high of $20,500, yielding an average of $17,732 for the 1990-1993 period. This average constitutes 79% of average household income. The number of households reported to have had home loans in this group varied from 21% to 31%, representing 2% to 3% of all households in our sample. The average per household decrease in the size of home loans for this group during the years 1990-1993 was $108. The average size of home loans in 1985 and 1988 were $14,140 and $27,350 respectively. The percentages of households that had these loans for these years were 36% and 48% for the group representing 4% and 6% of all households in the sample.

$25,000 - $30,000

| | 1985 | 1988 | 1990 | 1991 | 1992 | 1993 |
|---|---|---|---|---|---|---|
| Average Size of Home Loan | $19,730 | $16,850 | $20,230 | $23,770 | $18,933 | $23,930 |
| Percentage of Indebted Households in this group | 65% | 59% | 46% | 56% | 44% | 32% |
| Indebted Households as % of All Households in Sample | 1% | 7% | 6% | 2% | 3% | 2% |
| Average Income | $27,522 | $27,892 | $26,951 | $28,080 | $27,273 | $27,475 |
| Average size of home loans of this income group for 1990-1993 period | | | | | | $21,716 |
| Average per year increase in the size of a home loan for this group during 1990-1993 | | | | | | $1,233 |
| Average household income for 1990-1993 period | | | | | | $27,445 |

The average size of home loans varied from a low of $18,933 to a high of $23,930, yielding an average of $21,716 for the 1990-1993 period. This average constitutes 79% of average household income. The number of households reported to have had home loans in this group varied from 32% to 56%, representing 2% to 3% of all households in our sample.

The average per household increase in the size of home loans for this group during the years 1990-1993 was $1,233. The average sizes of home loans in 1985 and 1988 were $16,850 and $19,730 respectively. The percentages of households that had these loans for these years were 59% and 65% for the group representing 7% and 1% of all households in the sample.

**$30,000 -$35,000**

| | 1985 | 1988 | 1990 | 1991 | 1992 | 1993 |
|---|---|---|---|---|---|---|
| Average Size of Home Loans | $13,730 | $25,090 | $22,960 | $17,080 | $19,746 | $19,941 |
| Percentage of Indebted Households in this group | 67% | 50% | 47% | 46% | 43% | 43% |
| Indebted Households as % of All Households in Sample | 9% | 5% | 4% | 3% | 3% | 3% |
| Average Income | $32,617 | $31,706 | $32,752 | $32,511 | $32,326 | $32,680 |
| Average size of home loans of this income group for 1990-1993 period | | | | | | $19,932 |
| Average per year increase in the size of a home loan for this group during 1990-1993 | | | | | | $1,006 |
| Average household income for 1990-1993 period | | | | | | $32,567 |

The average size of home loans varied from a low of $17,080 to a high of $22,960, yielding an average of $19,932 for the 1990-1993 period. This average constitutes 61% of average household income. The number of households reported to have had home loans in this group varied from 43% to 47%, representing 3% to 4% of all households in our sample.

The average per household increase in the size of home loans for this group during the years 1990-1993 was $1,006. The average sizes of home loans in 1985 and 1988 were $13,730 and $25,090 respectively. The percentages of households that had these loans for these years were 50% and 67% for the group representing 5% and 9% of all households in the sample.

$35,000 - $40,000

| | 1985 | 1988 | 1990 | 1991 | 1992 | 1993 |
|---|---|---|---|---|---|---|
| Average Size of Home Loans | $20,020 | $25,150 | $27,980 | $22,570 | $22,830 | $29,039 |
| Percentage of Indebted Households in this group | 82% | 7% | 65% | 59% | 62% | 60% |
| Indebted Households as % of All Households in Sample | 5% | 7% | 3% | 4% | 20% | 23% |
| Average Income | $38,617 | $39,048 | $37,604 | $37,397 | $37,200 | $37,052 |
| Average size of home loans of this income group for 1990-1993 period | | | | | | $25,605 |
| Average per year increase in the size of a home loan for this group during 1990-1993 | | | | | | $353 |
| Average household income for 1990-1993 period | | | | | | $37,313 |

The average size of home loans varied from a low of $22,570 to a high of $29,039, yielding an average of $25,605 for the 1990-1993 period. This average constitutes 69% of average household income. The number of households reported to have had home loans in this group varied from 59% to 65%, representing 3% to 23% of all households in our sample.

The average per household increase in the size of home loans for this group during the years 1990-1993 was $353. The average sizes of home loans in 1985 and 1988 were $20,020 and $25,150 respectively. The percentages of households that had these loans for these years were 82% and 7% for the group representing 5% and 7% of all households in the sample.

$40,000 - $45,000

| | 1985 | 1988 | 1990 | 1991 | 1992 | 1993 |
|---|---|---|---|---|---|---|
| Average Size of Home Loan | $22,460 | $26,490 | $27,350 | $21,340 | $18,368 | $20,092 |
| Percentage of Indebted Households in this group | 64% | 69% | 71% | 75% | 67% | 21% |
| Indebted Households as % of All Households in Sample | 5% | 5% | 5% | 5% | 4% | 3% |
| Average Income | $42,884 | $42,474 | $43,006 | $42,282 | $42,317 | $42,214 |
| Average size of home loans of this income group for 1990-1993 period | | | | | | $21,788 |
| The average per year decrease in the size of a home loan for this group during 1990-1993: | | | | | | ($2,419) |
| The average household income for the 1990-1993 period was: | | | | | | $42,455 |

The average size of home loans in this group varied from a low of $18,368 to a high of $27,350, yielding an average of $21,788 for the 1990-1993 period. This constitutes 51% of the group's average income for the last four years of the survey. The number of households in this group that paid interest on home loans varied from 21% to 75%. This frequency represents 3% to 5% of all households in the sample.

The average decrease in the size of home loans for this group during the years 1990-1993 was $2,419 per household per year. The sizes of home loans in 1985 and 1988 were $22,460 and $26,490 respectively. The percentage of households having these loans for these two years were 64% and 69% for the group and accounted for 5% and 7% of all households in the sample.

**$45,000 - $50,000**

| | 1985 | 1988 | 1990 | 1991 | 1992 | 1993 |
|---|---|---|---|---|---|---|
| Average Size of Home Loans | $19,900 | $17,630 | $28,480 | $29,420 | $28,792 | $29,364 |
| Percentage of Indebted Households in this group | 79% | 40% | 75% | 37% | 68% | 81% |
| Indebted Households as % of All Households in Sample | 4% | 1% | 5% | 4% | 4% | 4% |
| Average Income | $47,994 | $54,749 | $47,071 | $47,697 | $47,933 | $47,660 |
| Average size of home loans of this income group for 1990-1993 period | | | | | | $29,014 |
| Average per year increase in the size of a home loan for this group during 1990-1993 | | | | | | $295 |
| Average household income for the 1990-1993 period | | | | | | $47,590 |

The average size of home loans varied from a low of $28,480 to a high of $29,420, yielding an average of $29,014 for the 1990-1993 period. This average constitutes 61% of average household income. The number of households reported to have had home loans in this group varied from 37% to 81%, representing 4% of all households in our sample.

The average per household increase in the size of home loans for this group during the years 1990-1993 was $295. The average sizes of home loans in 1985 and 1988 were $19,900 and $17,630 respectively. The percentages of households that had these loans for these years were 40% and 79% for the group representing 1% and 4% of all households in the sample.

$50,000 - $55,000

| | 1985 | 1988 | 1990 | 1991 | 1992 | 1993 |
|---|---|---|---|---|---|---|
| Average Size of Home Loans | $23,820 | $29,420 | $39,130 | $61,990 | $33,140 | $20,431 |
| Percentage of Indebted Households in this group | 1% | 75% | 56% | 38% | 75% | 53% |
| Indebted Households as % of All Households in Sample | 1% | 1% | 2% | 1% | 2% | 2% |
| Average Income | $51,847 | $52,671 | $52,682 | $52,159 | $52,343 | $52,802 |
| Average size of home loans of this income group for 1990-1993 period | | | | | | $36,602 |
| Average per year decrease in the size of a home loan for this group during 1990-1993 | | | | | | ($6,233) |
| Average household income for the 1990-1993 period | | | | | | $52,497 |

The average size of home loans varied from a low of $20,431 to a high of $61,990, yielding an average of $36,602 for the 1990-1993 period. This average constitutes 70% of average household income. The number of households reported to have had home loans in this group varied from 38% to 75%, representing 1% to 2% of all households in our sample.

The average per household decrease in the size of home loans for this group during the years 1990-1993 was $6,233. The average sizes of home loans in 1985 and 1988 were $23,820 and $29,420 respectively. The percentages of households that had these loans for these years were 1% and 75% for the group and representing 1% of all households in the sample.

$55,000 - $60,000

| | 1985 | 1988 | 1990 | 1991 | 1992 | 1993 |
|---|---|---|---|---|---|---|
| Average Size of Home Loan | $12,870 | $6,170 | $36,310 | $27,130 | $18,192 | $36,119 |
| Percentage of Indebted Households in this group | 1% | 50% | 7% | 61% | 38% | 71% |
| Indebted Households as % of All Households in Sample | 2% | 4% | 5% | 3% | 1% | 3% |
| Average Income | $56,898 | $55,524 | $57,806 | $57,387 | $57,491 | $57,463 |
| Average size of home loans of this income group for 1990-1993 period | | | | | | $29,635 |
| The average per year decrease in the size of a home loan for this group during 1990-1993 | | | | | | ($64) |
| The average household income for the 1990-1993 period was: | | | | | | $57,537 |

The average size of home loans varied from a low of $18,192 to a high of $36,310, yielding an average of $29,635 for the 1990-1993 period. This average constitutes 52% of average household income. The number of households reported to have had home loans in this group varied from 7% to 71%, representing 1% to 5% of all households in our sample.

The average per household decrease in the size of home loans for this group during the years 1990-1993 was $64. The average sizes of home loans in 1985 and 1988 were $12,870 and $6,170 respectively. The percentages of households that had these loans for these years were 1% and 50% for the group representing 2% and 4% of all households in the sample.

$60,000 - $102,000

| | 1985 | 1988 | 1990 | 1991 | 1992 | 1993 |
|---|---|---|---|---|---|---|
| Average Size of Home Loans | $6,930 | $9,120 | $36,200 | $34,190 | $34,501 | $31,695 |
| Percentage of Indebted Households in this group | 1% | 75% | 61% | 78% | 69% | 77% |
| Indebted Households as % of All Households in this Sample | 1% | 1% | 3% | 7% | 6% | 8% |
| Average Income | $60,175 | $62,659 | $63,454 | $62,149 | $63,114 | $62,266 |
| Average size of home loans of this income group for 1990-1993 period | | | | | | $33,564 |
| Average per year decrease in the size of a home loan for this group during 1990-1993 | | | | | | ($1,502) |
| Average household income for the 1990-1993 period | | | | | | $62,746 |

The average size of home loans varied from a low of $31,695 to a high of $36,200, yielding an average of $33,564 for the 1990-1993 period. This average constitutes 53% of average household income. The number of households reported to have had home loans in this group varied from 61% to 78%, representing 3% to 8% of all households in our sample.

The average per household increase in the size of home loans for this group during the years 1990-1993 was $1,502. The average sizes of home loans in 1985 and 1988 were $6,930 and $9,120 respectively. The percentage of households that had these loans for these years was 1% representing about 1% of all households in the sample.

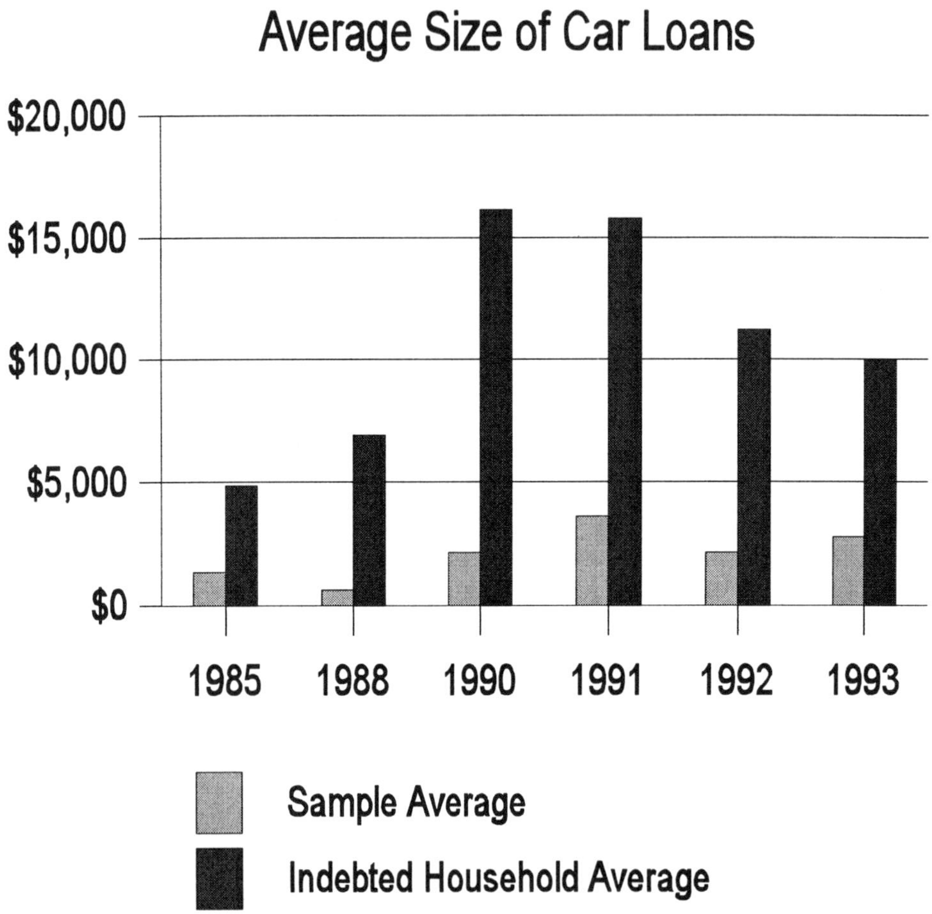
Average Size of Car Loans
$20,000
$15,000
$10,000
$5,000
$0
1985
1988
1990
1991
1992
1993
Sample Average
Indebted Household Average

**Figure 7**

Average Size of Car Loan

| Income | 1985 | | | 1988 | | | 1990 | | | 1991 | | |
|---|---|---|---|---|---|---|---|---|---|---|---|---|
| | Average Size of Car Loan | f/n[1] | f/N[2] | Average Size of Car Loan | f/n[1] | f/N[2] | Average Size of Car Loan | f/n[1] | f/N[2] | Average Size of Car Loan | f/n[1] | f/N[2] |
| $ 0-4,999 | $0 | 0.00 | 0.00 | $0 | 0.00 | 0.00 | $0 | 0.00 | 0.00 | $0 | 0.00 | 0.00 |
| $5,000-9,999 | $3,700 | 0.10 | 0.01 | $0 | 0.00 | 0.00 | $0 | 0.00 | 0.00 | $0 | 0.00 | 0.00 |
| $10,000-14,999 | $4,730 | 0.21 | 0.02 | $5,680 | 0.03 | 0.004 | $0 | 0.00 | 0.00 | $7,030 | 0.1 | 0.01 |
| $15,000-19,999 | $4,840 | 0.18 | 0.02 | $5,880 | 0.12 | 0.01 | $24,910 | 0.02 | 0.00 | $7,280 | 0.05 | 0.01 |
| $20,000-24,999 | $5,630 | 0.24 | 0.03 | $7,610 | 0.07 | 0.01 | $13,060 | 0.1 | 0.01 | $11,880 | 0.14 | 0.01 |
| $25,000-29,999 | $5,170 | 0.35 | 0.05 | $9,100 | 0.07 | 0.01 | $0 | 0.00 | 0.00 | $16,690 | 0.25 | 0.01 |
| $30,000-34,999 | $4,630 | 0.42 | 0.06 | $8,010 | 0.2 | 0.02 | $12,380 | 0.13 | 0.01 | $12,920 | 0.42 | 0.03 |
| $35,000-39,999 | $4,410 | 0.45 | 0.03 | $2,870 | 0.13 | 0.01 | $15,820 | 0.15 | 0.01 | $16,960 | 0.18 | 0.01 |
| $40,000-44,999 | $7,830 | 0.29 | 0.02 | $9,420 | 0.13 | 0.01 | $16,950 | 0.39 | 0.03 | $16,150 | 0.5 | 0.03 |
| $45,000-49,999 | $2,180 | 0.33 | 0.02 | $0 | 0.00 | 0.00 | $14,130 | 0.42 | 0.03 | $15,980 | 0.2 | 0.02 |
| $50,000-54,999 | $4,560 | 0.01 | 0.01 | $0 | 0.00 | 0.00 | $19,030 | 0.31 | 0.01 | $15,400 | 0.46 | 0.02 |
| $55,000-59,999 | $1,920 | 0.33 | 0.01 | $0 | 0.00 | 0.00 | $13,910 | 0.11 | 0.01 | $13,870 | 0.39 | 0.02 |
| $60,000-64,999 | $0 | 0.00 | 0.00 | $0 | 0.00 | 0.00 | $18,080 | 0.38 | 0.03 | $20,660 | 0.69 | 0.06 |

*f/n[1]:* *frequencies of indebted households*
*f/N[2]:* *frequencies among sampled households*

## Size of Car Loan

The average size of car loans, for all income groups and for all years of the survey, varied between $1,920 and $20,660. Interestingly enough, in 1985 and 1988, the outstanding average size of a car loan varied between $1,920 and $9,620. Most outstanding loans during this period were below $10,000, but the situation has changed rapidly since then.

We noticed that between 1990 and 1991, the outstanding size of car loans (of the reported cases) varied between $7,030 and $24,910. In different income groups, the percent of households having outstanding car loans in 1990-1991 varied between 1% and 69%. In 1985 and 1988, the percentages of households having car loans, were 11% and 45%. For the entire sample, the percentages of households having outstanding car loans varied between 1% and 6%.

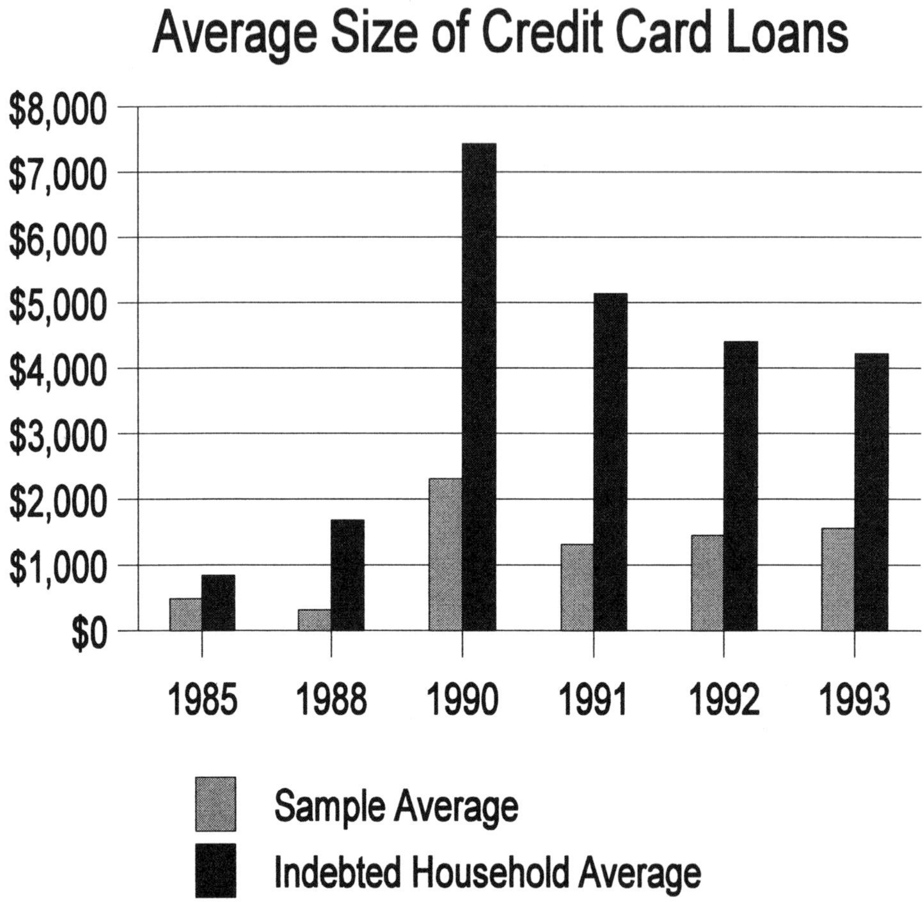
Average Size of Credit Card Loans
$8,000
$7,000
$6,000
$5,000
$4,000
$3,000
$2,000
$1,000
$0
1985
1988
1990
1991
1992
1993
Sample Average
Indebted Household Average

**Figure 8**

Average Size of Credit Card Loan

| Income | 1985 | | | 1988 | | | 1990 | | | 1991 | | |
|---|---|---|---|---|---|---|---|---|---|---|---|---|
| | Average Size of Credit Card Loan | f/n[1] | f/N[2] | Average Size of Credit Card Loan | f/n[1] | f/N[2] | Average Size of Credit Card Loan | f/n[1] | f/N[2] | Average Size of Credit Card Loan | f/n[1] | f/N[2] |
| $ 0-4,999 | $0 | 0.00 | 0.00 | $0 | 0.00 | 0.00 | $0 | 0.00 | 0.00 | $0 | 0.00 | 0.00 |
| $5,000-9,999- | $460 | 0.50 | 0.06 | $410 | 0.10 | 0.01 | $5,340 | 0.13 | 0.02 | $0 | 0.00 | 0.00 |
| $10,000-14,999 | $920 | 0.47 | 0.05 | $11,410 | 0.06 | 0.01 | $6,400 | 0.05 | 0.01 | $4,090 | 0.10 | 0.01 |
| $15,000-19,999 | $1,160 | 0.41 | 0.05 | $2,130 | 0.23 | 0.03 | $7,300 | 0.45 | 0.06 | $2,740 | 0.10 | 0.01 |
| $20,000-24,999 | $2,160 | 0.81 | 0.10 | $3,330 | 0.32 | 0.03 | $2,180 | 0.44 | 0.04 | $2,080 | 0.25 | 0.02 |
| $25,000-29,999 | $1,050 | 0.70 | 0.10 | $2,880 | 0.32 | 0.03 | $540 | 0.38 | 0.02 | $2,080 | 0.19 | 0.01 |
| $30,000-34,999 | $2,700 | 0.50 | 0.07 | $3,140 | 0.35 | 0.03 | $3,180 | 0.56 | 0.05 | $3,520 | 0.33 | 0.02 |
| $35,000-39,999 | $1,460 | 0.45 | 0.03 | $2,190 | 0.26 | 0.03 | $3,370 | 0.70 | 0.04 | $5,940 | 0.27 | 0.02 |
| $40,000-44,999 | $950 | 0.79 | 0.06 | $330 | 0.06 | 0.00 | $7,330 | 0.79 | 0.06 | $5,010 | 0.50 | 0.03 |
| $45,000-49,999 | $2,860 | 0.89 | 0.05 | $0 | 0.00 | 0.00 | $7,640 | 0.88 | 0.06 | $5,310 | 0.34 | 0.03 |
| $50,000-54,999 | $500 | 0.50 | 0.01 | $0 | 0.00 | 0.00 | $7,290 | 0.63 | 0.03 | $5,360 | 0.54 | 0.02 |
| $55,000-59,999 | $960 | 0.33 | 0.01 | $3,570 | 0.50 | 0.00 | $7,430 | 0.78 | 0.06 | $8,850 | 0.33 | 0.02 |
| $60,000-64,999 | $0 | 0.01 | 0.01 | $2,250 | 0.25 | 0.00 | $4,980 | 0.71 | 0.04 | $6,460 | 0.69 | 0.06 |

*f/n[1]:* *frequencies of indebted households*
*f/N[2]:* *frequencies among sampled households*

## Average Size of Credit Card Loan

The average size of credit card loans (of the reported cases) for all income groups and for all the years of the survey varied between $330 and $8850. In 1985, the average size of credit card loans was only $2860. With the passage of time, the average size of credit card loans began increasing in size to reach as high as $8850 in 1991 for some income groups.

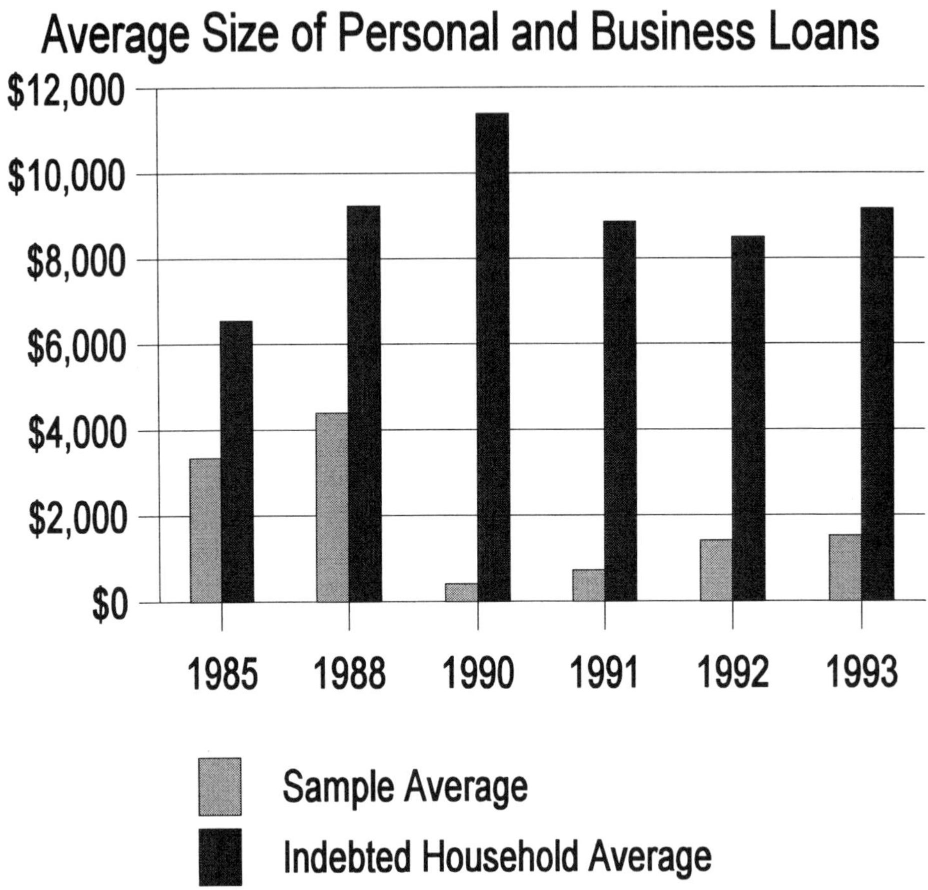
Average Size of Personal and Business Loans
$12,000
$10,000
$8,000
$6,000
$4,000
$2,000
$0
1985
1988
1990
1991
1992
1993
Sample Average
Indebted Household Average

Figure 9

Average Size of Personal & Business Loans

| Income | 1985 | | | 1988 | | | 1990 | | | 1991 | | |
|---|---|---|---|---|---|---|---|---|---|---|---|---|
| | Average Size of Personal & Business Loan | f/n[1] | f/N[2] | Average Size of Personal & Business Loan | f/n[1] | f/N[2] | Average Size of Personal & Business Loan | f/n[1] | f/N[2] | Average Size of Personal & Business Loan | f/n[1] | f/N[2] |
| $0-4,999 | $0 | 0.00 | 0.00 | $1,920 | 0.33 | 0.00 | $0 | 0.00 | 0.00 | $0 | 0.00 | 0.00 |
| $5,000-9,999 | $1,910 | 0.15 | 0.02 | $9,550 | 0.23 | 0.02 | $0 | 0.00 | 0.00 | $13,540 | 0.08 | 0.01 |
| $10,000-14,999 | $6,230 | 0.63 | 0.07 | $11,360 | 0.25 | 0.01 | $0 | 0.00 | 0.00 | $5,110 | 0.06 | 0.01 |
| $15,000-19,999 | $3,890 | 0.64 | 0.08 | $7,570 | 0.31 | 0.04 | $0 | 0.00 | 0.00 | $7,360 | 0.02 | 0.00 |
| $20,000-24,999 | $3,030 | 0.33 | 0.04 | $7,990 | 0.50 | 0.05 | $11,910 | 0.05 | 0.01 | $1,130 | 0.07 | 0.01 |
| $25,000-29,999 | $5,930 | 0.42 | 0.06 | $7,960 | 0.52 | 0.06 | $0 | 0.00 | 0.00 | $4,590 | 0.19 | 0.01 |
| $30,000-34,999 | $7,510 | 0.50 | 0.07 | $6,060 | 0.50 | 0.05 | $15,920 | 0.06 | 0.01 | $9,540 | 0.13 | 0.01 |
| $35,000-39,999 | $11,580 | 0.73 | 0.05 | $10,750 | 0.83 | 0.09 | $0 | 0.00 | 0.00 | $4,580 | 0.05 | 0.00 |
| $40,000-44,999 | $10,700 | 0.57 | 0.05 | $10,860 | 0.94 | 0.07 | $10,000 | 0.11 | 0.01 | $7,580 | 0.17 | 0.01 |
| $45,000-49,999 | $6,650 | 0.01 | 0.05 | $5,260 | 0.40 | 0.01 | $13,480 | 0.13 | 0.01 | $0 | 0.00 | 0.00 |
| $50,000-54,999 | $13,430 | 0.50 | 0.01 | $15,430 | 0.75 | 0.01 | $7,060 | 0.13 | 0.01 | $0 | 0.00 | 0.00 |
| $55,000-59,999 | $5,930 | 0.01 | 0.02 | $2,410 | 1.00 | 0.01 | $12,810 | 0.14 | 0.00 | $12,830 | 0.06 | 0.00 |
| $60,000-64,999 | $2,420 | 0.01 | 0.01 | $24,910 | 0.50 | 0.01 | $6,520 | 0.05 | 0.00 | $12,220 | 0.28 | 0.02 |

*f/n[1]:* *frequencies of indebted households*
*f/N[2]:* *frequencies among sampled households*

## Size of Personal and Business Loans

The average size of personal and business loans varied between $1,920 and $24,910 for 1985 and 1988. In 1985, the highest average for personal and business loans was $13,480. The average general size of personal and a business loans for the years 1985 and 1988 was between $1,910 and $10,860 for households with income levels varying from $5,000 to $45,000. Households with incomes of more than $45,000 (up to $65,000) had personal and business loans that averaged up to $24,910. The average size of personal and business loans varied between $1,130 and $13,480 during 1990 and 1991.

**The Size of Debt as % of Different Income Groups**

| | Income (In Thousands) | 1985 | 1988 | 1990 | 1991 | 1992 | 1993 |
|---|---|---|---|---|---|---|---|
| Group I | 0 - 5 | 742% | 49% | 0 | 0 | 0 | 0 |
| Group II | 5 - 10 | 101% | 158% | 86% | 152% | 0 | 0 |
| Group III | 10 - 15 | 122% | 109% | 93% | 69% | 188% | 136% |
| Group IV | 15 - 20 | 85% | 95% | 99% | 165% | 112% | 138% |
| Group V | 20 - 25 | 50% | 108% | 91% | 65% | 59% | 87% |
| Group VI | 25 -30 | 65% | 77.5% | 85% | 90% | 70% | 86% |
| Group VII | 30 - 35 | 52% | 77% | 86% | 76% | 66% | 61% |
| Group VIII | 35 - 40 | 78% | 84% | 82% | 72% | 62% | 82% |
| Group IX | 40 - 45 | 5% | 74% | 93% | 72% | 44% | 58% |
| Group X | 45 - 50 | 53% | 48% | 89% | 65% | 62% | 62% |
| Group XI | 50 - 55 | 70% | 53% | 101% | 122% | 63% | 39% |
| Group XII | 55 - 60 | 3% | 37% | 79% | 68% | 31% | 63% |
| Group XIII | 60 - 102 | 16% | 29% | 67% | 89% | 50% | 42% |

Group III, with income levels between $10 and 15 thousand, had debts that equaled 109% to 188% of their income during the years of the survey. Group IV, with income levels between $15 and 20 thousand, owed outstanding debt that equaled about 99% to 138% of their income during our survey years. Group V, with income levels between $20 and 25 thousand, owed debts that equaled 50% to 108% of their income. On the other hand, households with income levels exceeding $55 thousand had debts that equaled 31% to 89% of their income.

**Percentages of Households in Debt (For All Households) and Relation to Income**

| Size of the Debt as % of Income | Indebted Households 1985 | Indebted Households 1988 | Indebted Households 1990 | Indebted Households 1991 |
|---|---|---|---|---|
| 1% - 25% | 26% | 18% | 13% | 15% |
| 25% - 50% | 21% | 14% | 19% | 18% |
| 50% - 80% | 18% | 20% | 20% | 20% |
| 80% - 100% | 08% | 16% | 06% | 05% |
| More than 100% | 25% | 29% | 41% | 31% |

We notice that a significant number of households – 25% to 41% of indebted households during the period of our survey – had loans that equaled more than 100% of their income. Any loan that exceeds 100% of income is distressing. It is interesting to note that in all four years, about 20% of indebted households had loans that equaled 50% to 80% of their income.

The size of an outstanding debt, if equal to or exceeding a person's yearly income at any point of time, becomes psychologically depressing particularly for those who have to count every penny to keep afloat and out of debt-related problems. The large size of a debt is not a problem if it is invested in acceptable assets that yield adequate income to service and repay the debt.

Unfortunately, this is not the case with the household debts in mid-sized cities in the U.S. A significant part of the debt is used for consumption purposes, though a part is used to purchase assets such as homes, cars and other durable goods which are not liquid in character. A part of the debt may be used to buy financial assets that might give some kind of income in the form of interest earnings, but this is usually not adequate to cover the cost of credit on these household debts.

In view of the character and uses of this debt, we see that a larger debt size is regressive in its burden to households having a low income. Another interesting characteristic that emerges from the data is that households with low incomes or households living below the poverty level generally have debt sizes that exceed their yearly income. At times, outstanding debt averages equals almost 200% of their income.

We have expressed important national debts in terms of the average household debt and added them to get a glimpse of the immensity of debt that has kept the economy of this nation moving. As we stated earlier, the size of the debt itself is not something to worry about as long as it can be serviced or repaid. However, this is not happening with household debts. The present terms, conditions, and cost of debt have been matters of concern for households as well as for the present author. In addition to the present outstanding debt of households, the federal debt poses a real threat to households.

The constitution of this country prevents the federal government from printing dollar bills to cover the deficit of the federal government. Under these circumstances in order to pay their enormous debt the federal government may be forced to impose tax on its citizens. This move would amount to a shifting of the debt to households which will increase their already sizeable burden of debt. Household leverage in itself is not something to be overly concerned with as long as the household incomes permit the servicing of the debt efficiently, but this is not happening in small and mid-sized cities.

Households are compelled to borrow to supplement their incomes. There is nothing wrong with the borrowing, but what disturbs the present author are the terms and the conditions and the costs of borrowing, as well as the harassment by creditors and the economic hardship that the borrowers generally undergo, especially if they fail to keep up with their payments, not because of their own fault, but because of the unforseen circumstances that often confront them.

# CHAPTER FOUR
## THE BURDEN OF HOUSEHOLD DEBT

### Introduction

The monetary burden of household debt is essentially the monetary cost of servicing the debt. It includes interest rates, other costs of borrowing, late fees, and penalties that households are often required to pay. Interest payment is one of the important sources of income erosion for the households. A household budget cannot be conceived of without having some provision for the interest payments which are of paramount concern for the householders.

In our study, "interest" represents an amount of money that has to be removed from the household's discretionary outlays. Under the present credit environment, the cost of servicing debt in one form or another has become a major and painful drain on household income. This is more true of the low-income households than of the wealthy. Interest expenditure for some low-income households exceeds 25% of income, and we have shown in the case studies in Chapter Six that some farmers paid interest that equaled well over 50% of their income. The rate of interest on credit card, pawnshop, professional money lender and other indigenous sources of debt varies from 20% to 300%[1]. Finally the current official low interest rates are of no value to these households as they have been marked as credit-risks by the credit institutions of the country and they pay much higher interest rates than the official rates of interest.

In order to assess the burden of debt, the market interest rates of different years have been collected to show the changes that occurred in the cost of credit in different years. We have endeavored to determine the degree of influence that the discount rate of the Federal Reserve Bank and the prime rate of New York banks exert on the rates that the households pay on their loans.

---

[1]The interest rates of different loan giving agencies are discussed in detail in the prime rate and regional rates section of this study.

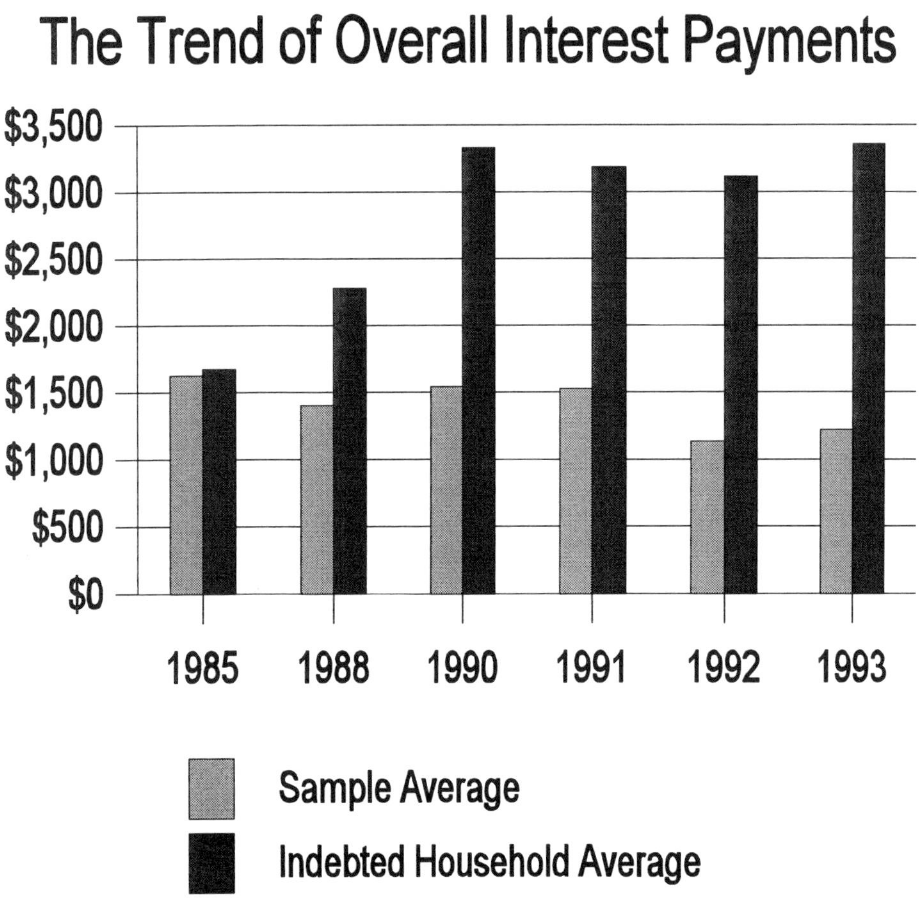


**Figure 10**

(Average is for all households)

**The Trend of Overall Interest Payments: Sample Averages**

| | 1985 | 1988 | 1990 | 1991 | 1992 | 1993 |
|---|---|---|---|---|---|---|
| The Sample Average Interest Payment[1] | $1,630 | $1,405 | $1,543 | $1,528 | $1,134 | $1,221 |
| The Average Size of Interest Paid by Indebted Households | $1,678 | $2,282 | $3,332 | $3,188 | $3,118 | $3,359 |
| The sample average interest payment for the 1990-1993 period | | | | | | $1,357 |
| Per year change[2] in sample average interest payment for the 1990-1993 period | | | | | | -$107 |
| The average interest payment by indebted household for the 1990-1993 period | | | | | | $3,249 |
| Per year changes in the average interest payment for the 1990-1993 period | | | | | | $9 |

The average interest payment by all households in the sample varied between $1,221 and $1,543, yielding an average interest payment of $1,357 per year for the 1990-1993 period. The interest payments made by indebted households gave a different picture.

The average size of interest payments varies between $3,118 and $3,332 (1990-1993 period) yielding an average of $3,249, which is almost twice as high as was the average interest payment in the beginning of this survey in 1985. This means that there has been an almost 100% increase in the interest payments of indebted households since we started collecting data. In short, the average interest payments of all households in the sample center around $1,360 while those of indebted households hover around $3,250 a year.

[1]The average for the 1990-1993 period has been calculated by adding the interest payments of these years and dividing it by four.

[2]Per year per household changes have been determined by finding net changes during the years and dividing it by three. This method has been followed throughout the book.

**Sample Average Size of Interest Paid (Item Wise)**[1]

| | 1985 | 1988 | 1990 | 1991 | 1992 | 1993 |
|---|---|---|---|---|---|---|
| Sample Average Size of Interest Paid on Home Loan | $1,070 | $844 | $1,053 | $960 | $769 | $886 |
| Sample Average Size of Interest Paid on Car Loan | $137 | $64 | $217 | $363 | $217 | $280 |
| Sample Average Size of Interest Paid on Personal & Business Loan | $335 | $440 | $420 | $740 | $142 | $153 |
| Sample Average Size of Interest Paid on Credit Card Loan | $88 | $56 | $231 | $131 | $145 | $156 |

[1]Sample average represents the average of all households in the sample including those which did not pay interest. Figures for 1992 and 1993 are estimated. Excepting interest payments on home loans, other interest payments in 1992 and 1993 are under reported.

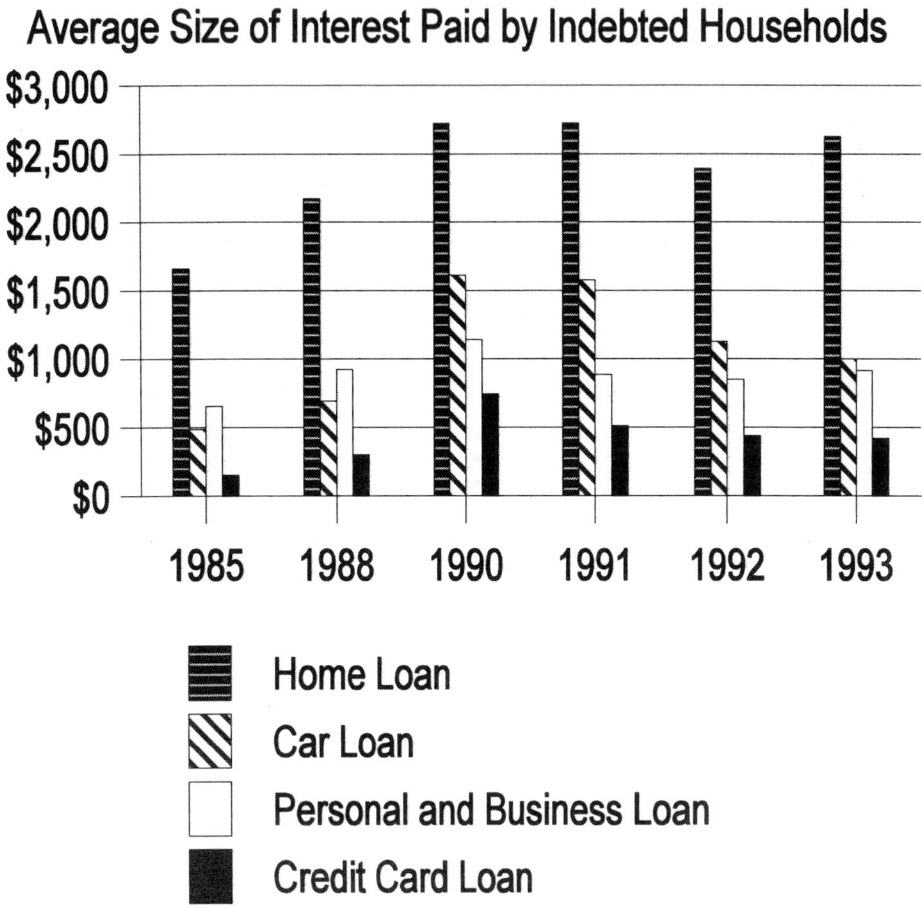
Average Size of Interest Paid by Indebted Households
$3,000
$2,500
$2,000
$1,500
$1,000
$500
$0
1985
1988
1990
1991
1992
1993
Home Loan
Car Loan
Personal and Business Loan
Credit Card Loan

Figure 11

**Average Size of Interest Paid by Indebted Household (Item Wise)[1]**

| Indebted Households | 1985 | 1988 | 1990 | 1991 | 1992 | 1993 |
|---|---|---|---|---|---|---|
| Home Loan Average Interest Paid | $1,663 (64%) | $2,172 (39%) | $2,723 (39%) | $2,728 (35%) | $2,394 (32%) | $2,629 (33%) |
| Car Loan Average Interest Paid | $485 (28%) | $693 (9%) | $1,613 (13%) | $1,579 (23%) | $1,126 (8%) | $1,000 (15%) |
| Personal and Business Loan Average Interest Paid | $655 (51%) | $923 (48%) | $1,139 (4%) | $886 (8%) | $850 N/A[2] | $915 N/A |
| Credit Card Loan Average Interest Paid | $152 (84%) | $303 (19%) | $743 (31%) | $514 (25%) | $440 (13%) | $422 (20%) |

| | |
|---|---|
| The average interest payment per household on home loan for the 1990-1993 period was | $2,619 |
| The average interest payment on car loan for the 1990-1993 period (per household) was | $1,330 |
| The average interest payment on personal and business loan for the 1990-1993 period (per household) was | $948 |
| The average interest payment on credit card loan for the 1990-1993 period (per household) was | $530 |

The average interest payment on home loans for the 1990-1993 period varied from a low of $2,394 to a high of $2,728, yielding an average of $2,619 and a decrease in interest payments of $31 per year per indebted household. Average interest payments on home loans for 1985 and 1988 were $1,663 and $2,172 respectively. Average interest paid on car loans varied between $1,000 and $1,613, yielding an average of $1,330 and a decrease of $204 per year for the 1990-1993 period. The average interest payment on car loan varied between $1,000 and $1,613 for the years 1985 and 1988 respectively.

[1]Percentages in parenthesis indicate the proportion of indebted households in the sample paying interest on this type of loan.

[2]Adequate data on these items during these two years were not available. The averages of these two years are bound to be underestimated.

Interest payments on personal and business loans varied between $850 and $1,139, yielding an average $948 and a decrease in interest payments of $74 per year for the same period. The average interest payment on personal and business loans varied between $655 and $923 for the years 1985 and 1988 respectively. Interest payments on credit card loans varied between $422 and $743 yielding an average of $530, with an average decrease in interest payment of $107 per year for 1990-1993 period.

The average interest payments on credit cards were $152 and $303 for 1985 and 1988 respectively, showing an increasing trend in interest payment on credit card loans for the same period. Having shown the general trend of interest payments in the survey area, we will now analyze the trend of interest payment by households in different income groups. This takes us close to the reality of the households' position with respect to interest payments.

## GROUP ANALYSIS[1]

### Interest Payments by Different Income Groups

(for all items of interest payment)

**$10,000 - $15,000**

| | 1985 | 1988 | 1990 | 1991 | 1992 | 1993 |
|---|---|---|---|---|---|---|
| Average Size of Interest Paid | $1,508 | $1,362 | $1,242 | $868 | $2,594 | $1,575 |
| Percentage of Households Paying Interest in this Group | 100% | 40% | 13% | 5% | 1% | 7% |
| Interest Paying Households as % of All Households in the Sample | 10% | 5% | 2% | 1% | 0% | 1% |
| Average Income | $12,231 | $12,787 | $12,152 | $12,232 | $12,113 | $12,390 |
| Average size of interest paid by households for 1990-1993 was | | | | | | $1,570 |
| Average increase in interest paid for this group during 1990-1993 | | | | | | $111 |
| Average income of the group for the 1990-1993 years was | | | | | | $12,222 |

The average amount of interest paid by households in this income group varied from $868 to $2,594, yielding an average of $1,570. This constitutes 13% of the group's average income of the last four years of the survey. The number of households that paid interest in this group varied from 1% to 13%, representing 1% to 2% of all households in the sample.

The average increase in interest payments for this group during the 1990-1993 period was $111. The average interest payment in 1985 and 1988 were $1,508 and $1,362 respectively. The percentages of interest-

---

[1]Note to Readers: As stated in Chapter Three, all group analysis are meant for future researchers. The size of debt, level of income, and interest payments in the future for different income groups can be compared with our findings to determine what changes have occurred to them. The pattern of analysis has a repetitive format and may not be interesting to general readers, but researchers may find our estimates as valuable reference materials. General readers may find a summary of all group analysis in Chapter Ten.

paying households for these two years were 100% and 40% for the group, and 10% and 5% for all households in the sample.

**$15,000 - $20,000**

| | 1985 | 1988 | 1990 | 1991 | 1992 | 1993 |
|---|---|---|---|---|---|---|
| Average Size of Interest Paid | $1,490 | $1,719 | $1,742 | $2,830 | $1,976 | $2,502 |
| Percentage of Households Paying Interest in this Group | 100% | 50% | 25% | 33% | 27% | 13% |
| Interest Paying Households as % of All Households in the Sample | 13% | 6% | 3% | 4% | 3% | 2% |
| Average Income | $17,361 | $18,756 | $17,190 | $17,285 | $17,446 | $17,464 |
| Average interest paid by households for the 1990-1993 period was | | | | | | $2,263 |
| Average change in interest paid for this group during 1990-1993 | | | | | | $253 |
| Average income of the group for the years 1990-1993 was | | | | | | $17,346 |

The average amount of interest paid by households in this income group varied from $1,742 to $2,830, yielding an average of $2,263 for the 1990-1993 period. This constitutes 13% of the group's average income of the last four years of the survey. The number of households that paid interest in this group varied from 13% to 33% for the 1990-1993 period representing 2% to 3% of all households in the sample.

The average increase in interest payments for this group during the same period was $253. The average interest payment in 1985 and 1988 were $1,490 and $1,719 respectively. The percentages of interest paying households for these two years were 100% and 50% for the group and 13% and 6% for all households in the sample.

$20,000 - $25,000

| | 1985 | 1988 | 1990 | 1991 | 1992 | 1993 |
|---|---|---|---|---|---|---|
| Average Size of Interest Paid | $1,110 | $2,520 | $1,995 | $1,434 | $1,374 | $1,995 |
| Percentage of Households Paying Interest in this Group | 100% | 63% | 50% | 50% | 20% | 29% |
| Interest Paying Households as % of All Households in the Sample | 12% | 6% | 4% | 4% | 2% | 2% |
| Average Income | $22,164 | $23,301 | $21,927 | $22,270 | $22,732 | $22,793 |
| Average interest paid by households for the 1990-1993 period was | | | | | | $1,700 |
| Average increase in interest paid for this group during 1990-1993 | | | | | | $0 |
| The average income of the group for the 1990-1993 period year was | | | | | | $22,431 |

The average amount of interest paid by households in this income group varied form $1,374 to $1,995, yielding an average of $1,700 for the 1990-1993 period. This constitutes 7.58% of the group's average income of the last four years of the survey. The number of households that paid interest in this group varied from 20% to 50%, representing 2% to 4% of all households in the sample. There was no change in the average of interest payment for this group during this period.

The average interest payments in 1985 and 1988 were $1,110 and $2,520 respectively. The percentages of interest paying households for these two years were 100% and 63% for the group and 12% and 6% for all households in the sample.

$25,000 - $30,000

| | 1985 | 1988 | 1990 | 1991 | 1992 | 1993 |
|---|---|---|---|---|---|---|
| Average Size of Interest Paid | $1,796 | $1,997 | $2,261 | $2,506 | $1,937 | $2,393 |
| Percentage of Households Paying Interest in this Group | 100% | 80% | 50% | 80% | 41% | 32% |
| Interest Paying Households as % of All Households in the Sample | 14% | 10% | 3% | 3% | 3% | 2% |
| Average Income | $27,522 | $27,892 | $26,951 | $28,080 | $27,273 | $27,475 |
| Average interest paid by households for the 1990-1993 period was | | | | | | $2,274 |
| The average increase in interest paid for this group during 1990-1993 | | | | | | $44 |
| The average income of the group for the 1990-1993 period was | | | | | | $27,445 |

The average amount of interest paid by households in this income group varied from $1,937 to $2,506, yielding an average of $2,274 for the 1990-1993 period. This constitutes 8.28% of the group's average income-of the last four years of the survey. The number of households that paid interest in this group varied from 32% to 80% for the same period, representing 2% to 3% of all households in our sample.

The average increase in interest payments for this group during the same period was $44. The average interest payments in 1985 and 1988 were $1,796 and 1,997 respectively. The percentages of interest paying households for these two years were 100% and 80% for the group and 14% and 10% for all households in the sample.

$30,000 - $35,000

| | 1985 | 1988 | 1990 | 1991 | 1992 | 1993 |
|---|---|---|---|---|---|---|
| Average Size of Interest Paid | $1,687 | $2,437 | $2,853 | $2,492 | $2,127 | $1,994 |
| Percentage of Households Paying Interest in this Group | 100% | 50% | 50% | 60% | 42% | 43% |
| Interest Paying Household as % of All Households in the Sample | 13% | 6% | 4% | 4% | 3% | 3% |
| Average Income | $32,617 | $31,706 | $32,752 | $32,511 | $32,326 | $32,680 |
| Average interest paid by households for the 1990-1993 period was | | | | | | $2,367 |
| Average decrease in interest paid for this group during 1990-1993 | | | | | | ($286) |
| The average income of the group for the 1990-1993 period was | | | | | | $32,567 |

The average amount of interest paid by households in this income group varied from $1,994 to $2,853, yielding an average of $2,367 for the 1990-1993 period. This constitutes 7.27% of the group's average income of the last four years of the survey. The number of households that paid interest in this group varied from 42% to 60% for the same period, representing 3% to 4% of all households in our sample.

The average decrease in interest payments of this group for the period was $286. The average interest payments in 1985-1988 were $1,687 and 2,437 respectively. The percentage of interest paying households for these two years were 100% and 50% for the group and 13% and 6% for all households in the sample.

$35,000 - $40,000

| | 1985 | 1988 | 1990 | 1991 | 1992 | 1993 |
|---|---|---|---|---|---|---|
| Average Size of Interest Paid | $3,022 | $3,142 | $3,056 | $2,676 | $2,283 | $3,043 |
| Percentage of Households Paying Interest in this Group | 90% | 90% | 80% | 70% | 5% | 32% |
| Interest Paying Households as % of All Households in the Sample | 5% | 9% | 3% | 4% | 2% | 3% |
| Average Income | $38,617 | $39,048 | $37,604 | $37,397 | $37,200 | $37,052 |
| The average interest paid by households for the 1990-1993 period was | | | | | | $2,765 |
| The average decrease in interest paid for this group during 1990-1993 | | | | | | ($4) |
| The average income of the group for the 1990-1993 period was | | | | | | $37,313 |

The average amount of interest paid by households in this income group varied from $2,283 to $3,056, yielding an average of $2,765 for the 1990-1993 period. This constitutes 7.41% of the groups average income of the last four years of the survey. The number of households that paid interest in this group varied from 5% to 80% during the same period, representing 2% to 4% of all households in our sample.

The average interest payments in 1985-1988 were $3,022 and $3,142 respectively. The percentages of interest paying households for both these two years were 90% for the group and 5% and 9% for all households in the sample.

$40,000 - 45,000

| | 1985 | 1988 | 1990 | 1991 | 1992 | 1993 |
|---|---|---|---|---|---|---|
| Average Size of Interest Paid | $2,354 | $3,157 | $4,020 | $3,038 | $1,870 | $2,009 |
| Percentage of Households Paying Interest in this Group | 100% | 90% | 80% | 90% | 62% | 46% |
| Interest Paying Households as % of All Households in Sample | 8% | 6% | 6% | 6% | 4% | 3% |
| Average Income | $42,884 | $42,474 | $43,006 | $42,282 | $42,317 | $42,214 |
| Average interest paid by households for the 1990-1993 period was | | | | | | $2,734 |
| The average decrease in interest paid for this group during 1990-1993 | | | | | | ($670) |
| The average income of the group for the 1990-1993 period was | | | | | | $42,455 |

The average amount of interest paid by households in this income group varied from $1,870 to $4,020, yielding an average of $2,734. This constitutes 6.44% of the group's average income of the last four years of the survey. The number of households that paid interest in this group, varied from 46% to 90% during the 1990-1993 period representing 3% to 6% of all households in our sample.

The average decrease in interest payments in this group during the same period was $670. The average interest payments in 1985 and 1988 were $2,354 and $3,157 respectively. The percentages of interest paying households for these two years were 100% and 90% for the group and 5% for all households in the sample.

$45,000 - 50,000

| | 1985 | 1988 | 1990 | 1991 | 1992 | 1993 |
|---|---|---|---|---|---|---|
| Average Size of Interest Paid | $2,539 | $2,236 | $4,274 | $3,100 | $2,951 | $2,936 |
| Percentage of Households Paying Interest in this Group | 100% | 80% | 80% | 70% | 70% | 80% |
| Interest Paying Households as % of All Households in Sample | 5% | 5% | 5% | 5% | 4% | 4% |
| Average Income | $47,994 | $54,749 | $47,071 | $47,697 | $47,933 | $47,660 |
| Average interest paid by households for the 1990-1993 period was | | | | | | $3,315 |
| The average decrease in interest paid for this group during 1990-1993 | | | | | | ($446) |
| The average income of the group for the 1990-1993 period was | | | | | | $47,590 |

The average amount of interest paid by households for this income group varied from $2,936 to $4,274, yielding an average of $3,315. This constitutes 6.96% of the group's average income of the last four years of the survey. The number of households that paid interest in this group varied from 70% to 80% for the 1990-1993 period, representing 4% to 5% of all households in the sample.

The average decrease in interest payments for this group during the same period was $446. The average interest payments in 1985 and 1988 were $2,539 and $2,236 respectively. The percentages of interest paying households for these two years were 100% and 80% respectively for the group and 5% for all house holds in the sample.

$50,000 - 55,000

| | 1985 | 1988 | 1990 | 1991 | 1992 | 1993 |
|---|---|---|---|---|---|---|
| Average Size of Interest Paid | $3,618 | $2,783 | $5,344 | $6,272 | $3,314 | $2,043 |
| Percentage of Households Paying Interest in this Group | 100% | 100% | 60% | 60% | 80% | 53% |
| Interest Paying Households as % of All Households in Sample | 1% | 1% | 2% | 2% | 3% | 2% |
| Average Income | $51,847 | $52,671 | $52,682 | $52,159 | $52,343 | $52,802 |
| Average interest paid by households for the 1990-1993 period was | | | | | | $4,243 |
| The average decrease in interest paid for this group during 1990-1993 | | | | | | ($1,100) |
| The average income of the group for the 1990-1993 period was | | | | | | $52,497 |

The average amount of interest paid by households in this income group varied from $2,043 to $6,272, yielding an average of $4,243. This constitutes 8.08% of the group's average income of the last four years of the survey. The number of households that paid interest in this group varied from 53% to 80% during the 1990-1993 period. This group represents 2% to 3% of all households in our sample.

The average decrease in interest payments for this group during the same period was $1,100. The average interest payments in 1985 and 1988 were $3,618 and $2,783 respectively. The percentage of interest paying households for these two years were 100% for the group and 1% for all households in the sample.

**$55,000 - 60,000**

| | 1985 | 1988 | 1990 | 1991 | 1992 | 1993 |
|---|---|---|---|---|---|---|
| Average Size of Interest Paid | $1,976 | $2,055 | $4,583 | $3,919 | $1,819 | $3,612 |
| Percentage of Households Paying Interest in this Group | 100% | 100% | 80% | 70% | 40% | 71% |
| Interest Paying Households as % of All Households in Sample | 2% | 1% | 5% | 6% | 1% | 3% |
| Average Income | $56,898 | $55,924 | $57,806 | $57,387 | $57,491 | $57,463 |
| Average interest paid by households for the 1990-1993 period was | | | | | | $3,483 |
| The average decrease in interest paid for this group during 1990-1993 | | | | | | ($324) |
| The average income of the group for the 1990-1993 period was | | | | | | $57,537 |

The average amount of interest paid by households in this income group varied from $1,819 to $4,583, yielding an average of $3,483. This constitutes 6.05% of the group's average income of the last four years of the survey. The number of households that paid interest in this group varied from 40% to 80% for the 1990-1993 period, representing 1% to 6% of all households in the sample. The average decrease in interest payments for the group during the same period was $324. The average interest payments in 1985 and 1988 were $1,976 and $2,055 respectively. The percentage of interest paying households for these two years were 100% for the group and 2% and 1% for all households in the sample.

$60,000 and Over

| | 1985 | 1988 | 1990 | 1991 | 1992 | 1993 |
|---|---|---|---|---|---|---|
| Average Size of Interest Paid | $935 | $1,916 | $4,814 | $6,059 | $3,612 | $3,191 |
| Percentage of Households Paying Interest in this Group | 100% | 100% | 70% | 90% | 70% | 80% |
| Interest Paying Households as % of All Households in the Sample | 0% | 1% | 4% | 3% | 5% | 8% |
| Average Income | $60,175 | $62,659 | $63,454 | $62,146 | $63,114 | $62,266 |
| Average interest paid by households for the 1990-1993 period was | | | | | | $4,419 |
| The average decrease in interest paid for this group during 1990-1993 | | | | | | ($541) |
| The average income of the group for the 1990-1993 period was | | | | | | $62,745 |

The average amount of interest paid by households in this income group varied from $3,191 to $6,059, yielding an average of $4,419. This constitutes 7.04% of the group's average income of the last four years of the survey. The number of households that paid interest in this group varied from 70% to 90% during the 1990-1993 period, representing 3% to 8% of all households in the sample. The average decrease in interest payments for this group during the same period was $541. The average interest payment in 1985 and 1988 were $935 and $1,916 respectively. The percentages of interest paying households for these two years were 100% for the group.

Summary: Three groups with income levels of 10-15, 15-20 and 25-30 thousand dollars experienced increases in interest payments which varied from $44 to $253 per year for the period 1990-1993.

On the other hand, eight groups with income levels of 20-25, 30-35, 35-40, 40-45, 45-50, 50-55, 55-60, and more than 60 thousand dollars, experienced decreases in their interest payments. The amount of decrease varied from a low of $4 to a high of $1,100 per year for the 1990-1993 period.

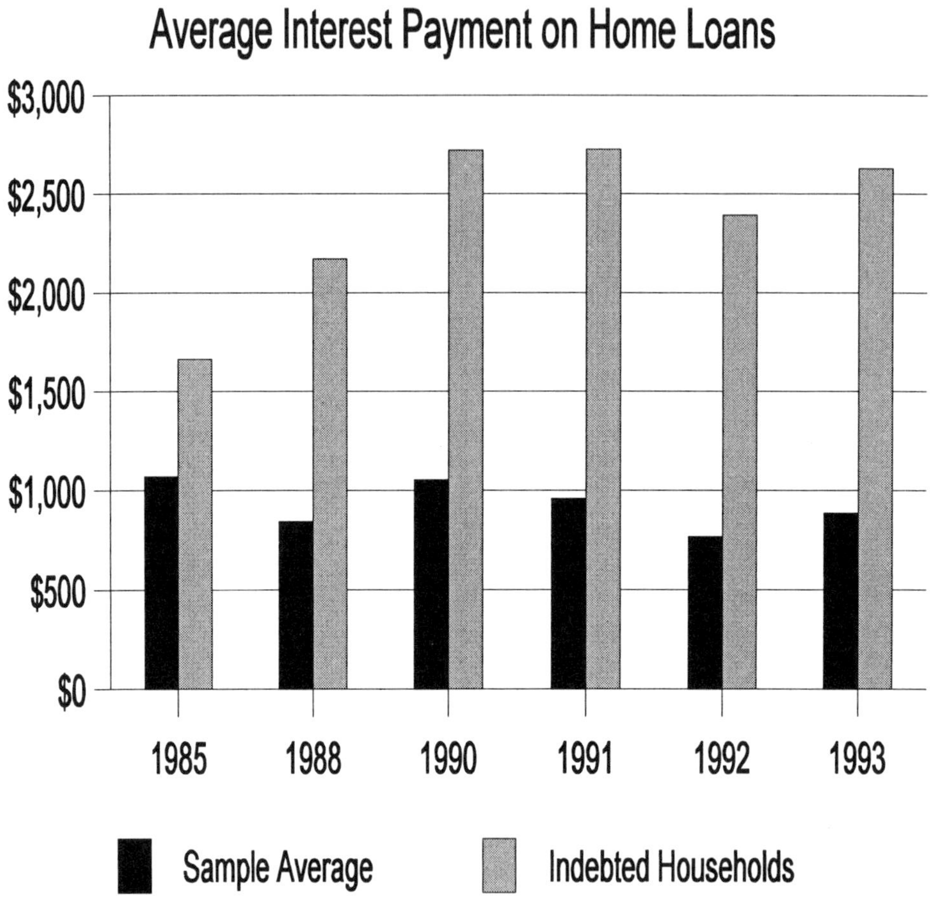
Average Interest Payment on Home Loans
$3,000
$2,500
$2,000
$1,500
$1,000
$500
$0
1985
1988
1990
1991
1992
1993
Sample Average
Indebted Households

Figure 12

Interest Paid on Home Loan

| Income | 1985 | | | 1988 | | | 1990 | | | 1991 | | |
|---|---|---|---|---|---|---|---|---|---|---|---|---|
| | Average Amount of Interest Paid | f/n[1] | f/N[2] | Average Amount of Interest Paid | f/n[1] | f/N[2] | Average Amount of Interest Paid | f/n[1] | f/N[2] | Average Amount of Interest Paid | f/n[1] | f/N[2] |
| $0-4,999 | $1,936 | .50 | .01 | $0 | .00 | .00 | $0 | .00 | .00 | $0 | .00 | .00 |
| $5,000-9,999 | $1,194 | .40 | .05 | $1,227 | .14 | .01 | $917 | .04 | .01 | $0 | .00 | .00 |
| $10,000-14,999 | $1,857 | .53 | .06 | $926 | .14 | .02 | $1,233 | .09 | .01 | $1,396 | .06 | .01 |
| $15,000-19,999 | $1,351 | .82 | .10 | $2,138 | .27 | .03 | $1,679 | .22 | .03 | $3,303 | .26 | .03 |
| $20,000-24,999 | $1,414 | .48 | .06 | $2,735 | .36 | .04 | $2,050 | .31 | .03 | $1,744 | .25 | .02 |
| $25,000-29,999 | $1,973 | .65 | .10 | $1,685 | .59 | .07 | $2,023 | .46 | .06 | $2,377 | .56 | .02 |
| $30,000-34,999 | $1,373 | .67 | .09 | $2,509 | .50 | .05 | $2,296 | .47 | .04 | $1,708 | .46 | .03 |
| $35,000-39,999 | $2,002 | .82 | .05 | $2,515 | .70 | .07 | $2,798 | .65 | .03 | $2,257 | .59 | .04 |
| $40,000-44,999 | $2,246 | .64 | .05 | $2,649 | .69 | .05 | $2,735 | .71 | .05 | $2,134 | .75 | .05 |
| $45,000-49,999 | $1,990 | .79 | .04 | $1,844 | .40 | .01 | $2,848 | .75 | .05 | $2,942 | .37 | .04 |
| $50,000-54,999 | $2,382 | .01 | .01 | $2,942 | .75 | .01 | $3,913 | .56 | .02 | $6,199 | .38 | .01 |
| $55,000-59,999 | $1,287 | .01 | .02 | $617 | .50 | .00 | $3,631 | .70 | .05 | $2,792 | .61 | .03 |
| $60,000-64,999 | $693 | .01 | .01 | $912 | .75 | .01 | $3,620 | .61 | .03 | $3,186 | .78 | .07 |

*f/n[1]:* *Frequencies of the indebted households*
*f/N[2]:* *Frequencies in the entire sample*

### Interest Paid on Home Loans

Interest payments on home loans varied from a low of $693 to a high of $6,199 for all income groups and for all the years of the survey. It is interesting to note that in 1985, interest payments on home loans in the survey area did not exceed the $2,000 level, but interest payments on home loans during the 1990-1991 period were between $1,000 and $3,000. The percentages of households that paid interest on home loans from all income groups and for all the years of the survey varied between 1% and 83%.

Interest Paid on Car Loan

| Income | 1985 | | | 1988 | | | 1990 | | | 1991 | | |
|---|---|---|---|---|---|---|---|---|---|---|---|---|
| | Average Amount of Interest Paid | f/n[1] | f/N[2] | Average Amount of Interest Paid | f/n[1] | f/N[2] | Average Amount of Interest Paid | f/n[1] | f/N[2] | Average Amount of Interest Paid | f/n[1] | f/N[2] |
| $0-4,999 | $0 | .00 | .00 | $0 | .00 | .00 | $0 | .00 | .00 | $0 | .00 | .00 |
| $5,000-9,999 | $370 | .10 | .01 | $0 | .00 | .00 | $0 | .00 | .00 | $0 | .00 | .00 |
| $10,000-14,999 | $473 | .21 | .02 | $568 | .03 | .004 | $0 | .00 | .00 | $703 | .10 | .01 |
| $15,000-19,999 | $484 | .18 | .02 | $588 | .12 | .01 | $2,491 | .02 | .00 | $728 | .05 | .01 |
| $20,000-24,999 | $563 | .24 | .03 | $761 | .07 | .01 | $1,306 | .10 | .01 | $1,188 | .14 | .01 |
| $25,000-29,999 | $517 | .35 | .05 | $910 | .07 | .01 | $0 | .00 | .00 | $1,669 | .25 | .01 |
| $30,000-34,999 | $463 | .42 | .06 | $801 | .20 | .02 | $1,238 | .13 | .01 | $1,292 | .42 | .03 |
| $35,000-39,999 | $441 | .45 | .03 | $287 | .13 | .01 | $1,582 | .15 | .01 | $1,696 | .18 | .01 |
| $40,000-44,999 | $783 | .29 | .02 | $942 | .13 | .01 | $1,695 | .39 | .03 | $1,615 | .50 | .03 |
| $45,000-49,999 | $218 | .33 | .02 | $0 | .00 | .00 | $1,413 | .42 | .03 | $1,598 | .20 | .02 |
| $50,000-54,999 | $456 | .01 | .01 | $0 | .00 | .00 | $1,903 | .31 | .01 | $1,540 | .46 | .02 |
| $55,000-59,999 | $192 | .33 | .01 | $0 | .00 | .00 | $1,391 | .11 | .01 | $1,387 | .39 | .02 |
| $60,000-64,999 | $0 | .00 | .00 | $0 | .00 | .00 | $1,808 | .38 | .03 | $2,066 | .69 | .06 |

*f/n[1]:* *Frequencies of the indebted households*
*f/N[2]:* *Frequencies in the entire sample*

### Interest Paid on Car Loans

For all the years of the survey (1985, 1988, 1990, 1991), interest paid on car loans varied between $192 and $2,491. We noted that during 1985-1988, interest payments on car loans for all groups were below the $1,000 level, but since 1990 interest payments for most groups exceeded the $1,000 mark.

It appears that the income levels between $10,000 and $45,000 contained the largest number of households paying interest on car loans — the frequencies of these households varied from 10% to 50%. For the entire sample, households paying interest on car loans varied from 1% to 6%.

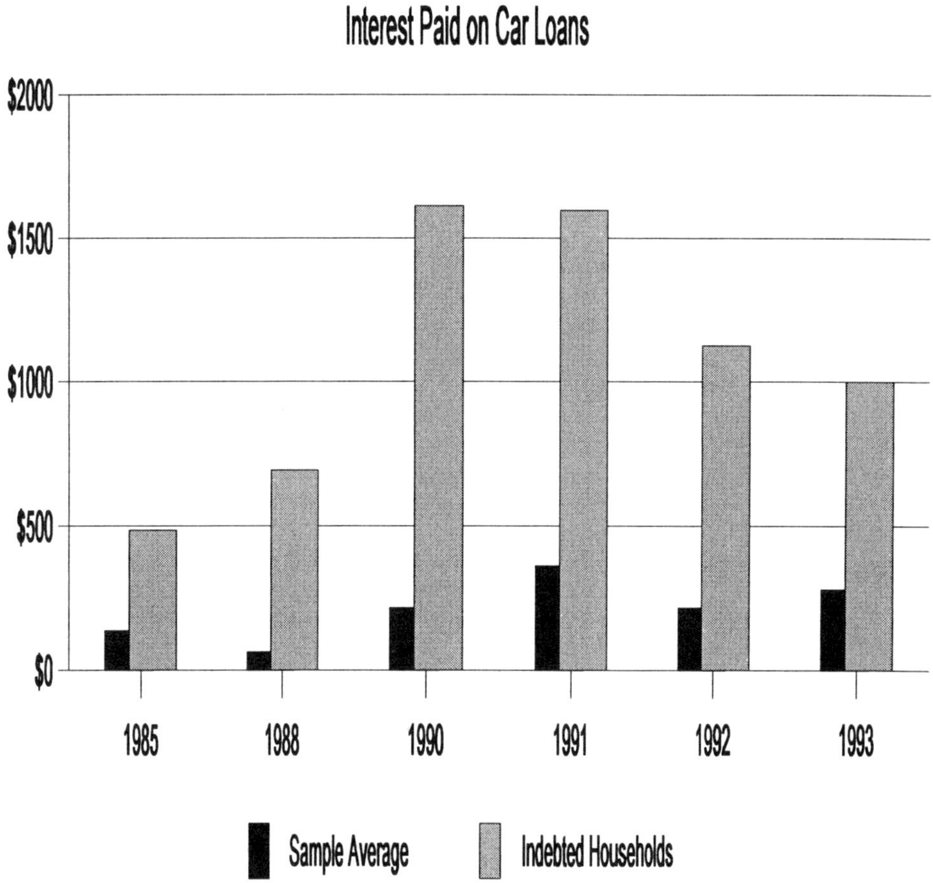
Interest Paid on Car Loans
$2000
$1500
$1000
$500
$0
1985
1988
1990
1991
1992
1993
Sample Average
Indebted Households

**Figure 13**

Interest Paid on Credit Card

| Income | 1985 | | | 1988 | | | 1990 | | | $1,991 | | |
|---|---|---|---|---|---|---|---|---|---|---|---|---|
| | Average Amount of Interest Paid | f/n[1] | f/N[2] | Average Amount of Interest Paid | f/n[1] | f/N[2] | Average Amount of Interest Paid | f/n[1] | f/N[2] | Average Amount of Interest Paid | f/n[1] | f/n[2] |
| $0-4,999 | $0 | .00 | .00 | $0 | .00 | .00 | $0 | .00 | .00 | $0 | .00 | .00 |
| $5,000-9,999 | $46 | .50 | .06 | $41 | .10 | .01 | $534 | .13 | .02 | $0 | .00 | .00 |
| $10,000-14,999 | $92 | .47 | .05 | $1,141 | .06 | .01 | $640 | .05 | .01 | $409 | .10 | .01 |
| $15,000-19,999 | $116 | .41 | .05 | $213 | .23 | .03 | $73 | .45 | .06 | $274 | .10 | .01 |
| $20,000-24,999 | $216 | .81 | .10 | $333 | .32 | .03 | $218 | .44 | .04 | $208 | .25 | .02 |
| $25,000-29,999 | $105 | .70 | .10 | $288 | .32 | .03 | $54 | .38 | .02 | $208 | .19 | .01 |
| $30,000-34,999 | $270 | .50 | .07 | $314 | .35 | .03 | $318 | .56 | .05 | $352 | .33 | .02 |
| $35,000-39,999 | $146 | .45 | .03 | $219 | .26 | .03 | $337 | .70 | .04 | $594 | .27 | .02 |
| $40,000-44,999 | $95 | .79 | .06 | $33 | .06 | .00 | $733 | .79 | .06 | $501 | .50 | .03 |
| $45,000-49,999 | $286 | .89 | .05 | $0 | .00 | .00 | $764 | .88 | .06 | $531 | .34 | .03 |
| $50,000-54,999 | $50 | .50 | .01 | $0 | .00 | .00 | $729 | .63 | .03 | $536 | .54 | .02 |
| $55,000-59,999 | $96 | .33 | .01 | $357 | .50 | .00 | $743 | .78 | .06 | $885 | .33 | .02 |
| $60,000-64,999 | $0 | .01 | .01 | $225 | .25 | .00 | $498 | .71 | .04 | $646 | .69 | .06 |

*f/n[1]:* *Frequencies of the indebted households*
*f/N[2]:* *Frequencies in the entire sample*

### Interest Paid on Credit Card Loans

In our surveys of 1985, 1988, 1990 and 1991, the average amount of interest paid on credit cards varied between $46 and $885. The percentages of households which paid interest on credit cards for all income groups and for all the years of the survey varied between 1% and 89%. A large number of households belonging to income groups between $5,000 and $45,000 had credit card loans. For the entire sample, the percentages of households paying interest on credit card loans varied from 1% to 6% of all households.

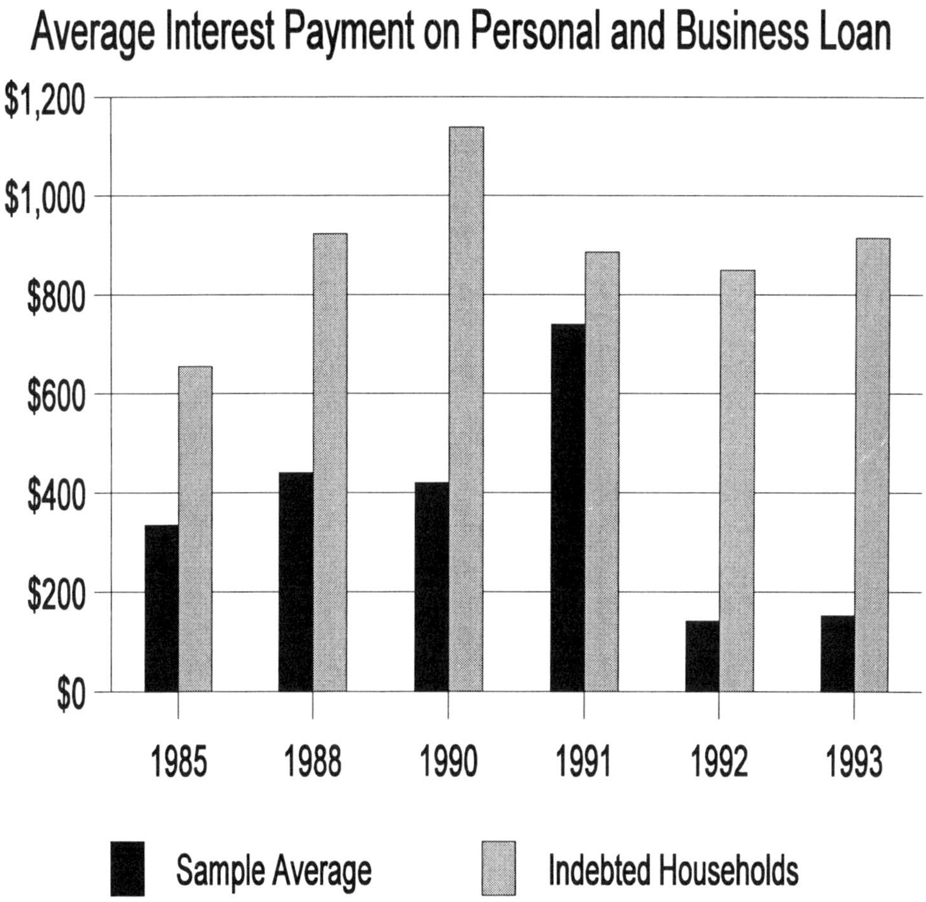
Average Interest Payment on Personal and Business Loan
$1,200
$1,000
$800
$600
$400
$200
$0
1985
1988
1990
1991
1992
1993
Sample Average
Indebted Households

**Figure 14**

Interest Paid on Personal & Business Loans

| Income | 1985 | | | 1988 | | | 1990 | | | 1991 | | |
|---|---|---|---|---|---|---|---|---|---|---|---|---|
| | Average Amount of Interest Paid | f/n¹ | f/n² | Average Amount of Interest Paid | f/n¹ | f/n² | Average Amount of Interest Paid | f/n¹ | f/n² | Average Amount of Interest Paid | f/n¹ | f/n² |
| $0-4,999 | $0 | .00 | .00 | $192 | .33 | .00 | $0 | .00 | .00 | $0 | .00 | .00 |
| $5,000-9,999 | $191 | .15 | .02 | $955 | .23 | .02 | $0 | .00 | .00 | $1,354 | .08 | .01 |
| $10,000-14,999 | $623 | .63 | .07 | $1,136 | .25 | .01 | $0 | .00 | .00 | $511 | .06 | .01 |
| $15,000-19,999 | $389 | .64 | .08 | $757 | .31 | .04 | $0 | .00 | .00 | $736 | .02 | .00 |
| $20,000-24,999 | $303 | .33 | .04 | $799 | .50 | .05 | $1,191 | .05 | .01 | $113 | .07 | .01 |
| $25,000-29,999 | $593 | .42 | .06 | $796 | .52 | .06 | $0 | .00 | .00 | $459 | .19 | .01 |
| $30,000-34,999 | $751 | .50 | .07 | $606 | .50 | .05 | $1,592 | .06 | .01 | $954 | .13 | .01 |
| $35,000-39,999 | $1,158 | .73 | .05 | $1,075 | .83 | .09 | $0 | .00 | .00 | $458 | .05 | .00 |
| $40,000-44,999 | $1,070 | .57 | .05 | $1,086 | .94 | .07 | $1,000 | .11 | .01 | $758 | .17 | .01 |
| $45,000-49,999 | $665 | .01 | .05 | $526 | .40 | .01 | $1,348 | .13 | .01 | $0 | .00 | .00 |
| $50,000-54,999 | $1,343 | .50 | .01 | $1,543 | .75 | .01 | $706 | .13 | .01 | $0 | .00 | .00 |
| $55,000-59,999 | $593 | .01 | .02 | $241 | 1.00 | .01 | $1,281 | .14 | .00 | $1,283 | .06 | .00 |
| $60,000-64,999 | $242 | .01 | .01 | $2,491 | .50 | .01 | $652 | .05 | .00 | $1,222 | .28 | .02 |

*f/n¹:* *Frequencies of the indebted households*

*f/N²:* *Frequencies in the entire sample*

## Interest Paid on Personal and Business Loans

The average amount of interest paid on personal and business loans for all groups and for all the years of the survey (1985, 1988, 1990 and 1991) varied between $1,592 and $1,910. Group frequencies or the percentages of households paying interest on personal business loans varied from 1% to 94%. A large number of households belonging to income groups between $5,000 and $45,000 contracted these loans.

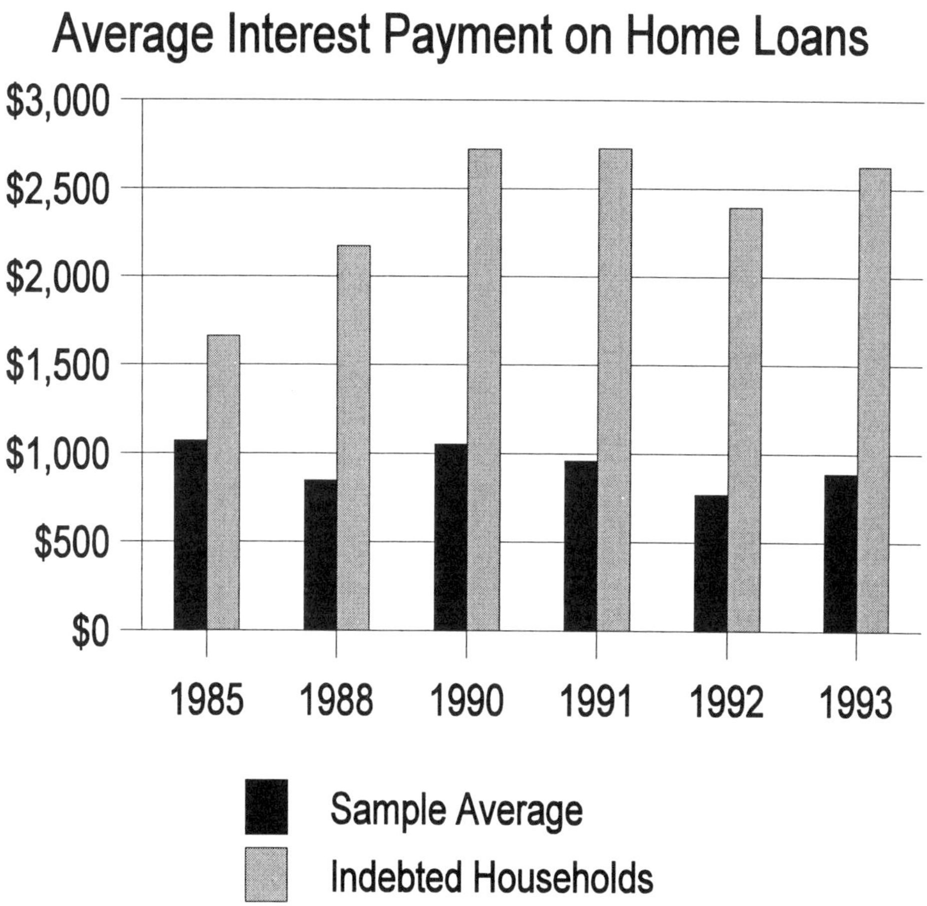
Average Interest Payment on Home Loans
$3,000
$2,500
$2,000
$1,500
$1,000
$500
$0
1985
1988
1990
1991
1992
1993
Sample Average
Indebted Households

Figure 15

**Interest Paid on Home Loan and Car Loan Together**

| | 1985 | 1988 | 1990 | 1991 | 1992 | 1993 |
|---|---|---|---|---|---|---|
| Average Interest Paid on Home Loan and Car Loan Together | $2,380 | $3,494 | $5,095 | $4,888 | $3,733 | $3,580 |
| Average Income of Those Who Paid Interest Both on Home and Car Loan | $30,357 | $29,480 | $48,558 | $49,314 | $54,694 | $51,516 |
| Interest Paid on Home Loan & Car Loan Together as % of Average Income (of those who paid interest on a home & car loan) | 8% | 12% | 10.5% | 10% | 7% | 7% |
| The average interest payment on both home and a car loan together for the 1990-1993 period was: | | | | | | $4,324 |
| The average percentage of income paid as interest on a home and car loan together for the 1990-1993 period was: | | | | | | 8.62% |

The interest paid on home loans and car loans together rose from $2,380 in 1985 to $5,095 in 1990. The average interest payment per year, for the survey period, amounted to $4,324. The average income of those who had these loans varied from $30,357 in 1985 to $54,694 in 1992. Interest payments equaled between 8% and 12% of the income of those households which had both home and car loans. It can be claimed that these households expend a little more than 10% of income as interest payments on these loans.

Trend of Interest Payments on Household Debts and Other National Debts

| | 1985 | 1988 | 1990 | 1991 | 1992 | 1993 |
|---|---|---|---|---|---|---|
| Average Size of Interest Paid by Indebted Household in the Survey Area | $1,695 | $2,282 | $3,332 | $3,188 | $3,118 | $3,359 |
| Average Interest Paid on Federal Debt (Per Household)[1] | $2,002 | $2,352 | $2,838 | $3,026 | $3,057 | $3,037 |
| Interest Paid on Household Debt as % of Average Household GNP | 4% | 4% | 6% | 5% | 5% | 4% |
| Interest Paid on Federal Debt as % of Average Household GNP | 4% | 4% | 5% | 5% | 5% | 5% |
| Average Household GNP | $46,260 | $53,550 | $58,570 | $59,510 | $63,031 | $65,916 |

The average interest paid on household debts grew at a pace akin to that of interest paid on the federal debt. In the six years of our survey, the interest paid on household debts varied between $1,695 and $3,359. Per household, the interest paid on the federal debt varied between $2,002 and $3,057 for the 1985 to 1993 period. When expressed in terms of average household GNP, interest paid on household debts varied between 4% and 6% of average household GNP, and interest paid on federal debt varied between 4% and 5% of average household GNP for the same period.

Except for the year of 1990, interest paid as a percentage of household GNP varied between 4% and 5% of average household GNP for both the household and federal debts. It is interesting to note that interest paid on household debt increased from 1985 to 1993 by 98%. Interest paid on the federal debt increased during the same period by 52%. It is worth mentioning here that GNP increased by 42% but household income increased in mid-sized cities by only 17% during the same period.

[1] Per household interest payment on federal debt has been found by dividing the total interest payments on federal debt by the total number of households in the U.S. economy.

### Interest Paid on Household Debt and Other Debt

| | |
|---|---|
| Average interest paid by indebted households for the 1990-1993 period | $3,249 |
| Average interest paid on federal debt (per household) for 1990-1993 period | $2,990 |

### Interest Paid as Percent of Income

| | |
|---|---|
| Average of overall interest payments as a percent (%) of household income for 1990-1993 period | 8% |
| Average of interest payments on a home loans as a percent (%) of household income for 1990-1993 period | 7% |
| Average of interest payments on a car loans as a percent (%) of household income for 1990-1993 period | 5% |
| The average of interest payments on a credit card loans as a percent (%) of household income for the 1990-1993 period was: | 2% |

### Interest Paid (item wise) as Percent of Income[1]

| | 1985 | 1988 | 1990 | 1991 | 1992 | 1993 |
|---|---|---|---|---|---|---|
| Interest Paid on all items | 7% | 9% | 9% | 8% | 6% | 8% |
| Home Loan | 8% | 8% | 7% | 7% | 6% | 7% |
| Car Loan | 2% | 3% | 4% | 4% | 5% | 5% |
| Personal and Business Loans | 3% | 4% | 3% | 4% | 3% | 3% |
| Credit Card Loan | 1% | 1% | 2% | 1% | 2% | 1% |

Except for the year 1992, in all the years of the survey, we notice that the interest payments of indebted households constituted between 6% and 9% of their income. We may claim that the interest payments of households in small and mid-sized cities constituted, on an average, approximately 8% of their income. Interest payments on home loans alone comprised about 6.75% of their income. Interest paid on personal and business loans equaled 3% of income, and that of credit card loans equaled 1% of household income in these cities.

[1]In reading these charts, we should note that all households did not pay interest on all items.

**Percentage of Households Paying Interest (For All Interest Paying Households)**

| Interest Paid as % of Income | 1985 | 1988 | 1990 | 1991 |
|---|---|---|---|---|
| 1% - 5% | 36% | 27% | 27% | 27% |
| 5% - 10% | 33% | 33% | 31% | 36% |
| 10% - 15% | 15% | 16% | 23% | 20% |
| 15% - 20% | 5% | 7% | 13% | 8% |
| 20% - 30% | 30% | 7% | 2% | 5% |
| 30% and over | 2% | 2% | 1% | 2% |

A large percentage of households (31% to 36%) paid interest that equaled 5% to 10% of their income. Interestingly enough, this feature prevailed in all four years of the study. The percentages of households that paid interest in the range of 5% to 10% of their income were 33%, 33%, 31%, and 36% in the years 1985, 1988, 1990, and 1991 respectively. We may claim that a little over 1/3 of all indebted households paid 5% to 10% of their income as interest. In 1985, 30% of households paid interest that equaled 20-30% of their income. In 1988, 1990 and 1991, 2% to 7% of households paid interest that equaled 20-30% of their incomes.

For many American families, the burden of debt is a real economic hardship. Many households have loans larger than the average annual income of the family. Bigger-than-income loans are psychologically depressing for low-income households. The burden of debt has reduced many families to the status of the poverty-stricken and has forced family members to make choices under very adverse economic conditions.

Debt, combined with adverse economic circumstances, has forced millions of households to choose between unpleasant alternatives. Out of economic necessity, families have had to forego better education and training for themselves and their children and have accepted jobs that did not match their education and experience. Many have resigned themselves to being numbered among America's poverty stricken after having been forced to divest themselves of businesses and household assets to satisfy their creditors. On top of the personal misfortune, their effective dropping out of the economic system reduces the total amount of expenditure thereby adversely affecting the aggregate demand side of the economy.

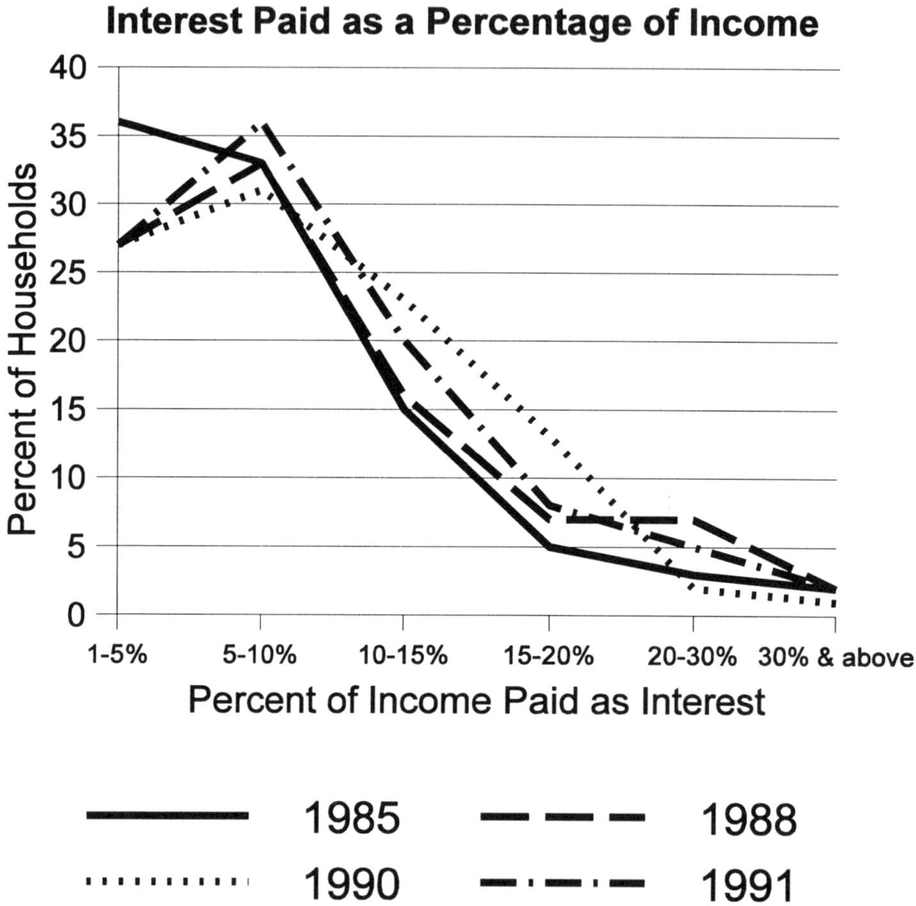
Interest Paid as a Percentage of Income
40
35
30
25
20
15
10
5
0
Percent of Households
1-5%
5-10%
10-15%
15-20%
20-30%
30% & above
Percent of Income Paid as Interest
1985
1988
1990
1991

Figure 16

Percentage of Households Paying Interest

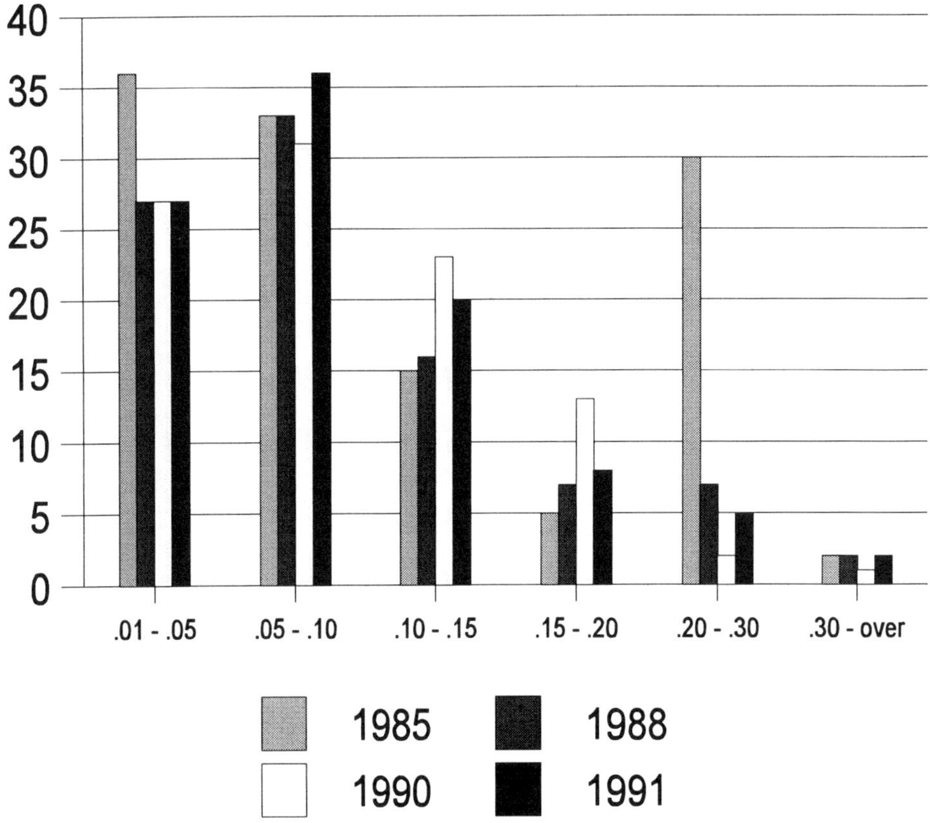


**Figure 17**

# CHAPTER FIVE
## INTEREST PAYMENTS & SIMPLE REGRESSION

Our walk with Jay has shown us that "emergencies," "urgencies," and the "unavoidable necessities" of life force households to buy goods and services on credit and in the process they incur debts. The transaction costs and costs of servicing loans are, in general, a drag on the household's efforts to attain a decent life and have proved to be major impediments to improving the household's economic condition. High interest on loans[1] and the present credit culture have made both the monetary and the real cost of servicing debt much higher than it appears to be. This has been hurting millions of low-income households in the U.S.

Most households are not really aware of the degree of erosion of their income which results from high interest payments on outstanding debts. One of the important objectives of this study has been to determine the portion of household income that is being spent in the form of interest or, more precisely, how much of each household dollar is spent as interest on household leverage. The slope estimate of our regression of interest payments on income reveals the degree of closeness that exists between these two variables.

The regression of the prime rate of New York banks on the discount rate of the Federal Reserve Bank and other money market rates, enables us to identify and determine the degree of influence that one rate exerts over the other. We ran several regressions of interest payments on income to build simple models aimed at finding mathematical relationships that exist between interest payment and income. This helps us focus on the average change in interest payments per unit change in income. The regression results and the equation that we have derived are given below.

---

[1] Despite the fact that the discount rate of the Federal Reserve Bank and other money market rates are low these days, low-income households can not avail themselves of these rates because of their poor credit reports.

## Models of Interest Payments on Home, Car and Credit Card Loans (Cross-Section Data)

A model was constructed to estimate how much of a dollar is spent in the form of interest for each additional dollar increase in household income.

### Interest Paid on Home Loan Regressed on Income

The model fitted was: $I_{ph}^{1} = B_0 + B_1$ income + error

**Regression Results**

| | 1990 | 1991 | 1992 | 1993 |
|---|---|---|---|---|
| **Constant** | -248.7<br>(1532.9) | -214.7<br>(1638.2) | -245.35<br>1230.4 | -177.71<br>1457.5 |
| **X Coefficient (s)** | 0.0433<br>(0.0041) | 0.0403<br>(0.0043) | 0.035<br>0.0033 | 0.0348<br>0.0036 |
| **R-Squared** | 0.23 | 0.20 | 0.2444 | 0.2096 |
| **No. of Observations** | 380 | 361 | 361 | 359 |

**Equations From Regression Results**

$$\textbf{1990: } I_{pH}^{1} = -248.7 + .043_Y$$
$$\textbf{1991: } I_{pH} = -214.7 + .040_Y$$
$$\textbf{1992: } I_{pH} = -245.35 + .035_Y$$
$$\textbf{1993: } I_{pH} = -177.71 + .0348_Y$$

The estimated coefficient of interest payments on home loans is positive and statistically significant at the 95 percent confidence level for the last four years of the survey. The goodness of the fit of this cross sectional data is reasonably satisfactory. As expected, a positive relationship exists between household income and the interest paid on home loans. For each additional dollar increase in household income, interest payments were 4.33 cents in 1990, 4.03 cents in 1991 and about four cents in 1992 and 1993.

[1] $I_{pH}$: Interest paid on home loan.

The results clearly demonstrate that the estimated slope of the regression line is remarkably consistent and demonstrates the viability of the model. Finally it can be claimed that the current interest payment on home loans for per dollar increase in income amounts to about four cents.

**Interest Paid on Car Loan Regressed on Income**

Model fitted was: $I_{pc}^{2} = C_0 + C_1 y^{1} + \text{error}$

Regression Results

| | | | |
|---|---|---|---|
| 1988 | Interest on Car Loan | = | $I_{pc}^{2}$ = 14.0 + .02Y |
| 1990 | Interest on Car Loan | = | - 017.7 + 0.0108 Income |
| | | | (557.0) (0.0015) |
| 1991 | Interest on Car Loan | = | -198.7 + 0.0193 Income |
| | | | (657.4) (0.0017) |
| | $R^2$ | = | 0.26 |
| | No. of Observations | = | 361 |

The percentages of income paid as interest on car loans were 2%, 1%, and 2% in 1988, 1990, and 1991 respectively. This means that interest payments on car loans for each dollar increase in income were two cents in 1988, one cent in 1990 and two cents in 1991. On average, we claim that for each $1 increase in income more than one cent was paid in the form of interest on car loan by households in small and mid-sized cities in the U.S.

---

[1]y: income

[2]$I_{pc}$: Interest paid on car loan.

**Interest Paid on Credit Card Regressed on Income**

The model fitted was:

1. Ipcc = Xo + $X_1$ y + error
   Regression Results:

1990 Interest on Credit Card = -51.74 + 0.0094 Income
(395) (0.0010)

$R^2$ = 0.18

No. Of observations = 380

1991 Interest on Credit Card = -69.13 + 0.0069 Income
(244) (0.0006)

$R^2$ = 0.24

No. Of observations = 361

2. The Equations derived from the regression results are:

1990 Ipcc[1] = -51.74 + .009y (where Ipcc = Interest paid on Credit Card Loan)

1991 Ipcc = -69.13 + .0069y Y: Income of household

The "t" ratios of the slopes of the equations for 1990 and 1991 were significant at the 95% confidence level indicating that the relationship between income and interest payments on credit card loans was statistically significant for the cross sectional data and that the goodness of the fit is satisfactory. The equations imply that in the early nineties, households spent about 1 percent of their income as interest on credit cards.

**A Model of Interest Payment on Different Income Groups (Households were divided into thirteen different income groups)**

Each group's interest payment was regressed on each group's average income. Our sample data was divided into thirteen income groups and for each group the average interest paid and the group's mean incomes were estimated. The regression results obtained were as follows:

---

[1]Ipcc: Interest paid on credit card.

| | 1985 | 1988 | 1990 |
|---|---|---|---|
| **Slope** | 0.0510 | 0.0775 | 0.0925 |
| **R-Squared** | 0.25 | 0.27 | 0.33 |
| **No. of Groups** | 13 | 13 | 13 |

The results clearly indicate that for every additional dollar increment in household income interest payment varied between of 3.1 cents and 9.2 cents. This generally supports our estimate arrived at by using the ungrouped data. The goodness of fit has improved, although the number of groups was small.

**Models on Total Interest Paid**
**Total Interest Paid Regressed on Income**

The model fitted was:

1. $I_p^1 = A_0 + A_1$ Income + Error

2. Regression Results

   Total interest paid was regressed on income. The regression results were as follows:

   1990 Total Interest Paid = -412.3 + 0.0650 Income
   (2071) (0.0054)

   $R^2 = 0.12$
   No. Of Observations = 361

   1991 Total Interest Paid = -491 + 0.0694 Income
   (2109) (0.0056)

   $R^2 = 0.30$
   No. Of Observations = 361

   1992 Total Interest paid = -438.9 + 0.0650 Income
   $R^2 = 0.38$
   No. Of Observations = 369

---

[1]$I_p$: Total Interest Paid
y: Income of households

3. Equations from Regression results are as follows:

| | | | |
|---|---|---|---|
| 1988 | $I_p$ | = | $57.6 + .05y$ |
| 1990 | $I_p$ | = | $412.3 + .069y$ |
| 1991 | $I_p$ | = | $491.4 + .069y$ |
| 1992 | $I_p$ | = | $-438.88 + .065y$ |

Where $I_p$ = Total Interest paid
$y$ = Income of the Household

The "t" ratio of the slopes of the equations for 1988, 1990, and 1991 are significant at the 95% confidence level indicating that the relationship between income and interest payment is statistically significant. The equations imply that for each dollar increase in income, households spent five cents in 1988, six and a half cents in 1990, and seven cents in 1991 as interest payment. All the estimated coefficients are of the expected signs and are statistically significant at the 95 percent confidence level. At this point, we extend our model to include interest earned as another explanatory variable.

## Extended Model of Total Interest Paid

A regression model of total interest payment was constructed taking household income and interest earned as explanatory variables.
The Model fitted was:

1. $D_0 + D_1 I_E + D_2$ income + error.

2. Regression Results
   Extended Model

1988 INT. PAID[1] = 78.6 - 0.11 INT. EARNED[2] + 0.06 INCOME[3]

(1600) (0.03) (0.01)

$R^2 = 0.20$
Number of observations = 216

1990 INT. PAID = -298.5 - 0.097 INT. EARNED + .0674 INCOME
(2036) (0.026) (0.0054)

$R^2 = 0.30$
Number of observations = 380

1991 INT PAID = -436.4 - 0.059 INT. EARNED + .0715 INCOME
(2083) (0.0188) (0.0055)

$R^2 = 0.32$
Number of observations = 361

3. Equations from the regression results are as follows:

| | |
|---|---|
| 1988 | $I_p = 78.6 - .11\ IE + .064y$ |
| 1990 | $I_p = 298.5 - .097\ IE + .067y$ |
| 1991 | $I_p = -436.4 - .059\ IE + .071y$ |

The estimated coefficient of income supports the hypothesis that the higher the level of income, the larger the size of interest payment. For

[1]Ip = Interest Paid

[2]Ie = Interest Earned

[3]Y = Income of Households

each additional dollar increase in income there were interest payments of about 6 cents in 1988, 7 cents in 1990 and 7 cents in 1991. All the estimated coefficients are of the correct signs and statistically significant at the 95 percent confidence level. Secondly, it can be noted that the estimated coefficient of interest earned is negative and statistically significant. This demonstrates the negative impact that interest earnings have on the size of total interest payments. Thus households with interest income have to pay less interest on household leverage than those which have no interest income. The goodness of the fit for the cross section data is satisfactory and the size of the sample is relatively large.

## Models on Prime Rates and Regional Rates: Models on Prime Rates

At this point we are interested in finding the impact of changes of the discount rate of the Federal Reserve Bank and the prime rate of the New York banks on other important interest rates. First, the prime rate of the New York banks was regressed on the discount rate of the Federal Reserve Bank.

The model fitted was

$P_r = P_o + P_1 \, DR + e$

[1]PR = prime rate of New York banks

[2]DR = discount rate of Federal Reserve Bank

The Regression Results:

New York prime rate regressed on the FRB discount rate

| | Regression Output: |
|---|---|
| Constant | 1.8704607 |
| Std Err of Y Est | (0.9094264) |
| $R^2$ | 0.9216101 |
| No. of Observations | 22 |
| Degrees of Freedom | 20 |
| X Coefficient(s) | 1.15522413 |
| Std Err of Coef. | (0.075338) |

[1]PR = prime rate of New York banks.

[2]DR = discount rate of the Federal Reserve Bank. This rate has been expressed just as the "discount rate."

The equation derived from the regression results is:

$$PR = 1.87 + 1.16\ DR$$

"T" ratios of the slope of the regression line are statistically significant at the 95% confidence level. The goodness of the fit is .92. As the slope is positive, the prime rate can be expected to increase with the increase in the discount rate.

The model implies that for a 1% change in the discount rate of the Federal Reserve Bank, there has been on an average 1.16% increase in the prime rate of the New York banks. For example, if the discount rate is at 5%, the prime rate is expected to be around 7.67% and if the discount rate changes to 6%, the prime rate would change to 8.83%. Our data show that the prime rate of the New York banks remained (more than 99% of the time) greater than the discount rate of the Federal Reserve Bank by more than 1%.

The average annual difference of the prime rate regressed on the average annual difference of the discount rate of Federal Reserve Bank. The fitted model was:

$$\Delta\ PR = P_o \ + \ P_1 \quad \Delta\ DR \ + \ \text{error.}$$

The regression result was:

$$\Delta\ \text{prime rate} = -0.113 + 0.8917 \quad \Delta DR$$
$$(1.72) \quad (0.230)$$

The equation follows: $\Delta PR = .113 + .8917\ PR\Delta DR$

where $\Delta$ represents first difference of annual values

Prime = prime rate of year t – prime rate of year t-1

DRSC = discount rate of year t – discount rate of year t-1

If the current annual difference in the discount rate deviates from the mean level by 1 percent, the annual change in the prime rate would deviate from the mean by 0.89 percent. The estimated coefficient is significant and the associated coefficient of determination is 0.37. The number of observations is 20 and the period of observation covers the 1961 to 1991 period.

## The Impact of the Frequent "Discount Rate" Change on the Prime Rate of the New York Banks

The estimated coefficients of the model is as follows:

The regression result was:

$$\Delta PRIME = \underset{(1.25)}{0.476} + \underset{(0.214)}{0.7760}\ DR - \underset{(0.028)}{0.0813}\ FREQ$$

$R^2 = 0.59$

Number of observations = 20

As the frequencies of the changes in the discount rate increase, the estimated coefficient of the prime rate decreases. This demonstrates that the higher the frequency of the discount rate change, the smaller the size of the prime rate change. The estimated coefficients are significant at the 95% confidence level.

Now we regress consumer loan rates and other business loan rates known in our book as the "regional rates"[1] on the prime rates of New York banks and the discount rates of the Federal Reserve Bank. This enables us to determine the degree of influence that national rates exert on regional or local rates.

## The Average Regional Rates Regressed on Prime Rates of New York Banks

The Model Fitted was:

$$RR = R_0 + R_1RR + \text{error}$$

Regional rates were regressed on the prime rate of the New York banks. Regression results were as follows:

$$\text{Regional Rate} = \underset{(0.8188)}{3.8302} + \underset{(0.0641)}{0.7624}\ \text{prime rate}$$

$R^2 = 0.904$

Number of observations = 17

The Equation from regression output:

$$RR = 3.83 + .76\ PR$$

[1]The terms regional rates and local rates have been used inter-changeably in this book. The average regional rate represents the average business loan rate at local levels.

For each one percent increase in the prime rate, there has been on an average of .76 of 1 percent increase in a regional rate. The estimated coefficient is statistically significant at a 95% percent confidence level and the goodness of the fit is 90%.

The model for the regional rate demonstrates that the prime rate of the New York banks exerts a strong influence in determining the regional rates. It simply means that regional banks change their rates of interest in response to changes in the prime rate of the New York banks. Now we intend to see the impact of the changes of the discount rate of Federal Reserve Bank on regional rates.

**Average Regional Rates Regressed on Discount Rates of FRB (1975 - 1991)**

**Regression Output**

| | |
|---|---|
| Constant | 4.172609 |
| Std Err of Y Est | (1.063812) |
| $R^2$ | 0.837941 |
| No. of Observations | 17 |
| Degrees of Freedom | 15 |
| X Coefficient (s) | 1.005161 |
| Std Err of Coefficient | (0.114135) |

$$\text{Avg RR} = 4.17 + 1.0 \text{ DR}$$

At a 95% confidence level, the regression of the average regional rates on the discount rates of the Federal Reserve Bank shows that for a 1% increase in the discount rate, there has been more than 1% increase in the average regional rates. The "t" ratio of the slope is significant and the goodness of the fit is 83%.

**Arkansas Consumer Rates Regressed on Discount Rates of FRB (1975 - 1996)**

**Regression Output**

| | |
|---|---|
| Constant | 6.182156 |
| Std Err of Y Est | (1.017976) |
| $R^2$ | 0.841943 |
| No. of Observations | 22 |
| Degrees of Freedom | 20 |
| X Coefficient | 0.870431 |
| Std Err of Coefficient | (0.08433) |

$$ArkCR = 6.18 + .87\ DR$$

The regression of the Arkansas consumer rate on the discount rate of the Federal Reserve Bank shows that for a 1% increase in the discount rate there has been .87 of 1% increase in the Arkansas consumer rate.

**Arkansas Consumer Rates Regressed on Prime Rates of New York Banks (1975 - 1996)**

**Regression Output**

| | |
|---|---|
| Constant | 1.987863 |
| Std Err of Y Est | (0.933184) |
| $R^2$ | 0.915998 |
| No. of Observations | 22 |
| Degrees of Freedom | 20 |
| X Coefficient | 1.141644 |
| Std Err of Coefficient | (0.077306) |

$$Ark\ CR = 1.98 + 1.14\ PR$$

We have just seen that the regression of the Arkansas consumer rate on the discount rate of the Federal Reserve Bank shows that for a 1% increase in discount rates, there has been .87 of 1% increase in the Arkansas consumer rate. The regression of the Arkansas consumer rate on the prime rate of New York banks shows that for a 1% increase in prime rates of New York banks, there has been a 1.4% increase in Arkansas consumer rates. At a 95% confidence interval the estimated coefficient is statistically significant with the goodness of the fit approximately .92.

**Michigan Consumer Rate Regressed on the Discount Rate of FRB (1980 - 1989)**

**Regression Output:**

| | |
|---|---|
| Constant | 7.799429 |
| Std Err of Y Est | (0.824067) |
| $R^2$ | 0.883193 |
| No. of Observations | 10 |
| Degrees of Freedom | 8 |
| X Coefficient (s) | 0.894253 |
| Std Err of Coefficient | (0.11498) |

Mich CR = 7.79 + .89 DR

**Michigan Consumer Rate**

**Regressed on the Prime Rate of New York Banks (1980 - 1989)**

**Regression Output:**

| | |
|---|---|
| Constant | 7.834305 |
| Std Err of Y Est | (0.933970) |
| $R^2$ | 0.849959 |
| No. of Observations | 10 |
| Degrees of Freedom | 8 |
| X Coefficient (s) | (0.639335) |
| Std Err of Coefficient | 0.094971 |

Mich CR = 7.83 + .63 PR

The regression of the Michigan consumer rate on the discount rate of the Fed shows that for each 1% increase in the discount rate, there has been .89 of 1% rise in the Michigan consumer rate. The "t" ratio of the slope is significant and the goodness of fit is .88. The regression results of Michigan consumer rates on prime rates of the New York banks show that for each 1% rise in prime rates of New York banks, there has been a .63 of 1% increase in the Consumer rate of interest. At a 95% confidence level, the estimated coefficient is statistically significant and the goodness of the fit is .84. This demonstrates that local consumer rates are greatly influenced by the discount rate of the Fed and the New York banks' prime rates.

The regression of the regional rate on the discount rate of the Federal Reserve Bank (DR) gives $R^2$ as .84, implying that 84% of the variances in regional rate are explained by the variance in the discount rate of the

Federal Reserve Bank. Similarly, this $R^2$ is .91 when RR was regressed on the prime rate of New York banks implies that 91% of the variance in the regional rate is due to the variation in PR. These higher $R^2$ confirm our theory that both the discount rate of the Federal Reserve Bank and New York banks function as important determinants of the regional rates.

These regression results confirm that a change in the discount rate brings changes in the prime rate of the New York banks which in turn affects regional rates. Had there been no traditional announcement of the of the New York banks' prime rate, the local rate would have been affected only by the changes of the discount rate. In the absence of the "prime rate tradition," the cost of credit at the regional level would have settled at a much lower rate than it has for the last several decades. The "prime rate" tradition has cost households and businesses billions of dollars since its invention during the Great Depression.

# CHAPTER SIX
## THE REAL BURDEN OF DEBT

We should not measure the burden of debt in monetary terms only. In obtaining and servicing debt, the debtors in small and mid-sized cities often undergo a tremendous amount of anguish, suffering and sacrifice. For instance, at the time of obtaining credit, a householder has to take time off from work, go to different places to obtain the required documents, and drive to different parts of the city to negotiate for a loan with bank officials. Often, a day's work and earnings are lost.

In servicing debts, unforeseen events such as the termination of jobs and the loss of income due to an economic recession, often occur. At times, death, sickness, and similar emergencies happen to the indebted households and render them unable to service their debts. Under these circumstances, delays and failures in payment are bound to happen, but the consequences of the delays and failures in payment are much more severe than we have generally assumed them to be. The usual bashing of the debtor by the creditor takes the following forms:

1. Frequent calls and registered letters from the creditors threatening to sue.
2. Threats of repossession of the debtor's home, car, appliances, and furniture by creditors.
3. Forced disinvestment and the pawning of household, business and personal assets, such as car, guns, and jewelry.

Other costs – such as late fees, penalties, and the high cost of credit itself – result in considerable erosion of the household income and make it impossible for the family to help their children obtain better education, training and skills. The deprivations, sacrifices, and woes of indebted households represent the real burden of debt.[1]

We enumerate below true stories of the sacrifices and sufferings that households in mid-sized cities have undergone in obtaining and servicing

---

[1]For details, please read the chapter "The Economic Saga of Jay."

debts. Students who interviewed householders collected these reports of true cases, most of whom happen to work on farms. We have reproduced their reports with few editorial changes. The reporting households requested that their identities be kept confidential. Some of these cases date to the late eighties.

## FIELD REPORTS[1]

### Case 1
### A Man's Inability to Buy a Gift for His Wife May Have Sparked Robbery, Suicide[2]

In Kenner, Louisiana, a man had been out of a job for nine months. His car was broken. He was about to lose his house. As a desperate measure he robbed a bank. As he ran back to his van, he tripped and dropped the money. Then, Jefferson Parish Sheriff's deputies and a witness cornered him in a nearby alley. While they begged him to drop the gun, the man yelled, "I have a letter for my wife in my pocket," dropped to his knees, put the gun in his mouth and pulled the trigger, sources told *The Times-Picayune* of New Orleans. At one time, he was making a lot of money, but after having lost his job, and having no other recourse to meet his financial need, he committed robbery and finally suicide.

### Case 2
### Episode Near Jonesboro, Arkansas in 1997

A head of household was unable to make payments for the treatment of his wife who was suffering from cancer. Observers noted that he "moved heaven and earth" to find financial help from banks and other possible sources without success; then he decided to rob a bank. They caught him and sent him to jail. Meanwhile, a well known, generous physician, Dr. Atique, from Jefferson Regional Medical Center in Pine Bluff, Arkansas agreed to treat his wife at no cost. As he came to know of this noble gesture by a physician, the householder expressed his gratitude and commented that he did not mind serving his term as long as his wife's treatment was assured.

---

[1]The first 2 cases were reported in the news papers and others by the students from the field.

[2]As reported in the Dallas Morning News

## (Student Reported Cases)

### Case 3

This case is about a good friend of mine named Mark. He and I grew up in the same neighborhood and graduated from high school together. After graduation, Mark and I started college, but after the first year, Mark dropped out because he felt school was not for him. He worked a year in a part-time job, saved a little money, then decided to try opening a club. He also tried to get a small business loan, but was turned down many times because he did not have collateral and his credit rating was poor.

Frustrated, he moved out to California with relatives thinking that he could make some quick money selling drugs. After a few months, he met with people who could get him started, and soon he was in the drug business. One summer Mark came home and told us how he enjoyed selling drugs and making easy money, and that in another year he would be ready to open his club. We did not hear from Mark for quite some time until one day his brother told us that they had arrested Mark in one of the biggest drug busts in Los Angeles County history. They sentenced him to ten years in prison.

### Case 4

Ricky was interested in buying a car but had bad credit. He had heard of car lots that would sell cars to buyers with bad credit, so he went to check them out. Each car lot would sell him a car, but at an inflated price, with high interest rates. He was required to make weekly or biweekly payments only. Though the payments were high, he bought a car on biweekly payments terms, financing it for a year and a half. After the first six months, it became more difficult for him to make payments on time and he had to borrow money to do so. Soon he started pawning things that he was not able to redeem. He started defaulting in payments, and eventually they repossessed his car. He had lost the car, the payments he had made and the articles he pawned.

### Case 5

A student reported that he had a friend named David who was here at this university and was a good student. His parents did not have adequate funds to send his children for higher education, so he worked to support himself and to pay for the cost of attending school. He did this for about two years and then decided to open a small clothing store to sell T-shirts. He dropped out of school and continued to work.

After about a year of working and saving a little money, he decided to start his own business. He found out that, in order to get a store in a nice area, he needed more money than he had available. He applied for a small loan but was turned down because he had bad credit. He withdrew his small savings and reluctantly used it to open his store in an affordable but less desirable area. The result was that he had to locate his business in a high crime neighborhood. A small loan from banks or other sources would have helped him operate the store in a safer area. As expected, there were repeated break-ins at the store forcing him to close his business. His dream to better his economic condition was nipped in the bud. A small financial accommodation could have made all the difference in his life.

### Case 6

Jim is a single man interviewed by a student. He currently has neither a job nor a home. He lives with friends and contributes toward paying rent and utilities when he finds work. He borrowed $5,000 at 10% interest from an uncle to help him along, but being jobless, he soon exhausted his borrowed fund in meeting the basic needs of life. Finally, the circumstances forced him to move in with his mother and aunt, where he does not have to pay rent. The thought that no opportunities exist to improve his situation continually depresses him. He hopes that he will find work overseas but sees few immediate avenues to improve his condition.

### Case 7

This case is about a young woman who lives alone and pays high interest on her car loan. She often falls behind in payments on her loan, rent, and utilities. At such times, she depends on her mother who helps her out from by lending her small sums – interest free. She has also borrowed from a local bank using a city lot her father left her. This has increased her debt burden as well as her miseries. She is desperately looking for a way out of this mess but does not know where to find help.

### Case 8

M.C. and his wife have two children. Their combined income is $26,000. Last year, they paid $10,267 in interest on loans on their car, house, and start-up business. When the business they tried to start failed, they began relying on interest free loans from their parents to make monthly payments. Their vehicles are now in their parents' names. M.C. often pawns or pledges property to pay utilities. Their home is now up for sale to meet their financial obligation. However, in the depressed housing market, it is unlikely that they will find a buyer and be able to satisfy creditors.

### Case 9

My friend, Carla, is from a poor family and had a job paying a little over the minimum wage. She couldn't afford a car, and tried to borrow money from the bank to buy one. The bank denied her loan on the ground that she had not been on the job long enough. A year later she went back to the same bank, and this time they stated that she needed a co-signer. Her father went to the bank to co-sign for her loan, but because her father had too many bills, the bank refused to approve the loan.

Carla tried to get food stamps but was refused because she did not have any children. About a year later, Carla had a little son. By the time Carla was twenty-three years old, she had four children. It was then that she became eligible to receive food stamps and satisfied the bank's requirements to get a loan.

### Case 10

My uncle, a college graduate, owns a small business in a rural area but found it hard to get a loan. On several occasions, he went to his bank to borrow some money, but was repeatedly turned down. Finally, he got an allotment which allowed new entrepreneurs to open their own businesses.

It took a while for his business to start booming and expanding. He did not realize, however, that the interest rate was at its highest and that he had to start repaying the loan back within a year. He finally reached the point where he had to sell half his business to pay off the amounts past due on his business loans. His business also started foundering as he raised prices to enable him to repay the loan. Because of the high interest rate, he ended up paying out more than he had gained in profits.

### Case 11

A student reports that some ethnic groups, overall, have difficulties in the business world because of their appearance, the way they talk, and the way they dress. When I visited California this summer, my half-black and half-white cousin recounted an experience that illustrates this. She had told me it was really hard to be of mixed race. She was a smart young lady but she usually wore jeans and dickeys and pulled her hair back in a ponytail.

My cousin worked in Beverly Hills at a clothing boutique and she needed money for a down payment on a BMW. She had tried to obtain a loan but had been turned down. One day, she decided to dress up and go downtown to the bank to reapply for the loan. She wore her hair straight and even decided to put on a little make-up. The same lady who had previously rejected her, called her to review her application. Without questioning her any further, the lady gave her a loan for $5,000.

**Case 12**

A householder took out a second mortgage on his home to finance a fast food restaurant. They gave the man one year's time to repay his loan or the finance company would take his property away. After three months in business, the owner became ill and did not have sufficient help to operate the business in his absence. The man was ill for six months during which time his business lost a substantial amount of money due to poor management. Being unable to repay his debt, the man was forced to sign over his business to his creditors to keep possession of his home. Left with only a home and no credit-standing, he was forced to start his life's struggle all over.

**Case 13**

The average pawnshop charges 25 cents on the dollar. For example, an article pawned for $150 costs the person $187.50 to regain it. This gives the pawnshop $37.50 a month for that pawned article. When one sells an article to a pawnshop, the pawnbroker often resells it for three times the price for which he bought it. For example, an article bought for $200 is sold for $600.

X[1] had a car accident with Y's automobile. As a result, X was liable for all damages. In order to pay for the damages, X sold all of his jewelry, valued at $925.00, to a pawnshop for $210.00. This amount was still not enough to pay for the damages to Y's car, therefore, X was forced to take out a loan from a loan shark. After all of this, X was still forced to borrow money from his family and his college fund to pay for all the damages. He continues to be constantly harassed by his creditors for payments.

[1] The person involved in the episode did not want to disclose his name.

### Case 14

X is a college student with debts from credit cards, telephone bills, and student loans totaling $12,000.00. He has no way to pay off these debts because he cannot find a good paying job. His only way out might be filing for bankruptcy and he is planning to do so.

### Case 15

The first farmer interviewed rented approximately 1,200 acres from two different landowners and obtained his financing by conventional means. As he described it "I do not depend on a government loan from the Farmers Home Administration. I get my own money from the First National Bank of McGhee ." This farmer's feeling is that the government is continuing to lend money to farmers who own their land so that the state can some day take over or nationalize farming on a large scale.

This may seem a radical view coming from some very patriotic "grass roots" Americans, but he cannot help feeling this way when he describes the impact interest rates are having on his life. The revenue he receives for his products does not meet the expenses required to produce them and pay for the cost of debt. He is currently paying 13 percent interest for his funds to run his farming operation and has lost money each year since 1981. He has indicated that this will be his last year farming.

### Case 16

The second farmer interviewed was a partner in a family-run operation consisting of two brothers and their father. They owned 960 acres in Lincoln, Arkansas. The interest rate had risen to around 14%. They had what was called a "floating loan" in which the interest rate on their loans is tied to the federal discount rate and can rise and fall during the term of the loan.

The price of equipment and chemicals have hurt most farmers, but they ran their operation with equipment that was at least 10 years old. They do not have the luxury of owning a new car or truck and the homes that they live in were built little by little and are now mortgaged. They own their lands but they are heavily mortgaged and the interest rate was overwhelming. It would be difficult to survive paying interest rates of 13 and 14 percent.

### Case 17

D.R. was once a farmer, but had to quit because the FHA foreclosed on his property. His debt was written off, but the government will not guarantee his loan if he wanted to farm again. He now works for the state and lives on his parents' land, rent-free. He still depends upon interest-free loans from his parents and often sells or pawns property just to get by. He is only paying interest on his car loan, but he must pay alimony and child support to his former wife every month. He wants to give his new wife some gifts, but it takes everything he makes just to pay the bills.

### Case 18

A farmer own 2,500 acres just south of Dermott, Arkansas and also owns a store that sells farm supplies. He is losing money on his business and is on the verge of bankruptcy. He feels that interest rates are so high that he will not be able to cover his expenses. The high rates are the major cause of his financial problems.

Every day, he sees that his customers cannot pay for the equipment they purchase, or they do not attempt to purchase necessary items because they cannot get loans. He and his customers believe that times are getting worse and may even reach the level of the Great Depression when banks lost their money and the farmers lost their lands.

### Case 19

This farmer leases 2,000 acres in Southeast Arkansas from his father. He gave up farming recently and sold all his equipment at a public auction. He is now forced to rent his land to other farmers.

He believes that Washington, D.C. is out of touch with farmers and says he never asks the FHA to lend him money. He believes that farmers should be able to earn a decent living for their families, but they can no longer achieve this. Because of increasing expenses and interest rates, he believes that farmers have no option other than to sell what is most important to them: their land.

### Case 20

This farmer claims that he now owes more interest to the banks than the principal amount that he had borrowed. He has been told that he cannot farm this year by using conventional financing. He will have to file for bankruptcy or the banks will repossess and auction his equipment.

He has been farming for twenty-five years and hopes that he can return to it some day, although he has nothing to show but many unpaid debts and endless heartache for himself and his family. He feels cheated because though he is a good farmer, the low prices he receives for his products cannot pay the unreasonable interest rates and outrageous prices for chemicals and equipment. According to him, it is a losing battle.

### Case 21

This case involves a young farm family whose interest payments last year totaled 72% of their income. They are being pulled from all directions, by the FHA, banks, and credit card companies to pay their bills. They feel that they will lose their home, car, and sanity. They now depend on loans from relatives to pay for the necessities of life.

### Case 22

This case is about a young farm family that is deeply in debt to the Farmer's Home Administration. The family's total income last year was $36,000, and 83% of this, or $29,884, was paid toward interest payments. The family is forced to live with the farmer's parents who help them pay some of the interest payments and utility bills; otherwise, this struggling family would not have survived.

### Concluding Remarks of a Student Reporter

It is evident from the interviews that the interest rates were the biggest problem for the farmers. They all seem to agree that the past few years had spelled doom for them in the rising cost of production, high interest rates, the climbing cost of equipment and the low prices paid for their products.

After hearing that his friend had committed suicide when he learned that the banks were taking his family farm this year, one individual summed it all up in this manner: "A man is dead, a good Christian and a good farmer. It is time to ask our government why this is happening to us farmers all over the nation."

"It is, indeed, happening all over the nation. To see it, one needs only to pick up the daily paper and read the legal section concerning bankruptcies and foreclosures on farmers and farm related industries. I think it is time that the lawmakers exercised their authority and begin to force our President and the Chair of the Federal Reserve Bank to do something about the farm situation before it is too late and we all suffer over time. Why not save our family farms that were the backbone of this country for many years and keep our country the "Bread Basket" of the world? If interest costs are not put in line soon, that the whole economy will be undermined and our great nation will lose its top place. Our elected officials should realize this now."

These few cases collected by student represent a very small sample of a large number of struggling farm families. Nevertheless, they illustrate a reality of life for millions of struggling households. Similar tales are recounted and comparable sad episodes are taking place on a daily basis in the U.S. economy.

All this points to the fact that many households pass through a variety of problems both in getting loans and servicing debts. The lack of stable jobs, low or nonexistent sources of income, high interest rates, and severe terms and conditions for obtaining credit or servicing debt account for the pains and woes that these households undergo during the tenure of their loans.

The credit environment is such that millions of households are being denied credit every day for one reason or another. At the same time, defaulting indebted households, for no fault of their own, pass through endless pains and sufferings with no relief in sight. It is a pity that the agonies of these indebted households have continued for decades, unnoticed and neglected, and have never been an issue of public debate.

# CHAPTER SEVEN
## INTEREST EARNED

"Interest Earned" is an important item of inquiry for any economic survey of households. Our information on this item indicates a household's ability to save under the given circumstances and the economic strength it enjoys over those who fail to do so. Very few of our surveyed households earn a large amount of interest though "interest earned" is a most crucial variable as it gives some measure of savings that are being generated in small and mid-sized cities.

The information gathered on interest earned can be used in estimating the amount and trend of savings made by the households, and it broadly reflects the economic status of households. In some quarters, it is assumed that the value of household assets far exceeds the amount of their outstanding debt. This statement does not establish which households owe debt and which ones are enjoying the fruits of the investments made out of their savings and borrowed money. Here we are interested in confirming our presumption that the indebted households in small and mid-sized cities are not the ones whose earnings from the acquired assets far exceed the debt incurred in acquiring the assets.

For a better understanding of this point, we compared the averages of interest earned and the averages of "interest paid" by interest paying households. This may give us insight into the economic strength of the indebted households and also their deficiencies. We estimated the sample average of "interest earned" for all households, and then the average of the "interest earned" by "interest earning households."

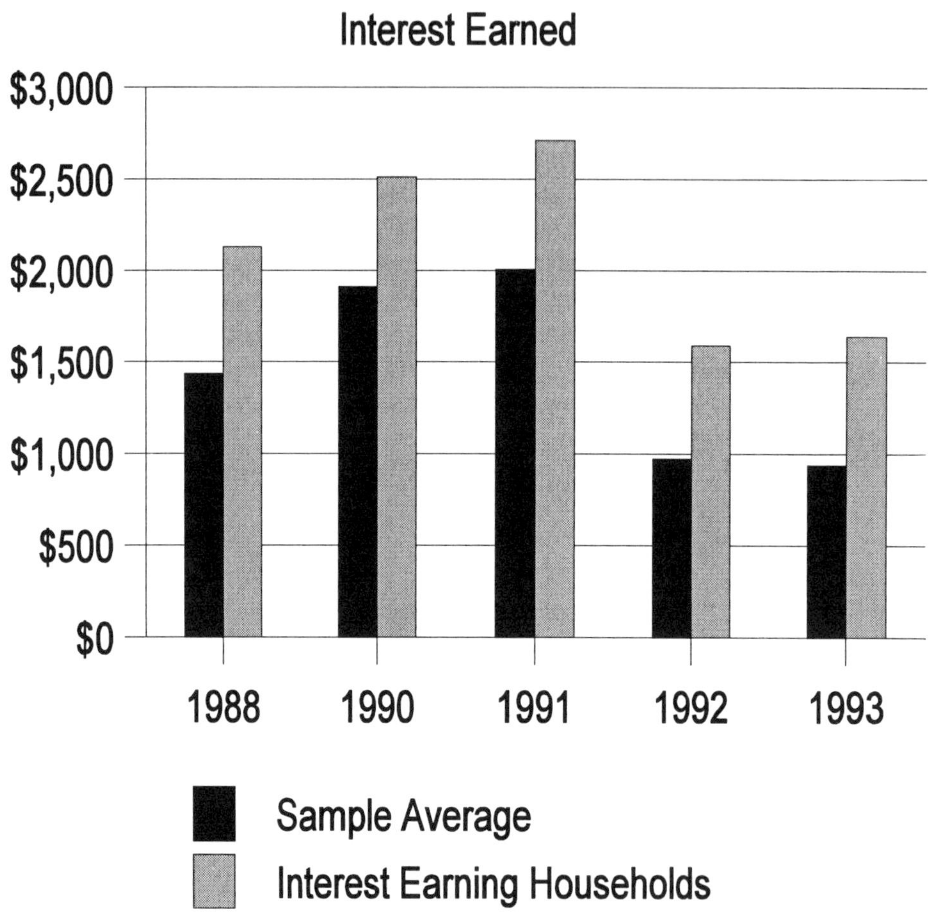
Interest Earned
$3,000
$2,500
$2,000
$1,500
$1,000
$500
$0
1988
1990
1991
1992
1993
Sample Average
Interest Earning Households

Figure 18

**The Trend of Average Size of Interest Earned by Households**

| | 1988 | 1990 | 1991 | 1992 | 1993 |
|---|---|---|---|---|---|
| Sample Average for all households | $1,435 | $1,911 | $2,006 | $974 | $936 |
| The Average of (only Interest Earning Households) | $2,128 | $2,513 | $2,712 | $1,590 | $1,639 |

The sample average of interest earned by households in this group varied between $936 and $2,000 during 1990-1993 period, yielding a decrease in the interest earnings by $325 per year. During the same period the average interest earned by interest-earning households varied between $1,590 and $2,712, yielding a decrease in interest earnings by $291 per year. The sample average of interest earned for the last four years of the survey was $1,457 and that of the interest earning households was $2,114.

| | |
|---|---|
| Average interest earned of by all households in our sample for 1990-1993 | $1,457 |
| Per household per year, average decrease in interest earned for 1990-1993 | $325 |
| Average interest earned by interest earning households for 1990-1993 | $2,114 |
| Per household per year, average decrease in interest earning for 1990-1993 | ($291) |

After describing the trend of interest earned by households, we intend to take a closer look at the trend of "interest earning" by different income groups. Below are the tables that show the trend.

## GROUP ANALYSIS[1]
### Interest Earned by Different Income Groups

**$0 - 5, 000**

| | 1988 | 1990 | 1991 | 1992 | 1993 |
|---|---|---|---|---|---|
| Average Size of Interest Earned | $3,194 | $19 | $4,206 | $778 | $267 |
| Percentage of Households Earning Interest in This Group | 1% | 1% | 4% | 11% | 1% |
| These Households as % of all Households in the Sample[2] | 1% | 1% | 3% | 18% | 13% |
| Average interest earned by households in this group for 1990-1993 | | | | | $1318 |
| Per household/year, average increase in interest earned for 1990-1993 | | | | | $83 |

The average interest earned by households in this group varied from a low of $19 to a high of $4,206, yielding an average of $1,318 for the 1990-1993 period. The average size of interest earned in this category shows a great deal of variation due to inheritances received by a limited number of households. The average interest earnings increased in 1991 to $4,206 but decreased in 1992 and 1993 to $778 and $267 respectively. The interest earnings by households in 1988 were $3,194. The percentages of households earning interest in this group varied from 1% to 11%, representing 1% to 18% of all households in the sample. Per household per year, the average increase in interest earnings for this group during the 1990-1993 period was $83.

[1]Note to Readers: As stated in Chapter Three, all group analysis are meant for future researchers. The "size of debt"," level of income," " interest payments," and "interest earnings" in the future for different income groups can be compared with our findings to determine what changes have occurred to them. The pattern of analysis has a repetitive format and may not be interesting to general readers, but researchers may find our estimates as valuable reference materials. General readers may find a summary of all group analysis in Chapter Ten.

[2]These households represent interest earning households.

$5,000 - 10, 000

| | 1988 | 1990 | 1991 | 1992 | 1993 |
|---|---|---|---|---|---|
| Average Size of Interest Earned | $1,128 | $1,558 | $1,856 | $1,022 | $1,988 |
| Percentage of Households Earning Interest | 7% | 10% | 7% | 27% | 14% |
| These Households as % of all Households in the Sample | 5% | 8% | 6% | 27% | 7% |
| Average interest earned by households in this group for 1990-1993 | | | | | $1,606 |
| Per household/year, average increase in interest earned for 1990-1993 | | | | | $143 |

The average interest earned by households varied from a low of $1,022 to a high of $1,988, yielding an average of $1,606 for the 1990-1993 period. The average interest earned by households in 1988 was $1,128. The percentages of households earning interest in this group varied from 7% to 27%, representing 6% to 27% of all households in the sample. Per household per year, the average increase in interest earning for this group during the 1990-1993 period was $143.

$10,000 - 15, 000

| | 1988 | 1990 | 1991 | 1992 | 1993 |
|---|---|---|---|---|---|
| Average Size of Interest Earned | $1,668 | $3,123 | $2,086 | $1,781 | $1,197 |
| Percentage of Households Earning Interest | 15% | 10% | 14% | 9% | 8% |
| These Households as % of all Households in the Sample | 10% | 7% | 10% | 5% | 4% |
| Average interest earned by households in this group for 1990-1993 | | | | | $2,047 |
| Per household/year, average decrease in interest earned for 1990-1993 | | | | | ($642) |

The average interest earned by households varied from a low of $1,197 to a high of $3,123, yielding an average of $2,047 for the 1990-1993 period. The average interest earned by households in 1988 was $1,668. The percentage of households earning this interest in this group varied from 8% to 14%, representing 4% to 10% of all households in the sample. Per household per year, the average decrease in interest earnings for this group during the 1990-1993 period was $642.

$15,000 - 20, 000

| | 1988 | 1990 | 1991 | 1992 | 1993 |
|---|---|---|---|---|---|
| Average Interest Earned | $928 | $2,921 | $2,281 | $1,110 | $2,210 |
| Percentage of Households Earning Interest | 11% | 11% | 10% | 12% | 9% |
| These Households as % of all Households in the Sample | 7% | 8% | 7% | 7% | 5% |
| Average interest earned by households in this group for 1990-1993 | | | | | $2,131 |
| Per household/year, average decrease in interest earned for 1990-1993 | | | | | ($237) |

The average interest earned by households varied from a low of $1,110 to a high of $2,921, yielding an average of $2,131 for the 1990-1993 period. The average interest earned by households in 1988 was $928. The percentages of households earning interest in this group varied from 9% to 12%, representing 5% to 8% of all households in the sample. Per household per year, the average decrease in interest earnings for this group during the1990-1993 period was $237.

$20,000 - 25, 000

| | 1988 | 1990 | 1991 | 1992 | 1993 |
|---|---|---|---|---|---|
| Average Size of Interest Earned | $1,146 | $3,194 | $1,626 | $1,029 | $1,650 |
| Percentage of Households Earning Interest | 9% | 9% | 9% | 10% | 8% |
| These Households as % of all Households in the Sample | 6% | 7% | 7% | 6% | 5% |
| The average interest earned by households in this group for 1990-1993 | | | | | $1,875 |
| Per household/year, the average decrease in interest earned for 1990-1993 | | | | | ($515) |

The average interest earned by households in this income group varied from a low of $1,029 to a high of $3,194, yielding an average of $1,875 for the 1990-1993 period. The average interest earned by households in 1988 was $1,146. The percentages of households earning interest in this group varied from 8% to 10%, representing 5% to 7% of all households in the sample. Per household per year, the average decrease in interest earnings for this group during the 1990-1993 period was $515.

$25,000 - 30, 000

| | 1988 | 1990 | 1991 | 1992 | 1993 |
|---|---|---|---|---|---|
| Average Size of Interest Earning | $2,546 | $3,336 | $439 | $1,539 | $1,521 |
| Percentage of Households Earning Interest | 13% | 7% | 4% | 10% | 8% |
| These Households as % of all Households in the Sample | 9% | 5% | 3% | 6% | 4% |
| The average interest earned by households in this group for 1990-1993 | | | | | $1,709 |
| Per household/year, average decrease in interest earned for 1990-1993 | | | | | ($605) |

The average interest earned by the households varied from a low of $439 to a high of $3,336, yielding an average of $1,709 for the1990-1993 period. The average interest earned by households in 1988 was $2,546. The percentages of households earning interest in this group varied from 4% to 10%, representing 3% to 6% of all households in the sample. Per household per year, the average decrease in interest earnings for this group during the 1990-1993 period was $605.

$30,000 - 35, 000

| | 1988 | 1990 | 1991 | 1992 | 1993 |
|---|---|---|---|---|---|
| Average Size of Interest Earned | $2,931 | $1,794 | $2,885 | $2,607 | $3,667 |
| Percentage of Households Earning Interest | 11% | 10% | 8% | 8% | 7% |
| These Households as % of all Households in the Sample | 7% | 8% | 6% | 5% | 4% |
| Average interest earned by households in this group for 1990-1993 | | | | | $2,738 |
| Per household/year, average increase in interest earned for 1990-1993 | | | | | $624 |

The average interest earned by households varied from a low of $1,794 to a high of $3,667, yielding an average of $2,738 for the 1990-1993 period. Interest earnings increased in 1991 to $2,885 but decreased to $2,607 in 1992. The average interest earned by households in 1988 was $2,931. The percentages of households earning interest in this group varied from 7% to 10% representing 4% to 8% of all households in the sample. Per household per year, the average increase in interest earnings for this group during the 1990-1993 period was $624.

### $35,000 - 40, 000

| | 1988 | 1990 | 1991 | 1992 | 1993 |
|---|---|---|---|---|---|
| Average Size of Interest Earned | $2,478 | $1,235 | $916 | $1,345 | $1,024 |
| Percentage of Households Earning Interest | 14% | 6% | 5% | 45% | 7% |
| These Households as % of all Households in the Sample | 9% | 4% | 4% | 28% | 4% |
| Average interest earned by households in this group for 1990-1993 | | | | | $1,130 |
| Per household/year, average increase in interest earned for 1990-1993 | | | | | ($70) |

The average interest earned by households varied from a low of $916 to a high of $1,345, yielding an average of $1,130 for the 1990-1993 period. The average interest earned by households in 1988 was $2,478. The percentages of households earning interest in this group varied from 5% to 45% representing 4% to 28% of all households in the sample. Per household per year, the average decrease in interest earnings for this group during the 1990-1993 period was $70.

### $40,000 - 45, 000

| | 1988 | 1990 | 1991 | 1992 | 1993 |
|---|---|---|---|---|---|
| Average Size of Interest Earned | $2,497 | $2,871 | $967 | $1,429 | $1,359 |
| Percentage of Households Earning Interest | 10% | 8% | 7% | 9% | 9% |
| These Households as % of all Households in the Sample | 6% | 6% | 6% | 6% | 6% |
| Average interest earned by households in this group for 1990-1993 | | | | | $1,657 |
| Per household/year, average decrease in interest earned for 1990-1993 | | | | | ($504) |

The average interest earned by households varied from a low of $967 to a high of $2,871, yielding an average of $1,657 for the 1990-1993 period. The average interest earned by households in 1988 was $2,497. The percentages of households earning interest in this group varied from 7% to 9%, representing 6% of all households in the sample. Per household per year, the average decrease in interest earnings for this group during the 1990-1993 period was $504.

$45,000 - 50, 000

| | 1988 | 1990 | 1991 | 1992 | 1993 |
|---|---|---|---|---|---|
| Average Size of Interest Earned | $4,647 | $1,566 | $5,073 | $2,578 | $566 |
| Percentage of Households Earning Interest | 100% | 100% | 96% | 77% | 73% |
| These Households as % of all Households in the Sample | 2% | 6% | 7% | 1% | 3% |
| Average interest earned by households in this group for 1990-1993 | | | | | $2,446 |
| Per household/year, average decrease in interest earned for 1990-1993 | | | | | ($333) |

The average interest earned by households varied from a low of $566 to a high of $5,073, yielding an average of $2,446 for the 1990-1993 period. The average interest earned by households in 1988 was $4,647. The percentages of households earning interest in this group varied from 73% to 100% representing 1% to 7% of all households in the sample. Per household per year, the average decrease in interest earnings for this group during the 1990-1993 period was $333.

$50,000 - 55, 000

| | 1988 | 1990 | 1991 | 1992 | 1993 |
|---|---|---|---|---|---|
| Average Size of Interest Earned | $1,535 | $3,505 | $3,314 | $1,968 | $299 |
| Percentage of Households Earning Interest | 100% | 81% | 92% | 100% | 80% |
| These Households as % of all Households in the Sample | 2% | 4% | 4% | 1% | 5% |
| Average interest earned by households in this group for 1990-1993 | | | | | $2,272 |
| Per household/year, average decrease in interest earned for 1990-1993 | | | | | ($1,069) |

The average interest earned by households varied from a low of $299 to a high of $3,505, yielding an average of $2,272 for the 1990-1993 period. The average interest earned by households in 1988 was $1,535. The percentages of households earning this interest in this group varied from 80% to 100%, representing 1% to 5% of all households in the sample. Per household per year, the average decrease in interest earnings for this group during the 1990-1993 period was $1,069.

**$55,000 - 60, 000**

| | 1988 | 1990 | 1991 | 1992 | 1993 |
|---|---|---|---|---|---|
| Average Size of Interest Earned | $4,652 | $1,203 | $2,287 | $1,821 | $1,994 |
| Percentage of Households Earning Interest | 100% | 100% | 77% | 85% | 77% |
| These Households as % of all Households in the Sample | 1% | 5% | 5% | 0% | 1% |
| Average interest earned by households in this group for 1990-1993 was | | | | | $1,826 |
| Per household/ year, average increase in interest earned for 1990-1993 | | | | | $264 |

The average interest earned by households varied from a low of $1,203 to a high of $2,287, yielding an average of $1,826 for the 1990-1993 period. The average interest earned by households in 1988 was $4,652. The percentages of households earning interest in this group varied from 77% to 100%, representing 1% to 5% of all households in the sample. Per household per year, the average increase in interest earnings for this group during the 1990-1993 period was $264.

**$60,000 - 65, 000**

| | 1988 | 1990 | 1991 | 1992 | 1993 |
|---|---|---|---|---|---|
| Average Size of Interest Earned | $3,806 | $649 | $2,038 | $1,045 | $2,189 |
| Percentage of Households Earning Interest | 100% | 100% | 100% | 100% | 97% |
| These Households as % of all Households in the Sample | 1% | 2% | 3% | 1% | 0% |
| Average interest earned by households in this group for 1990-1993 was | | | | | $1,480 |
| Per household/year, average increase in interest earned for 1990-1993 | | | | | $513 |

The average interest earned by households varied from a low of $649 to a high of $2,189, yielding an average of $1,480 for the 1990-1993 period. The average interest earned by households in 1988 was $3,806. The percentages of households earning interest in this group varied from 91% to 100%, representing less than 3% of all households in the sample. Per household per year, the average increase in interest earnings for this group during the 1990-1993 period was $513.

**Summary:** Out of the 13 groups of different income levels, 8 groups had net positive increases in interest earnings. The average of these earnings for these groups varied from a low of $64 to a high of $1,823 for the years 1990-1993. On the other hand, the remaining five groups reported to have had net negative interest earnings, the average of which varied from a low of $1,054 to a high of $2,194 for the years 1990-1993. Interest earnings by a larger number of groups should not mislead us into thinking that the households in general are doing well in acquiring some interest earning financial assets and that the value of these assets might have been exceeding the liabilities incurred in the form of borrowing. This point has been explained in the section on Interest Paying and Interest Earning Households.

### Interest Earned as % of Income

**Percentage of Households Earning Interest**

| Interest Earned as% of Income | | | |
|---|---|---|---|
| | 1988<br>f/n | 1990<br>f/n | 1991<br>f/n |
| .01 - .05 | 0.21 | 0.40 | 0.45 |
| .05 - .10 | 0.08 | 0.18 | 0.13 |
| .10 - .20 | 0.07 | 0.018 | 0.05 |
| .20 - .30 | 0.014 | 0.014 | 0.03 |
| .30 - More Than | 0.17 | 0.09 | 0.13 |

**Percentage of Households Earning Interest**

Interested earned as % of income

| | |
|---|---|
| .01 to .05 | 21% to 45% of households earned interest equal 1% to 5% of their income. |
| .05 to .10 | 18%, 14%, and 13% of households in 1988, 1990, and 1991 respectively earned interest equal to 5% to 10% of their income. |
| .10 to .20 | 07%, 18%, 5% of households in 1988, 1990, and 1991, respectively earned interest equal 10% to 20% of their income. |
| .20 to .30 | 1%, 1%, 3% of households In 1988, 1990, and 1991 earned interest that equaled 20% to 30% of their income. |
| More than .30 | 17%, 10%, 13% of households in 1988, 1990 and 1991 respectively earned interest that exceeded 30% of their income. |

This data shows that a sizeable number of households have a significant amount of savings on which they earned interest that equaled or exceeded 30% of their income. This data also speaks of concentration of wealth in few households.

**Interest Earned and Paid by Interest Paying Households**

| | 1988 | 1990 | 1991 | 1992 | 1993 | Average Interest Earned (1990-1993) |
|---|---|---|---|---|---|---|
| Average Income of Interest Paying Households | $29,463 | $39,360 | $39,918 | $42,437 | $46,369 | $42,021 |
| Average Interest Paid by Interest Paying Households | $2,267 | $3,332 | $3,188 | $2,429 | $2,864 | $2,953 |
| Average Interest Paid as % of Income | 8% | 8% | 8% | 6% | 6% | 7% |
| Average Interest Earned by Interest Paying Households | $880 | $1,448 | $1,193 | $1,087 | $555 | $1,070 |
| Average Interest Earned as % of Average Income | 3% | 4% | 3% | 3% | 1% | 3% |

The data shows that interest paying households' average income varied between $29,463 and $46,369, average interest paid varied between $2,267 and $3,332 and the average interest earned varied between $555 and $1,448 during our survey period (1985-1993). Interest paid by households for all the years of the survey varied from 6% to 8% of household income.

On the other hand, interest earned by households for all years of the survey varied from 1% to 4% of income: 3% being common for most of the years. This means that interest paid was, in a pragmatic sense, 100% larger than the interest earned by the interest-paying households in our survey. This also means that interest earned was not adequate to cover the interest payments on borrowed funds of households in small mid-sized cities.

**Average Debt, Interest Paid and Interest Earned Relationship**

| | 1988 | 1990 | 1991 | 1992 | 1993 |
|---|---|---|---|---|---|
| Average Size of Debt | $22,820 | $33,320 | $31,880 | $31,180 | $33,590 |
| Average Size of Interest Earned | $2,128 | $2,513 | $2,712 | $1,590 | $1,639 |
| Average Size of Interest Paid | $2,282 | $3,332 | $3,188 | $3,118 | $2,864 |
| Per One Dollar Debt Interest Earned | $0.09 | $0.08 | $0.09 | $0.07 | $0.06 |
| Per One Dollar Debt Interest Paid | $0.10 | $0.10 | $0.10 | $0.10 | $0.10 |
| Average interest earned by interest earning households in 1990-1993 | | | | | $2,114 |
| Average amount of interest paid for 1990-1993 was | | | | | $3,249 |
| Per one dollar debt average interest earned for 1990-1993 was | | | | | $.08 |
| Per one dollar debt average interest paid for 1990-1993 was | | | | | $.10 |

The data shows that per one dollar debt, interest earned varied from $.06 to $.09 for all the years of the survey. On the other hand, per one dollar of debt, the interest paid was $.10 for all the years of the survey. This demonstrates that the interest earnings of indebted households are not adequate to cover the servicing of the debt, much less paying off the debt.

Besides, as we mentioned elsewhere in this book, most borrowing is not always used to acquire assets that generate quick and adequate income for servicing and paying off the debt or to realize some excess over the borrowing. We have cited ample examples in our description of field reports of farmers and households who were unable to service their debts. Their properties were repossessed and many of them declared bankruptcy. The economic woes of the indebted households have been described in the chapter "Economic Saga of Jay."

# CHAPTER EIGHT
## TRACING THE CAUSES OF BURDENSOME DEBT

### A. PRIME RATE OF NEW YORK BANKS

The prime rate[1] is the basic short term loan rate which banks charge to their most credit-worthy customers. All banks may have their own prime rates, but we are interested in the prime rates of the big banks operating in the big cities, particularly in New York. This is because the prime rates of the New York banks influence the rates that most other banks in the country charge for business loans. A big bank in New York charges this rate in giving loans to customers and large corporations having high credit standing. This rate has a tremendous economic bearing both at home and abroad. Business loans involving billions of dollars as well as millions of corporations, businesses, and households are affected by the changes in this rate.

In the past, the prime rate of New York Banks has played an important role in worsening or improving the different phases of the business cycle. A surge in the prime rate during the period of our study contributed significantly to setting off the recession and devastating the economy in the early 80's.

As stated earlier, the prime rate, while meant for big corporations, affects other money market rates as well. Generally, all regional banks in the country respond to the pronouncement of prime rate changes of New York banks by changing their rates. The fact remains that, since its invention, the "prime rate tradition"[2] has continued to exert its influence on the rates of business loans and other rates in this country in one form or another until today. Over the years, it has become an important institution in itself. Unfortunately, the tradition of the pronouncement of the prime

---

[1]The term "prime rate" refers to the prime rate of New York banks.

[2]By "prime rate tradition" we mean the tradition of changing the local rates in response to changes in the prime rates of New York banks.

rate, and the usage of the rate by other banks as a base, has always resulted in a higher cost of credit at the regional and local levels, but this fact has seldom drawn our attention.[1]

Many of us are not well-acquainted with the underlying economic forces that gave birth to the "prime rate tradition," the motive that prompted the invention of this rate, the damages it inflicted on the national economy in the past, and, above all, the higher cost of credit it has been causing at the regional level. Our inquiries into these questions lead us to discuss the different facets of the "prime rate tradition." First, we will examine the impact of the high prime rates of New York banks on the United States economy in the early eighties.

In 1980, the prime rate of big banks in many cities, including New York, reached as high as 21%. In following the prime rate, the regional rates in some places were raised as high as 23%. This higher cost of credit severely constrained both consumption and investment spending by businesses and households, greatly accounting for the devastating recession of 1980. We describe below the magnitude of the devastation caused to the economy by this downturn of the economy.

### Adverse Affects of the Recession of 1980

As reflected in available government publications, the downturn in the economy threw 11,000,000 people out of jobs, the highest amount of unemployment since the Great Depression of 1930. In addition, tens of thousands of businesses were closed down: 82,216 businesses failed (1980-1983) and 642 businesses having yearly business of more than $1,000,000 declared bankruptcy (this number represented an all-time high). About 68% of businesses with liabilities varying from $100,000 to $1,000,000 failed or had serious difficulties in continuing their operation. More than 17,000 businesses in commercial areas failed (this number exceeded all past records).

At the same time, during the period of 1980-1983, over 3,000 business mergers took place. In most cases, small businesses were swallowed by big ones, giving the appearance that cannibalism was prevalent in the business world during this time.

The high prime rate and high regional rate accounted for a great number of these mergers and business failures. Banks were selective in approving loans to the more solvent customers who could afford to offer

---

[1]We elaborate on this point at a greater length in the section on regional rates.

collateral against their loans and borrow the minimum loan limit amount set by banks. The "minimum loan limit" was $3,000 or more in many places. Both "collateral" and "minimum loan limit" requirements literally prevented thousands of low and middle-income households in mid-sized cities from obtaining badly needed credit. These requirements also caused extreme hardships for households and made it very difficult for small businesses to continue their operations.

In a nutshell, the indices of economic variables, including unemployment, bankruptcies, failures of business, the swallowing of small businesses by big ones, and the disinvestment of assets increased rapidly in the wake of high interest rates. These high rates were the result of regional banks following the rates of the large New York banks in determining their loan rates.

In following the upward move of the prime rate, the lending institutions, in general, waste no time in raising their rates to several points greater than the prime rate of the New York banks. On the other hand, the pace is painfully and notoriously slow in lowering the loan rates when the prime rates of New York banks go down. However, it is clear that during the early 1980's, the prime rate of the large banks in New York assumed a pivotal role in bringing about the unprecedented rise in regional rates. These high rates in turn contributed significantly to bringing in the recession of the early 80's.

An economic variable has seldom done so much harm to households, businesses and financial institutions as did high prime rates of New York banks in the early 1980's. Since the induction of the New York banks' prime rate as an institution in the economy of the U.S. in the early 1930's, it has been the cause of higher cost of credit at the local level. It is against this background of damage done to the economy by high prime rates in the recent past and its potentiality of rendering harm to the economy in the future, that we intend to examine critically the background economic forces and the motives of large banks in New York that gave birth to the prime rate tradition in this country.

## The Birth of the Prime Rate

A severe depression engulfed the nation in the early thirties. The indices of the economy and the credit market started sinking. The demand for money was at its lowest level and the business loans constituted only 8% of the assets of all insured commercial banks. The loan deposit ratio had fallen from 68% in 1930 to 36% in 1935. The yield on treasury bills averaged only .25%. The rate of return on prime commercial paper was hardly above 1%. These indices of a depressed money market set the stage for cutthroat competitions among credit institutions.

Bitter rivalry among banks in attracting prospective borrowers was the order of the day. The prospect for profit on investment was bleak. Under these uncertainties and hopeless business conditions, a few banks in New York got together and came up with a great idea for their survival. They agreed not to compete in lowering interest rates, but to charge a minimum rate on their loans to future borrowers. They agreed that no bank should charge below 1/2% to business borrowers of high credit standing and this in turn dictated rates for non-prime borrowers as well.

This minimum rate was the so-called prime rate and this is how the historic "prime rate tradition" was born. This arrangement was clearly anti-competitive in spirit and anti-democratic in its pricing and decision-making process. Nevertheless, most banks adhered to these arrangements.

While following this agreement, a new "tradition" and new concept was brought into existence in the arena of money markets. Most banks started determining their rates on loans in view of changes in the prime rate of New York banks. With the passage of time, the tradition of following the prime rate of New York banks by other banks was firmly established. The chart below shows the relationship of prime rates of New York banks and the rates of other banks for the last two decades.

### The Trend and Relationship of the Prime Rates of New Banks with Other Rates[1]

| Year | Discount Rates | Average Rate of New York Banks | Regional Rates[2] |
|---|---|---|---|
| 1975 | 6.88 | 7.99 | 8.88 |
| 1976 | 5.25 | 6.81 | 7.38 |
| 1977 | 6.00 | 7.13 | 10.07 |
| 1978 | 7.79 | 9.78 | 11.11 |
| 1979 | 10.88 | 13.71 | 14.42 |
| 1980 | 11.50 | 15.53 | 15.68 |
| 1981 | 13.00 | 18.57 | 16.97 |
| 1982 | 10.00 | 14.44 | 15.74 |
| 1983 | 8.50 | 10.83 | 12.13 |
| 1984 | 8.50 | 11.95 | 13.24 |
| 1985 | 7.50 | 10.00 | 11.77 |
| 1986 | 6.25 | 8.25 | 11.38 |
| 1987 | 6.00 | 8.54 | 10.75 |
| 1988 | 6.50 | 9.50 | 11.69 |
| 1989 | 7.00 | 11.00 | 12.35 |
| 1990 | 6.50 | 10.00 | 11.58 |
| 1991 | 6.50 | 8.75 | 9.33 |
| 1992 | 3.00 | 6.00 | 8.80 |
| 1993 | 3.00 | 6.50 | 8.00 |
| 1994 | 4.08 | 7.30 | 9.08 |
| 1995 | 5.25 | 8.75 | 10.25 |
| 1996 | 5.00 | 8.25 | 10.00 |

[1]Throughout this book, the term "prime rate" refers to the rates of New York banks, while the term "discount rate" refers to the rates of the Federal Reserve Bank.

[2]These rates have been estimated by collecting the local rates prevailing in Arkansas and other neighboring states.

The chart also shows that the prime rates of New York banks remained greater than the discount rates of the Federal Reserve Bank while the regional rates remained greater than the prime rate of the New York banks, for most of the time during the last two decades. The chart gives the average figures only. In reality, in some places, the rates rose as high as 21%. The highest difference between the two rates occurred in 1981, when the regional rate rose to more than 21%.

The chart also demonstrates that there exist close relationships among these three rates: the discount rate of the Federal Reserve Bank, the prime rate of New York banks, and the regional rates of local banks. Households in mid-sized cities are mostly affected by regional rates. This led us to determine how the discount rate of the Federal Reserve Bank impacts the prime rate of New York banks and how the prime rate, in turn, impacts the regional rate. First, let us reflect on the "prime rate-discount rate" relationship.

**New York Prime Rates/Discount Rates (1975-1996)**

| | |
|---|---|
| **1.** Number of years the prime rate of New York banks remained greater than the discount rate of the Federal Reserve Bank | 21 |
| **2.** Number of times the prime rate of New York banks was at a higher level than the discount rate of the Federal Reserve Bank (at the time of discount rate changes) | 55 |
| **3.** The New York prime rate exceeded the discount rate of the Federal Reserve Bank by | 1.25% to 5.02% |
| **4.** The average percentage point at which the prime rate of New York banks was greater than the discount rate of the Federal Reserve Bank for the last 25 years | 2.96% |
| **5.** The range of variation in the prime rate of the New York banks during 1929 to 1996 | 1.5% to 21.5% |

## Determinants of the Prime Rates of New York Banks

The prime rate's behavior is shaped partly by market forces and partly by institutional factors. We have developed a hypothesis that the prime rate responds directly to the discount rate change of the Federal Reserve Bank. To test our hypothesis, we did simple regressions of the prime rate on the discount rate using time series data for a period of 50 years. The results are as follows:

$$PR = 1.87 + 1.16\ DR$$ [1]

The regression results demonstrate that a close relationship exists between the discount rate of the Federal Reserve Bank and the prime rate of New York banks. In reality, the prime rate, as discussed earlier, is greatly influenced by the discount rate and usually settles at a higher level than the level of the discount rate. Our model shows that for a 1% change in the discount rate, there has been, on an average, more than a 1% increase in the prime rate of New York banks. In fact, we would not be completely out of place if we were to assume that the New York banks use the discount rate as a base to determine rates for their customers.

The regression equation we have derived is not meant to make a prediction of the prime rate, but to establish the fact that a close relationship exists between the "discount rate" and the "prime rate." According to our findings, the prime rate follows the discount rate. Our regression of the changes in the discount rate on the prime rate confirms this relationship between discount rate and prime rate changes. We also attempted to determine if there exists some association between yield of three-month T bills and prime rates. We did regression of three-month T bills on the prime rate. The results were as follows.

$$\text{Prime} = 1.62 + 1.0143 = \text{3MTB (three month treasury bills)}$$
$$(1.71) \quad (.099)$$
$$R^2 = 0.80, \quad N = 29$$

---

[1]For details in deriving the equation, please see Chapter Five. Also, time series data (1960-1990) gives the similar equation, which is as follows:

$$PR = 0.261 + 1.2021\ DR$$
$$(1.569) \quad (0.1144)$$
$$R^2 = 0.83 \qquad N = 30$$

As we stated earlier, this regression equation is not meant to forecast the prime rate, but it helps us understand that there exist some associations between the yields of T bills and the prime rates of the New York banks. In other words, the yield of T bills influences the determination of the prime rate. Finally, our regression results confirm the fact that a change in the Federal Reserve Bank rate invariably causes changes in the prime rate of the New York banks.

However, we also observed that the gap between the prime rate and the discount rate, in the absolute and the relative sense, varied widely over various phases of the business cycle. Most of the time, the prime rates of New York City banks remain at a higher level than that of the Federal Reserve Bank rate, though the gap between these two rates may widen or shrink depending on the prevailing condition of the economy.

It has also been observed that there is a quick and strong response of the prime rate to a rise in the discount rate of the Federal Reserve Bank, but a delayed response by the prime rate to a fall in the discount rate. This means that higher costs of credit continue despite discount rate decreases. Often, the prime rate does not decrease proportionately to decreases in the discount rate. At times, the large gap between the two rates has devastating effects on the entire economy, as was observed in the early 1980's.

The behavior of regional banks in response to changes of the prime rate of New York banks also shows the oligopolistic nature of the nation's banking industry. The major New York banks administer the prime rate to influence the future economic climate of the country and other banks follow the lead of these banks in changing their rates. "The prime rate tradition" also accounts for the evolution of the dual allegiance of commercial banks - to the Federal Reserve Bank (by law) and to the New York banks by tradition.

## Dual Allegiance of Commercial Banks

In most nations, the discount rate of the central bank influences the lending rates of financial institutions. Large banks in such countries do not post or announce a separate rate, as is done in the United States, where New York City banks announce the so-called prime rate. Regional banks take the prime rate of New York banks as a base in determining their rates on most business loans and also accept the discount rate of Federal Reserve Bank as a base for determining their rates on consumer loans – showing allegiance to both the Federal Reserve Bank and to the banks of New York.

### The Future of Prime Rate

At present, the prime rate is being administered by New York bankers. The role of leadership in setting the lending rate was thrust upon the big banks in New York by the economic circumstances of the 1930's. Over the years, the pronouncement of the prime rate has become an important economic institution in the U.S. economy. To initiate a change in their interest rates, most banks in this country look forward to obtaining signals of changes from the New York bankers. Since 1934, no single bank, nor group of banks outside New York City, has ever questioned this rate-setting role assumed by the New York banks.

Households and businesses need credit badly. Excessive increases in the prime and regional rates cause bankruptcies and unemployment, as we noticed in the early 1980s. When the prime rate rose to 21%, unemployment rose to eleven million, and the number of bankruptcies reached its highest level since the depression of 1930. Unemployment and interest rates tend to follow a reciprocal relationship over different phases of business cycles. As unemployment decreases with economic expansion, the discount rate of the Federal Reserve Bank is raised to a higher level to avert episodes of inflation. In chasing the discount rate, the New York banks raise their prime rate. In following the prime rate of New York banks, regional banks raise their rates resulting in a higher cost of credit to households and businesses.

The prime rate announcements of the New York banks demonstrate that two parallel authorities exist in announcing influential national rates: one is the Federal Reserve Bank, the other is the New York banks. By announcing their rates and knowing that these impact the regional rate, the New York banks give the air of being the boss banks to regional banks. The "prime rate tradition" also accounts for the big difference that exists between the Federal Reserve Bank rate and regional lending rates in the country (as we have shown in our charts, graphs and equations).

The credit-standing of large corporations in New York City differ considerably from that of businesses and households in small and mid-sized cities – far away from New York. The needs, the size, and the kinds of loans required by thousands of small and medium-sized businesses are different from those of large corporations for whom the prime rate of New York is generally set.

This is the dilemma. The Federal Reserve Bank, an autonomous, nonprofit institution, is expected to determine its rate in the interests of the economy and the nation.[1] On the other hand, banks in New York, profit-earning institutions, set their prime rates in their own best interests. The interest of large banks and the interest of the economy may not be the same and may, indeed, be in conflict, at times. We would naturally prefer the Federal Reserve Bank's authority to that of the large banks in initiating changes in interest rates which have a profound impact on the entire economy. As previously mentioned, the discount rates of central banks in most nations greatly influence the lending rates of financial institutions and big banks do not post or announce a separate rate, as is done in the U.S.

The prevalence of the "prime rate tradition" has divided loan markets into two sectors – consumer loans and business loans. The rate of interest on the former is influenced by the discount rate of the Federal Reserve Bank while that of the latter is influenced by the prime rate of the large banks of New York. This division of authority over loan markets limits the effectiveness of the manipulation of the instruments of credit controlled by the Federal Reserve Bank.

In order to achieve the objectives of monetary policy, all areas of the loan market should be directly influenced by the changes in the discount rate of the Federal Reserve Bank, but presently this is not happening. The prime rates of New York banks are influencing the rates of business loans in the market. Thus, the institution of the "prime rate tradition" with its seemingly innocent facade, has been burdening the nation with an unwarranted, and undesired, higher cost of credit.

It is our opinion that the rate's continued announcement is unwarranted under changed socio-economic conditions, for it has outlived its utility and importance. In the interest of the economy and of millions of households, the rate's quiet burial should be accomplished by announcing that the big banks will no longer announce their prime rates. Regional

---

[1]The Federal Reserve System, or the "Fed," as the system is commonly called, is an independent governmental entity created by Congress in 1913 to serve as the central bank of the United States. It is responsible for formulating and executing monetary policy, supervising and regulating depository institutions, providing an elastic currency, assisting the federal government's financing operations and serving as the banker for the U.S. government. In addition, it has important roles in operating the nation's payment systems, protecting consumers' rights in their dealings with banks and promoting community development and reinvestment.

banks must part with their habit (tradition) of mechanically following the prime rate of the New York banks.

## B. FEDERAL RESERVE BANK AND DISCOUNT RATE

The discount rate of the Federal Reserve Bank is one of its most powerful instruments of credit control. By definition it is the rate at which the Federal Reserve Bank discounts first class negotiable bills and grants loans to commercial banks. Changes in this rate are watched both at home and abroad with great interest, since it affects the cost of borrowing and the aggregate expenditure of the economy. We are interested here in discussing the discount rate changes in the context of their past history and the way they impacted the economy, particularly households and businesses. The Federal Reserve Bank is, after all, an important source of money supply and its policy of raising or lowering the discount rate has a tremendous impact on income, employment, interest rates, inflation, and other economic variables.

Over the last eighty years, the Federal Reserve Bank has been working as a guardian of the financial institutions of our vast economy, engaged in organizing, restructuring, and establishing the work-ethics and guidelines among these institutions that have played an important role in mobilizing and channeling savings for investment and capital accumulation. The Federal Reserve Bank's contributions to the economic progress of this country, particularly in formulating guidelines and laws to establish discipline among the financial institutions, is extraordinary. The current levels of economic growth, the stable dollar and the low levels of unemployment, all point to the Bank's impressive accomplishments.

The Federal Reserve Bank has been a major partner in the gigantic effort of developing and organizing one of the largest economies in the world. How vast the U.S. economy is can be understood by looking into the Gross National Product (GNP), which, in recent years, has surpassed eight trillion dollars, while per capita income has risen above $28,000. In 1975, the GNP was less than two trillion dollars and per capita income was less than $7,500. Another significant feature of this economy is that the U.S. covers more than three million square miles and supports more than 250 million people. It is one of the most highly industrialized nations in the world. Its vast resources, inherent strength, and potentialities for future growth make the U.S. economy the leading and most impressive economy in the world.

These achievements, however, do not mean that the Federal Reserve Bank's policies and actions have always been flawless. Its policy of manipulating the discount rate should be examined and analyzed. For example, the frequency of discount rate changes during the last fifty years (although only the discount rate changes of a few typical years are given below) demonstrates that, practically, there were no legal limits in changing the discount rate at any time and that the Federal Reserve Bank has changed its rates almost at will.

**History of the Discount Rate**

| 1980 | | 1981 | |
|---|---|---|---|
| January 1, 1980 | 12% | January 1, 1981 | 13% |
| February 16, 1980 | 13% | May 5, 1981 | 14% |
| May 29, 1980 | 12% | September 22, 1981 | 13% |
| June 13, 1980 | 11% | December 4, 1981 | 12% |
| July 18, 1980 | 10% | | |
| September 26, 1980 | 11% | | |
| November 17, 1980 | 12% | | |
| December 5, 1980 | 13% | | |

| 1982 | | 1983 | |
|---|---|---|---|
| January 1, 1982 | 12% | January 1, 1983 | 8.5% |
| July 21, 1982 | 11.5% | December 31, 1983 | 8.5% |
| August 2, 1982 | 11% | | |
| August 16, 1982 | 10.5% | | |
| August 27, 1982 | 10% | | |
| October 12, 1982 | 9.5% | | |
| November 22, 1982 | 9% | | |
| December 14, 1982 | 8.5% | | |

| 1984 | | 1985 | |
|---|---|---|---|
| January 1, 1984 | 8.5% | January 1, 1985 | 8% |
| April 9, 1984 | 9% | May 21, 1985 | 7.5% |
| November 21, 1984 | 8.5% | | |
| December 24, 1984 | 8% | | |

| 1986 | | 1987 | |
|---|---|---|---|
| January 1, 1986 | 7.5% | January 1, 1987 | 5.5% |
| March 7, 1986 | 7% | September 9, 1987 | 6% |
| April 22, 1986 | 6.5% | | |
| July 11, 1986 | 6% | | |
| August 22, 1986 | 5.5% | | |

| 1988 | | 1989 | |
|---|---|---|---|
| January 1, 1988 | 6% | January 1, 1989 | 6.5% |
| August 9, 1988 | 6.5% | March 3, 1989 | 7% |

SOURCE: Arkansas Bankers Association.

The table points out the fact that the discount rate of the Federal Reserve Bank reached its historical peak when it was raised to 13% in 1980. This highest discount rate pushed interest rates in Arkansas to well over 17% and to more than 20% in other places. It may be mentioned here that in Arkansas interest rates on consumer loans, in general, rise 5% above the discount rate. In fact, when the Federal Reserve Bank raised the discount rate to 12%, interest rates on home loans in some states went as high as 18%. This caused a dramatic slowdown in the sale of cars, boats, appliances, and other durable goods and forced many layoffs. These layoffs, in turn, accounted for higher unemployment and higher deficits in the federal budget. Few new businesses were started when the interest rate approached 15%.

The trend of change in the discount rate of the Federal Reserve Bank shows that in ten years (1980-1989) the rate had changed thirty-nine times, averaging almost four times a year. In some months, the rate changed three times and, on occasions, the rate changed eight times a year. These frequencies in rate-change are high, and because financial institutions use the discount rate as a base to set their rates for loans, frequent rate changes destabilize the market. A bigger problem than eight changes in one year is the wide swings in the federal discount rate that took in the past.

Minor corrections and marginal changes have a bearable impact on the economy, but a change from 12% to 8.5% in one year spreads anxiety throughout the economy. A variation in the discount rate of high magnitude in either direction has a profound economic implication: it creates a kind of uncertainty and fear in the minds of businesses and households about the future.

Any changes in the range of five percentage points in one year cannot be looked upon as fine tuning of the economy. Such changes appear more like tampering with the economy. Businesses in general are not willing to spend $50,000 on a new plant which will generate a 10% return on investment, when the interest cost is 15% or more.[1] In a climate of rising interest rates, venture capital with risk premiums associated with it drives the interest rate up to the 20 - 25% range.

The life blood of American businesses is the availability of capital at acceptable costs. A high discount rate is an impediment to the accumulation of capital. Discount rate changes in modern economies generally stem from the demands of the economy, but this has not always

---

[1]As happened in the early eighties.

been the case when the Federal Reserve Bank changed the discount rate. In the past, some seasonal changes in the discount rate took the form of a ritual.

Some observers have commented that with the advent of the new year come new year prices which signal two months of inflationary pressure. According to this group, this first-quarter rise in prices is normal in the real world of business and the rate slows down each year after the initial increase. Yet it appears that, at times, the Federal Reserve Bank would take a February number and multiply it by twelve to come up with a yearly inflation index. It would then initiate an increase in the discount rate. This would raise the cost of credit causing more harm than good to businesses and households.

## Economic Episodes of the Early Seventies

### Collapse of the Gold Standard

Next, we turn briefly to the collapse of the gold link to the dollar, the subsequent changes in the discount rate, and their impact on the economy. In the early seventies, foreign central banks and businesses were allowed to exchange dollars for gold. The official exchange rate was around $38 an ounce. The gold pool centers in Europe facilitated the conversion of dollars into gold and helped keep the dollar's value stable in the international market, thus creating an impression to the outside world that the dollar was as good as gold and the strongest currency in the world.

Unfortunately, in the early seventies, the U.S. economy was passing through difficult times in its trade with other nations. The problems of the trade deficit were acute, especially during the Vietnam War. The continued deficit in the balance of payments and the outflow of gold for one reason or another resulted in the reduction of the official gold reserve of the U.S. This created panic among foreign central banks and others who were holding dollars thinking that the currency was as good as gold.

Holders of dollars rushed to the gold pool centers to surrender the dollars for gold, but they were frustrated at the inability of these centers to redeem dollars for gold. The doors of these centers were literally closed. This crisis in the conversion of the dollar into gold started during the presidency of Lyndon Johnson. Finally, during President Nixon's term, laws were enacted to sever the gold connection to the dollar - implying that dollars would no longer be redeemed for gold.

When the gold link to the dollar was cut off, foreign banks and businesses began surrendering dollars in the international market. The supply of dollars, as expected, far exceeded the demand for them. This depressed the value of the dollar in the international market considerably. At home, prices started soaring, creating turmoil among policy makers.

Alarmed and almost in panic, the Federal Reserve Bank increased the discount rate until it reached 13%. This checked the oversupply of dollars in foreign markets and stabilized the dollar's value, but the high discount rates set other rates galloping toward higher ceilings - particularly the prime rate of New York banks and the regional rates that follow the prime rate. The prime rate of the New York banks and other regional rates went as high as 21%. This tremendously constrained the aggregate demand side of the economy and ushered in the recession of the early 80's.

The impact of the recession on employment, on output and on prices, has been discussed earlier. We, however, feel that the high prime rates of New York banks, influenced by high discount rates of the Federal Reserve Bank, also contributed toward the higher rates of other credit institutions. These high interest rates resulted in the failure of thousands of borrowers to make payments and eventually led them to declare bankruptcy. These events subsequently led to the demise of a large number of credit institutions in this country.

The federal government then undertook a large rescue operation pouring billions of dollars into protecting these institutions.[1] Few economists linked the severing of the gold tie from the dollar with the high lending rates in this country, which in turn accounted for the demise of a significant number of financial institutions and businesses.

Another interesting observation during this period was that interest rates remained very high for a considerably long period of time. The entire nation was clamoring for the reduction of the high interest rates with no success. Even foreign heads of state from Canada, France and other countries visiting the U.S. voiced their protest against the abnormally high interest rates in the U.S. Unfortunately, sufferings at home and protest from the outside world moved neither government nor Federal Reserve Bank authorities to take any immediate action to reduce interest rates.

During this period, many felt as if no one was in charge who could provide leadership and offer much needed relief in the form of interest rates reduction. The economy was left largely to its own course. By the time

[1] When a large bank or a corporation is in financial trouble the government often comes to its rescue. Unfortunately, millions of households facing acute financial problems are left abandoned, helpless, and on their own.

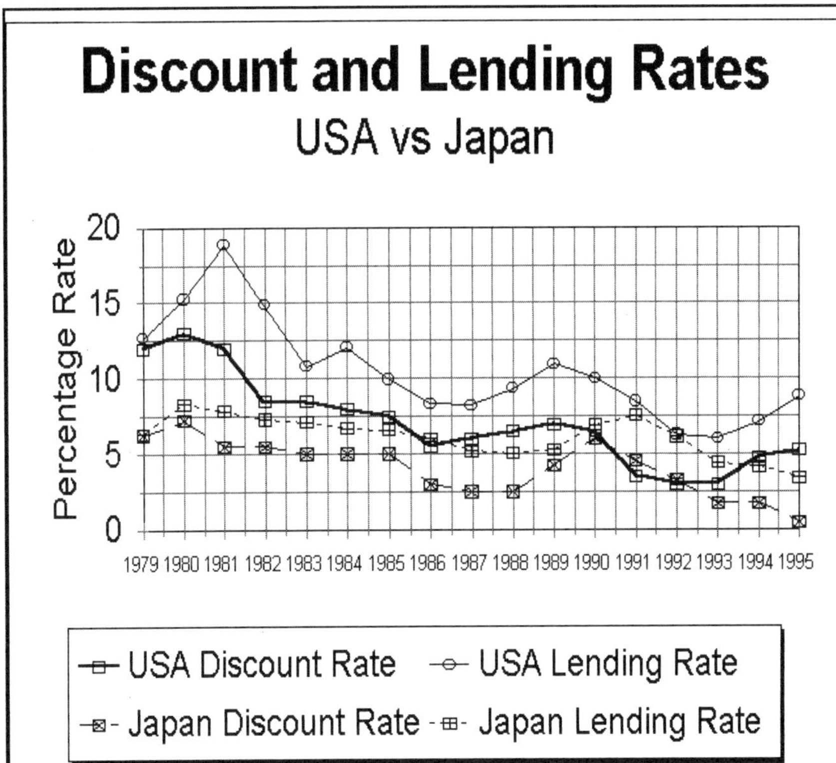


**Figure 19**

interest rates started dropping, the damage done to the economy by the high rates was extensive.

**Discount Rates and Lending Rates in the U.S. and Japan**[1]

In the future, under similar circumstances, prompt action by the Federal Reserve Bank would minimize the damage to the economy. Here it may be interesting to compare the Federal Reserve Bank rates and corresponding lending rates of commercial banks with Japan's central bank rates and corresponding lending rates of commercial banks in Japan.

---

[1]International Financial Statistics Yearbook, 1998

| | 1979 | 1980 | 1981 | 1982 | 1983 | 1984 | 1985 | 1986 | 1987 | 1988 | 1989 | 1990 | 1991 | 1992 | 1993 | 1994 | 1995 |
|---|---|---|---|---|---|---|---|---|---|---|---|---|---|---|---|---|---|
| **USA** | | | | | | | | | | | | | | | | | |
| Discount Rate | 12.0 | 13.0 | 12.0 | 8.50 | 8.50 | 8.00 | 7.50 | 5.50 | 6.00 | 6.50 | 7.00 | 6.50 | 3.50 | 3.00 | 3.00 | 4.75 | 5.25 |
| Lending Rate | 12.67 | 15.27 | 18.87 | 14.86 | 10.79 | 12.04 | 9.93 | 8.35 | 8.21 | 9.32 | 10.92 | 10.01 | 8.46 | 6.25 | 6.0 | 7.14 | 8.83 |
| **JAPAN** | | | | | | | | | | | | | | | | | |
| Discount Rate | 6.25 | 7.25 | 5.50 | 5.50 | 5.00 | 5.00 | 5.00 | 3.00 | 2.50 | 2.50 | 4.25 | 6.00 | 4.50 | 3.25 | 1.75 | 1.75 | .50 |
| Lending Rate | 6.37 | 8.35 | 7.86 | 7.31 | 7.13 | 6.75 | 6.60 | 6.02 | 5.21 | 5.03 | 5.29 | 6.95 | 7.53 | 6.15 | 4.41 | 4.13 | 3.40 |

The table shows that the discount rate of the Federal Reserve Bank during (1979-1995) varied between 3% and 13%, and that of Japan varied between 1/2% and 7.25%. The rate of the central bank of Japan has remained below 7.25% for almost the last two decades.

On the other hand the highest rate of the central bank in the U.S. reached 13%. It is interesting to note that the central bank in Japan did not hesitate to reduce its rate to as low as 1/2% during the same period. The other characteristics of these two central banks are as follows:

**Central Bank Rates**
**Federal Reserve Bank Rates vs. Bank of Japan Rates**

| | U.S.[1] (60yrs) | Japan (21yrs) |
|---|---|---|
| 1. The number of times the discount rate of the Federal Reserve Bank changed since 1934 . . . . . . . . . . . . . . . . | 114 | 14 |
| 2. The average rate of change of the Federal Reserve Bank made in the downward direction since 1934 . . . . . . . . | .51% | 1.33% |
| 3. The range of variation in the discount rate of the Federal Reserve Bank since 1970 . . . . . . . . . . . . . . . . . . . . . . | 3% to 13% | .50% to 7.25% |
| 4. The average number of times per year changes were made in the Federal Reserve Bank rate since 1970 . . . . . | 2.29 | |

[1] Sixty years data of the discount rate change of the Federal Reserve Bank has been used here to focus on the characteristics of the bank's rate changes; although for the sake of convenience, we have shown the data of only twenty years in the table.

The data above clearly show that in a little more than sixty years, the discount rate changed more than 114 times. In some years, the discount rate changed more than eight times. The variation in the rates ranged from a low of 3% to a high of 13%. The average rate of increase per year in the discount rate of the Federal Reserve Bank was .60%. The data shows that the discount rate of Japan changed approximately fourteen times over the last twenty-one years.

Japan's central bank rates varied from a low of .5% to a high of 7.25%. This shows that Japan's central bank rate over the years has been much less erratic than that of the Federal Reserve Bank. Japan's central bank maintained its low rate at times for several continuous years without being panicked by inflation invasion of the economy. The Bank of Japan does not suffer from inflation phobia as does the Federal Reserve Bank in the U.S. This also means that Japan's central bank policy has always aimed at preserving the climate of low-cost credit in the country.

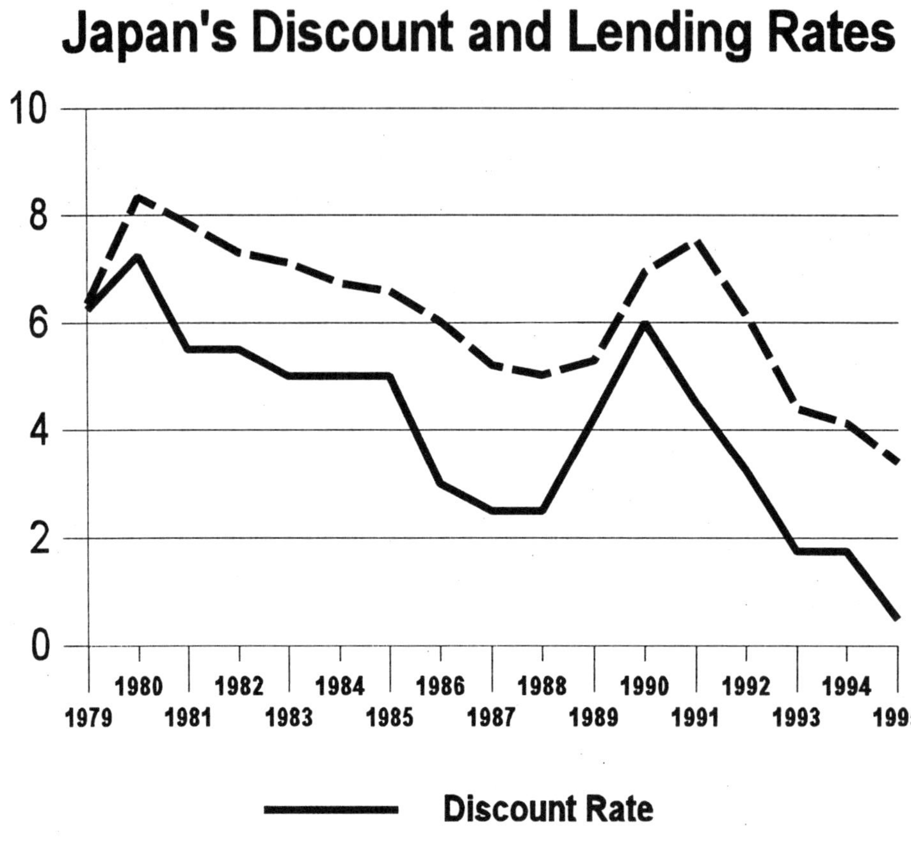
Japan's Discount and Lending Rates
10
8
6
4
2
0
1980
1982
1984
1986
1988
1990
1992
1994
1979
1981
1983
1985
1987
1989
1991
1993
1995
Discount Rate
Lending Rate

Figure 20

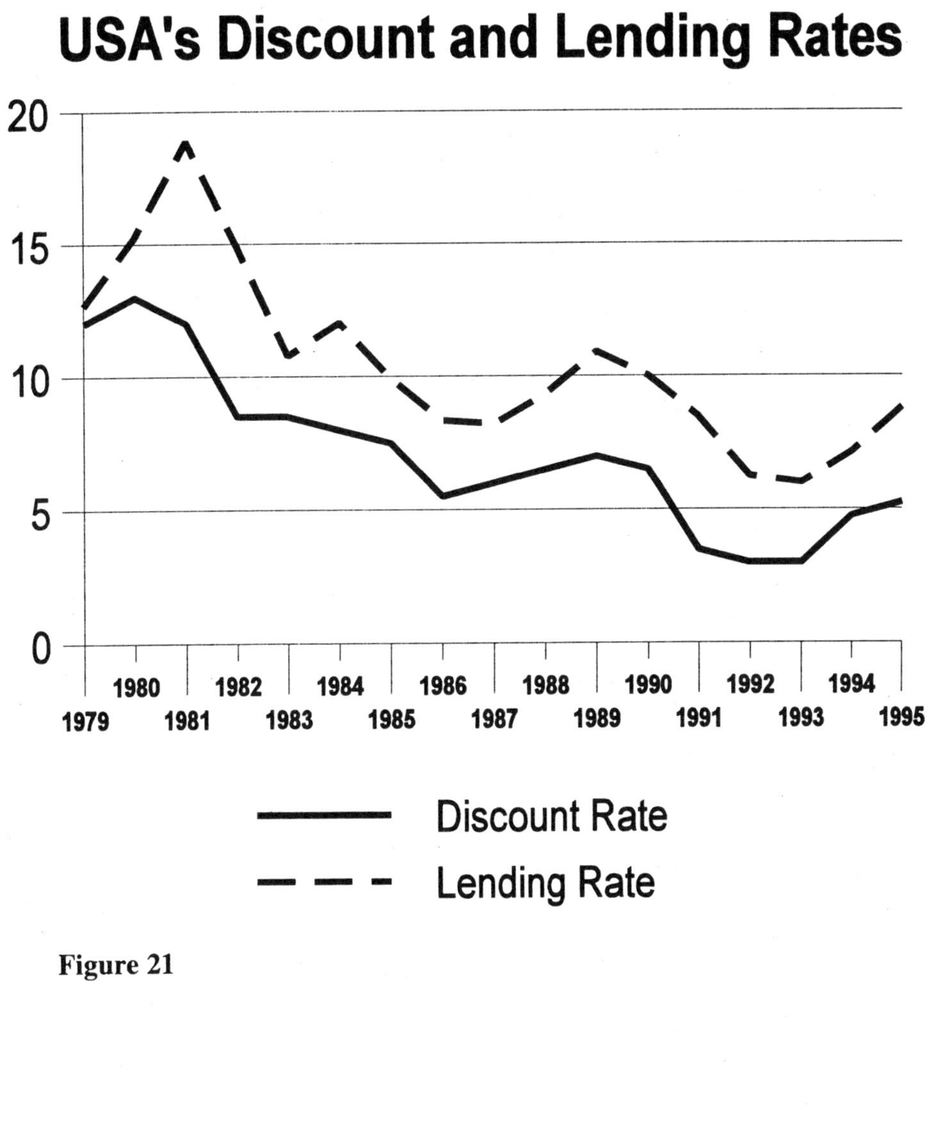
USA's Discount and Lending Rates
20
15
10
5
0
1980
1982
1984
1986
1988
1990
1992
1994
1979
1981
1983
1985
1987
1989
1991
1993
1995
Discount Rate
Lending Rate

Figure 21

**Commercial Bank Rates**

| | U.S. | JAPAN |
|---|---|---|
| The number of times the lending rate changed since 1975 | 20 | 20 |
| The average upward rate of change in the lending rate since 1975 | 2.09% | 1.12% |
| The average downward rate of change direction in the lending rate since 1975 | 1.62% | .64% |
| The range of variation in the lending rate since 1975 | 6.0% - 18.87% | 3.40% - 8.35% |

**Lending Rates in the U.S. and Japan**

The overall average lending rates in the U.S. varied from a low of 6% to a high of 18.87%[1] for the 1979 to 1996 period, whereas in Japan, lending rates varied from a low of 3.4% to a high of 8.3%. This shows that both the lowest and highest limits of lending rates in the U.S. over the last two decades were 50% more than they were in Japan; U.S. credit institutions were charging twice as much interest as the credit institutions in Japan.[2]

If we look at the history of the evolution of the banking system, we notice that bank failures in the early years of the development of credit institutions in this country were not uncommon. Such failures produced a general apprehension and mistrust in the public of losing money from these institutions.

The general public, from their experience with bank failures, voiced disapproval of concentration of money in one bank. This was, in part, the reason why the First Bank and Second Bank of the U.S.A. were not given renewed licenses for their operation, despite the fact that they functioned efficiently for twenty years. For the same reason, the country was divided into twelve banking districts, with one central bank operating in each

[1]This represents only the average rates. In reality, in many places in the U.S. during the period of the early 80's lending rates rose as high as 22%.

[2]It also means that the cost of credit on the average was two times higher in the United States than it was in Japan.

district. All other banks in the district became affiliated with their respective district Federal Reserve Bank.

The driving force behind the creation of the twelve Federal Reserve Banks was to remove the fear of concentration of money in one bank and to accommodate local needs. Thus, in creating the Federal Reserve System, the intention of the law makers was that local economic forces should influence Federal Reserve Bank policies. Unfortunately, with the passage of time, the importance of this Federal Reserve Bank policy consideration has diminished. Regional economic forces now have minimal influence in the Federal Reserve Bank policy making process. Also, there has been no initiative taken by the Federal Reserve Bank to alleviate the debt-burden problems of the low and middle-income households in these cities, nor has there been any Federal Reserve Bank policy to make cheap credit available to them.

In the past, the Federal Reserve Bank raised its rates to control inflation, but quantitative credit control alone often caused large-scale unemployment and deprived millions of households in mid-sized cities of badly needed credit. We have already discussed at length how high interest rates impacted the economy, especially low-income households in small and mid-sized cities of the U.S. Below are our comments and suggestions with regard to future Federal Reserve Bank policy:

1. The frequent changes in the discount rate causes uncertainties about the future and are not welcomed by the business community.

2. Past wide swings in changes of the discount rate have done more harm than good to the economy. These large variations created doubts about the future rates of interest and reduced investment, output, and employment.

3. At times, the Federal Reserve Bank has been less than prompt in acting to correct problems produced by high interest rates. This was apparent when the federal discount rate rose to 12%, the prime rate of (New York banks) rose to 21%, and regional rates rose to 23%. Such abnormally high rates ushered in the recession of 1980 and threw eleven million people out of their jobs. The Fed appeared to have delayed an abnormally long time before starting the process of reducing the discount rate. A quicker move could have minimized the damage done to the economy. At other times, the Fed has raised rates to achieve certain monetary targets with

little regard to the dire consequences that the policy would have on low and middle-income households. This was the case with the Federal Reserve Bank policy adopted immediately after the gold link to the dollar was severed.

4. We suggest that a combination of both quantitative and qualitative control may be adopted to benefit the entire society. When the Fed decides to raise its rate to control inflation or achieve some predetermined monetary aggregates, this invariably raises the cost of credit, driving thousands of low-income households out of the credit market. Unfortunately, if there is no provision in the Fed's policy for accommodating low-income groups, inflation may be controlled at the expense of the interest of millions of low-income households. In such a case, the job is not done well. This is why we recommend that a combination of quantitative and qualitative credit control policies be adopted in combating inflation.

5. Finally, the Federal Reserve Bank must continue to distance itself from the inflation phobia from which it apparently suffers: the raising of the discount rate should not take the form of a ritual.

The problem of the erratic rise in interest rates is not expected to disappear completely as long as there remains any prospect of a federal deficit of high magnitude. The current surplus in the federal budget does not guarantee that there will always be surpluses in the future. The most fundamental solution to the problem would be to balance the federal budget. A balanced budget should produce a discount rate of 3% to 5%, and commercial and consumer loans of 8% to 10%. This is a livable rate that would stimulate the economy and provide long-term stability, jobs, prosperity, and security. Most households and corporations in the U. S. are not able to withstand interest rates of 18% to 22% similar to those of the early 1980's.

The Federal Reserve Bank must have the power and means to prevent this and should remain alert and sensitive to unusually high levels of the prime rate of the New York banks. Finally, with these few suggestions and comments on Federal Reserve Bank policy, we acknowledge the outstanding contributions of the Federal Reserve System in making the U.S. economy the world's richest and most stable economy. Unfortunately, a large section of this society still has not been able to benefit fully from this prosperous U.S. economy.

## C. REGIONAL RATES

Regional rates are the rates of banks operating in places other than large cities such as New York, where the so-called prime rate originates. The announcement of changes in the New York prime rate has an immediate impact on all regional rates of interest. In a pragmatic sense, interest rates other than those of the big banks in New York may be broadly looked upon as regional rates. These rates may also be called local rates.

Regional loans constitute a significant part of the total credit volume in the country and comprise all of the commercial, consumer, and mortgage loans at the local level. In discussing the features of the regional rates, we intend to shed some light on the characteristics of consumer, business, and mortgage loans at the local level. These loans originate from buying homes, cars, boats, furniture, refrigerators, appliances and other necessary goods and services on credit. A large number of business loans are also contracted at the local level. Interest rates on these loans possess some peculiarities.

The trends of interest rates on different loans, along with the interest rates of different institutions are given below. The author is greatly concerned about the determinants of these rates. It is the regional rate that should influence the prime rate of the New York banks and the discount rate of the Federal Reserve Bank, but presently, it is the other way around. As a result, supply and demand forces for funds at the local level has only a minimal impact in determining regional rates.

**Discount Rate, Prime Rate and Regional Rate**[1]

| Year | Discount Rate of FRB | New York Prime Rate | Average Regional Rate | Mortgage Rate | Arkansas Consumer Rate | Michigan Consumer Rate |
|---|---|---|---|---|---|---|
| | % | % | % | % | % | % |
| 1975 | 6.56 | 8.25 | 8.88 | 9.04 | 13.08 | N/A |
| 1976 | 5.38 | 6.75 | 7.38 | 8.86 | 13.02 | N/A |
| 1977 | 5.88 | 7.13 | 10.07 | 8.84 | 12.97 | N/A |
| 1978 | 7.79 | 9.78 | 11.11 | 9.63 | 13.19 | N/A |
| 1979 | 10.88 | 13.44 | 14.42 | 11.19 | 13.85 | N/A |
| 1980 | 11.71 | 16.06 | 15.68 | 13.77 | 16.50 | 17.75 |
| 1981 | 13.00 | 18.02 | 18.8 | 16.63 | 17.00 | 18.75 |
| 1982 | 10.00 | 14.27 | 15.74 | 16.08 | 16.75 | 18.25 |
| 1983 | 8.50 | 10.75 | 12.13 | 13.23 | 13.50 | 15.50 |
| 1984 | 8.50 | 11.94 | 13.24 | 13.87 | 13.75 | 15.50 |
| 1985 | 7.50 | 10.00 | 11.77 | 12.42 | 13.00 | 15.51 |
| 1986 | 6.25 | 8.25 | 11.38 | 10.18 | 11.75 | 13.25 |
| 1987 | 6.00 | 8.50 | 10.75 | 10.20 | 10.50 | 12.00 |
| 1988 | 6.50 | 9.50 | 11.69 | 10.34 | 11.00 | 13.50 |
| 1989 | 7.00 | 11.00 | 12.35 | 10.32 | 11.75 | 14.00 |
| 1990 | 6.50 | 10.00 | 11.58 | 10.13 | 11.50 | N/A |
| 1991 | 4.90 | 8.17 | 9.33 | 9.25 | 9.90 | N/A |
| 1992 | 3.00 | 6.00 | 8.80 | 8.40 | 8.80 | N/A |
| 1993 | 3.00 | 6.50 | 8.00 | 7.33 | 8.00 | N/A |
| 1994 | 4.08 | 7.30 | 9.08 | 8.35 | 9.08 | N/A |
| 1995 | 5.25 | 8.75 | 10.25 | 7.95 | 10.25 | N/A |
| 1996 | 5.00 | 8.25 | 10.00 | 7.80 | 10.00 | N/A |

The chart shows the trend of influential rates and how they affect other rates. The average regional rates vary considerably depending upon the locations of the bank, the credit standing of the borrowers, and the supply and demand forces for funds at the local level. The range of variations in these rates at any point in time is significant.

[1]Discount rates are from Federal Reserve Bank publications; other rates are from statements of large banks in New York and from local banks.

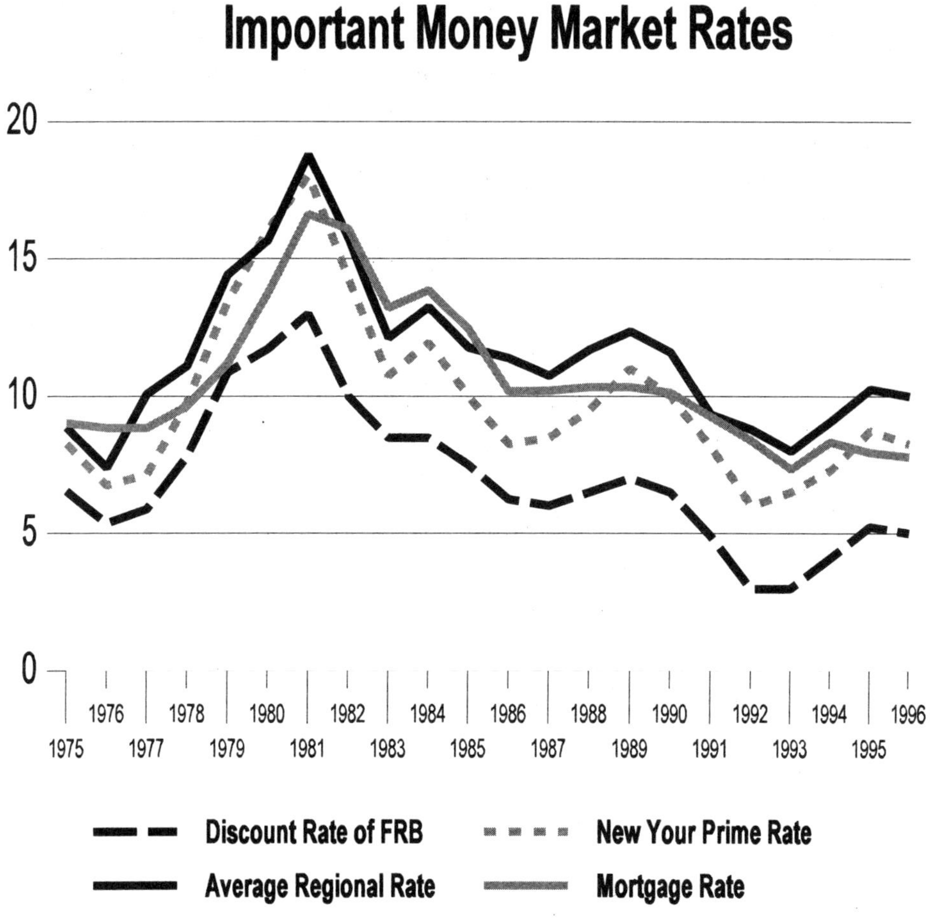
Important Money Market Rates
20
15
10
5
0
1976
1978
1980
1982
1984
1986
1988
1990
1992
1994
1996
1975
1977
1979
1981
1983
1985
1987
1989
1991
1993
1995
Discount Rate of FRB
New Your Prime Rate
Average Regional Rate
Mortgage Rate

Figure 22

It is interesting to note that there always exists a big difference in the officially announced prime rate of a bank (on any category of loan) and the rates that are actually charged on loans for most borrowers. To cite an example: if the official prime rate of a local bank is 8%, the actual interest rate charged to most borrowers may exceed this rate (the official prime rate) by two to three percentage points. This means that borrowers will be charged 10 to 11% interest on their loans. The rates we see in this chart are mostly the averages of the officially announced prime rates of local banks and are, in most cases, an underestimation of the actual interest rates that they charged to borrowers at the local level. Some important characteristics of each category of interest rates and their relationships to other interest rates, are described below:

**The Average Regional Rate**[1]
(its relation with other rates)

| | |
|---|---|
| The number of years the average regional rate remained greater than the discount rate of the Federal Reserve Bank between 1975-1996 was: | 22 |
| The number of years the average regional rate remained greater than the New York prime rate between 1975-1996 was: | 21 |
| The percentage points by which the average regional rate exceeded the discount rate of the Federal Reserve Bank between 1975-1990 were: | 1.472% to 11.15% |
| The percentage points by which the average regional rates were greater than the New York prime rates were: | 5.09% |
| The average percentage points by which the average regional rate was greater than the discount rate of the Federal Reserve Bank for the 1975-1996 period were: | 7.2% |

The data and the graphs show that the average regional rate[1] remained greater than the prime rate of New York banks except in 1980.

---

[1] These rates are estimated by taking the average of interest rates charged on personal and business loans by local banks.

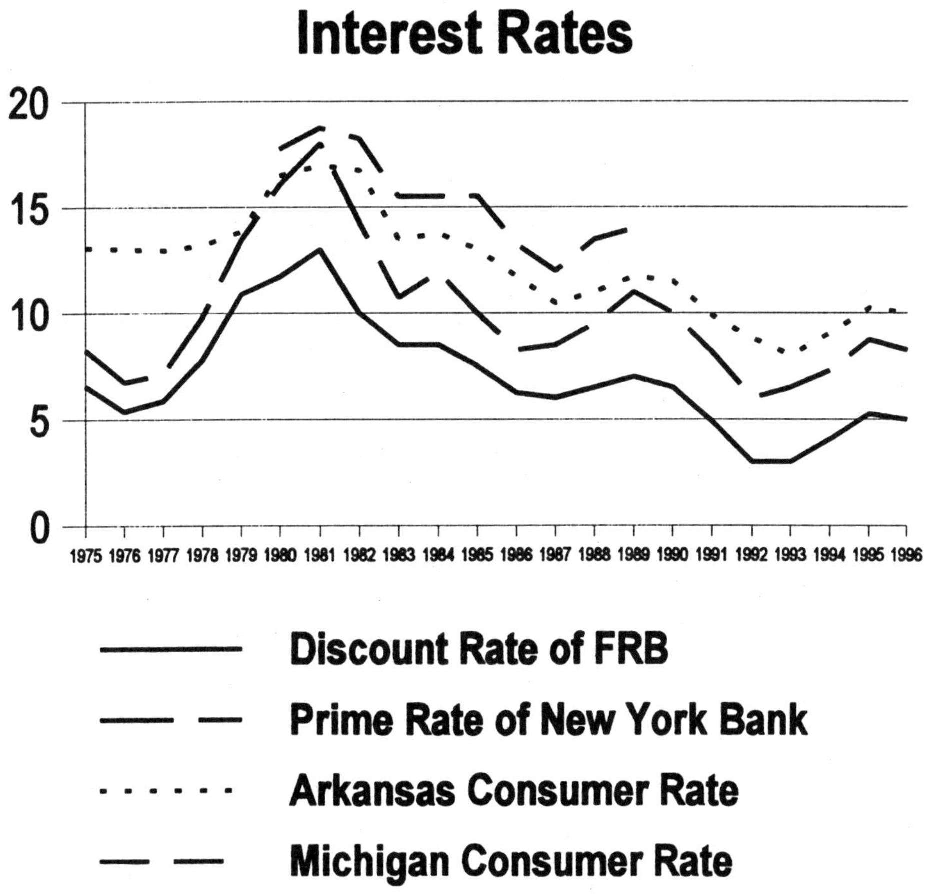
Interest Rates
20
15
10
5
0
1975 1976 1977 1978 1979 1980 1981 1982 1983 1984 1985 1986 1987 1988 1989 1990 1991 1992 1993 1994 1995 1996
Discount Rate of FRB
Prime Rate of New York Bank
Arkansas Consumer Rate
Michigan Consumer Rate

Figure 23

**Arkansas Consumer Rate**
(its relation with other rates)

| | |
|---|---|
| The number of years the Arkansas consumer rate remained higher than the discount rate of the Federal Reserve Bank between 1975-1996: | 22 |
| The number of years the Arkansas consumer rate remained higher that the New York prime rate between 1975-1996: | 21 |
| The percentage points by which Arkansas consumer rate exceeded the discount rate of the Federal Reserve Bank for the 1975-1990 period: | 2.97% to 7.64% |
| The percentage points by which the Arkansas consumer rates were greater than the New York prime rates: | .41% to 6.27% |
| The average percentage points by which the Arkansas consumer rate was greater than the discount rate of the Federal Reserve Bank for the 1975-1996 period: | 5.27% |
| The average percentage points by which the Arkansas consumer rate was greater than the New York prime rate: | 2.45% |

The Arkansas consumer rate of interest remained higher than the discount rate of the Federal Reserve Bank for all the years during the 1975-1996 period. The highest difference between these two rates was in 1976, when the consumer rate exceeded the discount rate of the Federal Reserve Bank by 7.46 percentage points. In most years during this period, the consumer rate remained higher than the discount rate of the Federal Reserve Bank by five percentage points.

**Michigan Consumer Rate**
**1980 - 1989**
(its relation with other rates)

| | |
|---|---|
| The number of years the Michigan consumer rate remained higher than the New York prime rate: | 10 |
| The number of years the Michigan consumer rate remained higher than the discount rate of the Federal Reserve Bank: | 10 |
| The percentage points by which the Michigan consumer rate exceeded the New York prime rate: | .73% to 5.50% |
| The percentage points by which the Michigan consumer rates exceeded discount rates of the Federal Reserve Bank: | 5.75% to 8.25% |
| The average percentage points by which the Michigan consumer rate was greater than the discount rate of the Federal Reserve Bank: | 6.90% |

The highest percentage point difference between the discount rate and the Michigan rate was 9.25% in 1983 when the Michigan consumer rate was 15.5% and the discount rate was at 8.5%. The Michigan consumer rate and the Arkansas consumer rate share the common characteristic of staying at rates that always exceed the discount rate of the Federal Reserve Bank and the prime rate of the New York banks.

The table shows that the consumer interest rate varied from 8% to 17% in the South, and from 12% to 18.75% in the North of the United States during the 1975-1995 period. During the same period, the discount rate of the Federal Reserve Bank varied between 3% and 13%. The table shows that consumer interest rates both in the South and in the North of the United States far exceeded the prevailing discount rate of the Federal Reserve Bank. At one time, it exceeded the discount rate by more than eight percentage points. The interesting similarities of these rates in the South and the North of the country point to the fact that a similar situation prevails throughout the nation.

**Mortgage Rate**
**1975 - 1996**
(its relation with other rates)

| | |
|---|---|
| The number of years the mortgage rate remained higher than the discount rate of the Federal Reserve Bank between 1975-1996: | 22 |
| The number of years the mortgage rate remained higher than the New York prime rate between 1975-1996: | 15 |
| The percentage points by which the mortgage rate exceeded the discount rate of the Federal Reserve Bank between 1975-1996: | .31% to 6.08% |
| The percentage points by which the mortgage rate exceeded the New York prime rate: | .13% to 2.48% |
| The average percentage point by which the mortgage rate was greater than the discount rate of the Federal Reserve Bank: | 3.67% |
| The average percentage points by which the mortgage rate was greater than the New York prime rate: | 1.55% |

Mortgage rates over the last two decades varied from a low of 7.33% in 1993 to a high of 16.63% in 1981. These rates exceeded the discount rate of the Federal Reserve Bank by 3.63 percentage points in 1980 and by 4.33 percentage points in 1993. These mortgage rates are averages for the nation and do not truly represent the much higher mortgage rates prevailing at local levels.

All these rates will be further discussed in the context of changes in the discount rate of the Federal Reserve Bank and the prime rate of the New York banks. These last two rates exert their influence in determining the regional rates. The prime rate, the consumer loan rate, the commercial loan rate, and the unemployment rate are all affected by changes in the discount rate of the Federal Reserve Bank and the prime rate of the New York banks.

Banks at the local level at times charge consumers almost twice as much as it costs them to borrow from the Federal Reserve Bank. Commercial banks in Arkansas charged about 17% interest on loans when the discount rate was 12% in the early 1980's. This high rate brought hardship to thousands of households and businesses. Sales for many businesses declined by 50%. Also, high rates, at times, accelerate unemployment rates in the country as we witnessed in the early 1980s.

**Civilian Unemployment and Bank Rate[1]**

| Year | Consumer Loan Rate | Unemployment Rate (%) | Number of Persons |
|---|---|---|---|
| 1975 | 13.08 | 8.5 | 7,929,000 |
| 1976 | 13.02 | 7.7 | 7,406,000 |
| 1977 | 12.97 | 7.1 | 6,991,000 |
| 1978 | 13.19 | 6.1 | 6,202,000 |
| 1979 | 13.85 | 5.8 | 6,137,000 |
| 1980 | 15.47 | 7.1 | 7,637,000 |
| 1981 | 18.09 | 7.6 | 8,237,000 |
| 1982 | 18.65 | 9.7 | 10,678,000 |
| 1983 | 16.68 | 9.6 | 10,717,000 |
| 1984 | 16.67 | 7.5 | 8,536,000 |
| 1985 | 16.09 | 7.3 | 8,413,000 |

The unemployment rate during the period 1982-1983 climbed to 10%, accounting for the unemployment of eleven million people, when regional interest rates were between 14 to 18%. During the years 1975 through 1995, the discount rate was at its lowest in 1992 and 1993 when it was at 3%. In 1976, regional banks were borrowing at 5.38% from the Federal Reserve Bank, but were refloating the money to consumers at 13.02%, a 242% increase over the rate at which the bank originally borrowed. Another interesting feature we noticed is that although consumer loan rates increase as the discount rate increases, the rate does not decrease as rapidly as it increases. In 1981, the discount rate dropped to 11.02 and the prime

[1]Statistical Abstract of the U.S. 1982-83, 1986

rate decreased to 14.86%; yet the consumer rate remained at 18.65% for some time.

Arkansas Law (Amendment 60) permits banks to charge 5% above the discount rate. This large margin allows banks to make sizeable profits by borrowing from the Federal Reserve Bank and lending the money to the members of the public at a considerably higher cost. By contrast, in many places of the world, rates on consumer loans fluctuate within a narrow band above the discount rate of the central bank. Another feature of the credit market is that during any downturn of the economy, a bank's policy of not granting loans of less than a certain amount may actually worsen the economic situation of low and middle-income households.

During the recession of the early 80's, the local banks' policy of not granting loans less than $3,000 to any borrower deprived thousands of households of needed credit. In fact, this limit prevented thousands of low-income households from applying for badly needed funds. The door of the bank was literally closed for those households.

We will now show the relationships between regional rates and other rates that influence the availability of capital funds both to consumers and businesses who are seeking funds for investment and consumption purposes. We will first show the relationship algebraically then we will analyze regression results when regional rates are regressed on other important rates. We have already shown in charts and graphs that the prime rate of the New York banks is always greater than the discount rate of the Federal Reserve Bank (DR) and the regional rate (RR) is always greater than PR. Here we intend to express RR and PR in terms of DR. This enables us to derive an equation that proves that the existence of the prime rate tradition makes the RR much higher in size than it would otherwise have been. We can write PR > DR; RR > PR.

Algebraically, PR[1] and RR[2] may be expressed in terms of DR[3] as follows:

DR: Exogenously determined by FRB

PR: This rate being higher than DR by E1 amount

PR=DR+ E1, where E1=(PR-DR)

$E_1$, Excess over DR. In determining E1, banks take into consideration variables such as the supply and demand forces for loans, cost of mobilizing funds, yields on T bills.

When $E_1$ is expressed in terms of DR  E1 = P.DR

PR = DR + P.DR

PR = DR (1 + P)  (1)

RR: This rate being higher than PR by E2 amount:

$RR = PR + E_2$

E2 = (RR - PR)

E2 excess over PR: In determining $E_2$, the regional banks give more weight to the demand side of the market forces.

When E2 is expressed in terms of DR this can be written as: E2 = r DR. The regional rate being higher than the prime rates of the New York banks by $E_2$ can be written as:  RR = PR + r DR

RR can be written as:  RR=DR+pDR+r·DR  (2)

From equation one and two, we can derive:  RR = DR (1 + P + r)

The magnitude of "p" depends on institutional goals. Banks set the DR first and then consider how far they can raise interest rates in view of supply and demand forces for the loans. The magnitude of "r" depends upon the customers' need for funds at the local levels. At any point in time, we can approximate regional rates, if we have the values of "p" and "r" using the simple equations presented above. The equation for RR demonstrates that the regional rates under present credit market practices always exceed the discount rate of the Federal Reserve Bank and the prime rate of New York banks.

We have shown earlier that, for twenty-five years, the prime rate of New York banks remained, on an average, 3% higher than the discount rate of the Federal Reserve Bank. The average regional rate remained greater

---

[1] PR = prime rate of New York banks.

[2] RR = regional rate or local rate

[3] DR = discount rate of the Federal Reserve Bank.

than all other rates most of the time (except for a few years) while the consumer interest rate tended to remain, on average, higher than the prime rate of New York banks by more than 2%.

We regressed regional rates on both the discount rate of the Federal Reserve Bank and the prime rate of the New York banks. The equation derived from the regression results confirms the fact that the discount rate of the Federal Reserve Bank functions as an important determiner for the prime rate of New York banks and both the discount rate and the prime rate influence the determination of regional rates. The equations are[1]:

| | |
|---|---|
| Average Regional Rate: | AV RR = 4.17 + 1.0 DR |
| Average Regional Rate: | AV RR = 3.83 + .76 PR |
| Arkansas Consumer Rate: | ARK CR= 6.18 + .87 DR |
| Arkansas Consumer Rate: | ARK CR= 1.98 + 1.14 PR |
| Michigan Consumer Rate: | MICH CR = 7.83 + .63 PR |
| Michigan Consumer Rate: | MICH CR = 7.79 + .89 DR |

These equations which we discussed in Chapter Five show that:

- a 1% rise in the discount rate on average causes a 1% rise in the average regional rate;
- a 1% rise in the prime rate on average causes a .76 of 1% rise in the average regional rate;
- a 1% rise in the discount rate causes an average .87 of 1% rise in the Arkansas consumer rate;
- a 1% rise in the prime rate causes, on an average, a 1.14% rise in the Arkansas consumer rate;
- a 1% rise in the discount rate causes a .89 of 1% rise in the Michigan consumer rate;
- a 1% rise in the prime rate causes a .93 of 1% rise in the Michigan consumer rate.

These regression results again confirm that a change in the discount rate of the Federal Reserve Bank brings about a change in the prime rate of the New York banks which in turn influences regional rates. Our equations

---

[1]The detailed analysis of these equations have been made in Chapter 5.

and simple examples also demonstrate that the regional rate settles at a much higher level than it would have done if the tradition of the prime rate announcement had been nonexistent.

From the invention of the "prime rate tradition" to the present day, millions of households have been paying much more interest on their loans than they would have been paying had this "tradition" not been invented. Millions of businesses and households located in small and mid-sized cities have been bearing higher burdens of debt because of the prevalence of the prime rate tradition. This "extra" over the prime rate charged by the regional banks yields billions of dollars in interest payments. A few households might be enjoying higher regional rates in the form of interest earnings, but a vast majority have been paying the higher price for the "tradition" and bearing heavier burdens of debt.

## D. RAY, CREDIT BUREAUS & CREDIT INSTITUTIONS

Most banks extend credit to households but it is the commercial banks that dominate the scene. Unfortunately, most of the beneficiaries of credit facilities have been the affluent households with high credit ratings. Credit institutions, in general, have done a good job for the low-risk customer, helping the country to accumulate vast capital resources. Earlier, our walk with Jay described how deeply overwhelmed he was by bills and debts. He was constantly bashed, thrashed and hounded by his creditors. Here, we are concerned about the credit institutions' policy of extending credit to less advantaged households and intend to analyze critically the information and the pedagogy that credit institutions use in granting credit. In doing this, we will now take another walk, this time with Ray.

Here is the story of Ray. He presents a different economic situation in the sense that Ray had paid off all his old debts and his current income equaled the mean income of his city's residents. With no debt, Ray felt confident that he would have easy access to credit to reinvigorate his small business, increase his income, and give his children the higher education, training and skills they need for better opportunities in life. In his attempt to obtain a new loan, the initial encounter between Ray and the bank officer was very pleasant, encouraging and full of promise. The loan officer appeared to be friendly and helpful. As the time for making a decision on the application arrived, the officer appeared grim-faced. A very anxious and nervous Ray inquired if his loan application was approved. The answer was a frustrating and a disappointing "No."

Stunned and angered by the answer, Ray wanted to know what had gone wrong. He had paid his old debts, was currently earning a decent income and was holding a respectable position as a teacher in a local school. Pressed by Ray, the officer explained that it was "nothing personal," but the "negatives" contained in his credit report recorded several years ago compelled him to deny credit. And he added, these "negatives" once entered into the records of the credit bureau would remain there for almost a decade. In a pragmatic sense, Ray will not be able to bypass these "negatives" during his lifetime. This is because, to some creditors, he will remain ineligible for credit for the rest of his life.

Inside Ray "felt" the sting of knowing that he was no longer welcomed in the credit market. This denial of credit suddenly caused Ray to realize that he commanded no respect from the credit institutions of his own city, where he was a productive, well respected, and responsible resident. The credit report had portrayed him as untrustworthy. This distrust challenged Ray's ego, honesty and sincerity. He felt devastated.

The credit report had made him "stink" in the credit market, alienated him from the system and punished him excessively by denying credit on grounds of the "delinquencies" which had occurred several years ago. Yet, the credit institutions completely ignored his paying off the debt in its entirety, his honesty, sincerity, current income and his ability to meet new credit obligations. This treatment deepened his anger against credit bureaus, credit reports and credit institutions.

Millions of households share Ray's feelings of anger and frustration against credit bureaus' repeatedly reporting past negatives in their accounts, thereby depriving them of the credit they deserve. Often, harmful inaccurate information is printed in the credit report year after year. There exists no simple way to correct it. Lack of organization and leadership among households affected by these policies prevent them from effectively voicing their protest against this kind of reporting.

Ray resigned himself to forget all his hopes for the economic uplifting of his family and a better education for his children. Above all, his long-cherished desire of regaining control of his life and of his financial future was lost. A life free of basic wants, debts, creditors and credit reports which contribute to branding a person a "credit-market outcast" was not within reach any longer. We share Ray's frustrations and anger.

Thousands of households experience similar frustrations and disappointments every day in the U.S. They feel deprived of their natural right to fair credit deals because of inaccurate reporting by credit bureaus. Hundreds of examples exist where even small private clinics would not provide emergency services on credit to persons like Ray who had once been branded as "poor credit risks" based on the credit report alone. The denial of credit to millions of households on the basis of credit reports leads us to critically examine the contents of the credit report.

Generally, a credit report is written in a language not easily intelligible to most American households. It seems like a sign language designed to communicate secret messages to credit supplying institutions. Credit bureaus have invented their own codes, signs and symbols to highlight the "negative" and "positive" aspects of accounts on which they are reporting.

Mostly, the report includes outstanding balances, names of credit grantors, delinquencies in accounts, past due amounts, late payments, information on cancellation of credit cards, public records such as tax liens by the IRS, liabilities of the debtors, and the number of times customers had asked for a credit report. Most households feel that the overall thrust and intent of the report is to focus more on the "negatives" of the accounts than on the "positives."

Credit reports also report accounts that were paid up many years ago. In many cases, the negative aspects of the report are placed at the outset, on the front page of the report. One or two "negatives" in the report are enough to destroy a person's attempts to obtain credit, although the applicant may have dozens of "positives" on the same report. The most common excuses shown by credit giving agencies in denying credit are as follows:

1) Lack of collateral
2) Lack of credit
3) Poor credit record
4) Low income
5) Loss of job
6) Loss of business
7) Current late payment status
8) Past due amount
9) Foreclosure of property
10) Lack of guarantor
11) Lien on property by IRS
12) Garnishing of wages by creditors
13) Too many requests for credit report
14) Too many open accounts
15) Bankruptcies
16) High debt ratio to income

As previously stated, low income, temporary jobs, excessive bills and open accounts render low and middle-income households vulnerable to these disqualifications and excuses for denial of credit. Summarized below are some important uses and features of credit reports.

### The Uses of the Credit Report

Goods and services worth billions of dollars are bought and sold on credit each day in the U.S. economy. In most of these transactions, credit reports are used to determine the eligibility for credit. Credit reports have helped many successful businesses but have also rendered thousands of individuals helpless, miserable, and devastated.

1. The credit report has become, over the years, a powerful instrument in the hands of creditors in granting or refusing credit.

2. Credit reports are used as a sole determinant of the credit-worthiness of low-income households which have no other assets to offer as collateral or guarantors to cover their loans.

3. Credit reports are used as shields by credit-supplying institutions, when credit has been denied.

4. One negative in the credit report can effectively block the granting of a loan, although the applicant may have dozens of positives.

5. The credit report perpetuates a continuous punishment of the debtor both during the currency of a loan and many years after the loan has been paid off. This is mainly because the credit bureau continues to print negatives of the account holder long after the debt has been settled.

6. In the approval of a loan application, the credit report assumes more importance than the personal character and integrity of the applicant.

7. Banks seldom ignore credit reports that portrays an applicant as a poor credit-risk, although the report might have been based on past negatives of the applicant. Frequently, "past negatives" outweigh the present ability of the applicant to meet his credit obligation.

Current credit reports are devoid of some pertinent information about the applicants such as:

1. Very often, the credit report is inaccurate and not updated. In the decision-making process, the credit report is taken as undisputed fact and the accuracy of the report is never questioned by the credit supplying institutions.

2. The credit report does not take into account information on the improved economic condition of the account holder such as increased salary or a better job obtained in the recent past.

3. To most credit-supplying institutions, one past "negative" outweighs dozens of "positives." The debtor's "sincerity," "honesty," "willingness," and "cooperation" with the creditor in paying off debts have little impact in the credit report.

If a debtor is late in payments, creditors are generally prompt to bring it to the notice of the credit reporting agencies. But, when the account is paid up, or updated, some creditors take a long pause to inform the credit reporting agencies about it. Some of them will not inform credit reporting agencies about the release of "liens" promptly, although the account had been paid off.

There is no effective and quick method to appeal a bad credit report, although inaccurate credit reports influence credit officials tremendously. It is interesting and puzzling that an otherwise soft-spoken, gentle-looking, polite official becomes a completely different individual at the sight of a credit report that highlights late payments, slow payments, past dues and delinquencies of the applicant's accounts. One can notice a 180-degree turn in the attitude of the loan officer.

To the official, the applicant appears to have committed a serious crime to have allowed his accounts to be "past due" and "delinquent." He, in reality, does not bear any malice against any prospective borrowers. His reaction to an adverse credit report is instinctive. The credit report portrays the account-holder as a high credit risk and the official cannot ignore it. This has become a part of the credit culture in the country.

Recent trends indicate that even some prospective employers inquire to see if an applicant is heavily indebted or sluggish in his payments. If the answer is yes, he is less desirable to the employer. Some insurance companies check credit records with employers before giving a policy to their prospective customers. This demonstrates the manifold uses of credit reports. We feel that the use of credit reports for purposes other than credit is highly questionable, despite their demonstrate d utility as multipurpose instruments. We feel that judging people on the basis of a credit report alone ignores other vital information about the character of the applicant, often resulting in decisions that are bound to be biased and unfair.

### Credit Reports and Credit Outcasts

We have explained how Ray was branded as a credit outcast. Millions of householders in Ray's situation throughout this nation have been similarly branded as "credit outcasts," implying that they are not welcome in the credit market. The credit culture and environment has been greatly influenced by the evolution of the credit reporting instrument, but the mechanical use and literal interpretation of credit codes prevent the credit-giving agencies from being fair, just, impartial, and above all, humane.

The society in which we live cannot guarantee stable and decent earnings or opportunities to all its citizens. The distribution of income is not fair and equitable. Households with low income and temporary jobs cannot compete with their more fortunate fellow workers. Fair and just allocations of credit could go a long way toward uplifting the economic condition of these households.

Lawmakers, motivated to protect the interests of the credit-supplying institutions, discipline and punish those borrowers who happen to fail in keeping their promises to the lenders. Legally or morally, there is nothing wrong in this arrangement, but what has gone wrong, and what concerns us most, is the abuse in the use of credit instruments and the subtle and systematic destruction of the credit-base of millions of low-income households on the basis of the credit report.

Many householders have unstable jobs and unreliable sources of income. Jobs are terminated or sources of income disappear not due to the householders' fault, but because of decisions of the employer or the overall conditions of the economy. Under these circumstances, the borrower is compelled to be late and is unable to keep promises made to his creditors. But, late payments destroy the household's credit base and the family's strategies for advancement. In some cases, defaults initiate the actual downfall of the family. Society has taken a "hands off" attitude toward the debt-trapped households and is indifferent to their sufferings. There is no one in the horizon to rescue them.

It cannot be repeated too often that this process of assessing credit-worthiness based on the credit report alone has deprived millions of households of the credit they need so badly. The "negatives" of credit reports have created a mass of "credit outcasts" in the credit market. Credit reports facilitate the continuous punishment of some debtors. During the currency of a loan, some indebted householders do not get any additional accommodation because of their late payment records, and after having paid off the outstanding balance they still remain ineligible for any external help because the credit report continues to focus on their past "negatives."

Credit bureaus also maintain information from public records, personnel investigation of employees, collection services, reports of fraud cases and the tracing of customers who left town without informing creditors. Nowadays, information is gathered and distributed electronically on a nationwide basis without paying any heed to the sanctity of confidentiality between creditors and borrowers. The privacy of a customer is in jeopardy.

The Fair Reporting Credit Act passed in 1971 gave a person the right to know what information about him is contained in a credit report and the name and address of the credit bureau whose information was used to deny credit. Very few households have the time, energy, or resources to correct inaccuracy in the report and to take advantage of this Fair Credit Act.[1]

We must understand that the denial of credit is the denial of one's natural and legitimate right to have access to opportunities that make an individual more productive in society. This raises the question of whether the credit report contains adequate information to determine a person's credit worthiness. Clearly, the answer is an emphatic "NO."

The credit bureau maintains information relating to the negatives of accounts for seven years or more, despite the fact that all those accounts might have been paid up for several years. The intent of this practice seems to tell credit supplying institutions to BEWARE of these "credit market outcasts." Their past defaulting is not forgivable and their present improved economic status is no valid ground to eradicate their past records of default.

Households think that the purpose of carrying this information long after the debts have been paid off is revengeful, harmful, and in utter disregard to the ideals of justice and fairness. The report blatantly ignores, or fails to take note of, pertinent information such as the improved economic condition of the applicant, the ratio between the negatives and positives in the account and, above all, the applicant's honesty, sincerity, reliability, and current high credit worthiness as a borrower. This goes contrary to the principles of fairness, justice, and the very grain of the American spirit of helping the needy. The impact of the credit report on low-income households can be summarized as follows:

---

[1]This Act has hardly helped low-income households obtain fair credit deals in the marketplace.

**The Vicious Cycle of Credit Reporting**

Low income or loss of jobs
leads to
Defaulting in payments
which leads to
Negative credit reports
which lead to
Denial of credit
which leads to
Denial of educational opportunities,
acquiring skills and undertaking business
which leads to
Denial of better jobs
which leads to
Poverty and low income

The bottom line in the decision-making process is that households are penalized for their past negatives, either by being denied credit or by being charged exorbitant rates of interest. The up-to-datedness of the current accounts and even a substantial income is of no value in erasing the past record. This reminds us of the story of the wolf and the lamb. The wolf was inventing an excuse to get the lamb, so he asked why the lamb was polluting the water he (the wolf) was drinking. The lamb replied, "How on earth can I pollute your drinking water by staying downstream from you?" The wolf retorted, "It was your great-great grandfather who polluted the drinking water and you must pay the price for it!" Many creditors believe that even if one's present income is decent and all accounts are up-to-date, one should still pay the price for what occurred to one's account in the past.

We know of a case where a householder with a yearly income of $100,000 was denied credit because he was late several times in the payments on one of his accounts, even though he had over three dozen accounts that were paid up or in "current status." Our credit culture prompts credit officials not to make any compromise with any record of past delays in payments.

The credit report digs deep into personal history, excavates and highlights the negatives that occurred in the past with the accounts, and disregards account holders' current high credit worthiness. In other words, the credit report suffers from the serious drawback of being inaccurate in reporting the current status of accounts. Apparently, the credit report is not well conceived device designed to insure fairness in allocating an important and scarce resource such as "credit" among households. Millions of households are denied access to credit and opportunities on inaccurate and incomplete information. This needs to be corrected.

The philosophies of credit reporting institutions and the analysis of credit reports by credit-supplying institutions need to be changed. The present practice of dangling the "negatives" before the eyes of prospective credit supplying agencies long after the debt has been paid off needs to be changed. In assessing the credit worthiness of a prospective borrower, credit institutions must give more weight to the ability and reliability of the applicant than to the so-called "negatives" of credit reports. Credit reporting in its present form has accentuated the burden of household debt.

### Pawnshops and Small Loan Companies

As we drive through U.S. cities, we encounter signs such as McDonald's, Kentucky Fried Chicken, Hardees, Taco Bell, etc. Along with these typical signs of U.S. cities, we also see the signs of pawnshops, mostly on busy avenues and streets. This indicates that pawnshops like motels and other businesses, occupy an important position in the daily life of Americans. But, seldom do we ask ourselves for whom they exist. The answer is, again, the low-income residents of these cities. Pawnshops that charge reasonable prices on their loans and provide a needed service are acceptable. But often, this is not happening. We are interested in assessing the cost of pawning and the nature of the burden of debt pawnshop customers are bearing.

A pawnshop's main operating principle is simple. Say a householder, namely Kay, needs funds badly but has no access to banks or other organized financial institutions due to lack of collateral or having been branded a credit outcast by credit bureau reports. Kay takes an old .22 rifle that was handed down to him by his father many years ago to a pawnshop. The pawnbroker then determines what he thinks the gun is worth and makes Kay an offer. If he says that he will loan Kay $100.00 on the item for 30 days and Kay agrees, they will then sign an agreement stating that, at the end of 30 days, when Kay returns to pick up the gun, he will pay 25% of the loan amount as storage fees. So, Kay will have to pay the pawnbroker $125.00 before he can take the gun home again. If Kay does not return after the 30-day period, the pawnbroker can then sell the gun in his shop to anyone, to recoup his $100 and the $25 storage fee.

This is a very simple but common operation that is done six days a week at pawnshops all over the country. The lifeblood of the pawnshop operation is, of course, the storage fee rate and the repeat customer who returns to pick up his pawned items. We are interested, of course, in the cost of obtaining a fair credit deal in the marketplace. Twenty-five dollars a month storage fee on a $100 loan amounts to a 300% rate of interest. Pawnshops are surviving on the desperate needs of hundreds of low-income households who have no alternatives to meet their credit needs. In similar fashion, some lending companies are extending funds to these low-income people for a period covering from one pay day to the next pay period at a rate of 30% to 35% on their loaned money.

### Debt Associated Other Costs

It is common for low-income families to experience such high interest rates when they have to pay late fees on their home and car payments, overdraft fees on checks and "over the limit" and past due penalties on their two or three credit cards. At times, they also pay fines and penalties for not paying taxes on time. The fines and penalties that households generally pay may be summarized as follows:

**Debt Associated Other Costs (Rough Estimate)**

| | |
|---|---|
| Late fees in paying home loan three times a year:<br>[at a rate of $25 a month = 25 x 3] | $75 |
| Late fees on a car loans (two cars at three times a year)<br>[at a rate of $15 a month = 15 x 3 x 2] | $90 |
| Late fees on two credit cards (three times a year) [20 x 3 x 2] | $120 |
| Over the limit charges<br>[at a rate of $20 a month for three months = 20 x 3 x 2] | $120 |
| At one time closing cost in buying a house ($2500/30) | $83 |
| Penalty for at least three return checks $20 x 3 | $60 |
| Penalty and interest on unpaid taxes of $1000 | $40 |
| **Total** | **$588** |

From the figures above, we notice that the interest payment is not the only cost of credit to the borrowers. There are other costs that a large number of borrowers bear without much protest. The rules to collect payment and impose penalties on those households that are able to make payments but are avoiding responsibilities deliberately are justified. But, what about those who lost their sources of income through no fault of their own and are forced to make all these additional payments in the form of late fees and penalties, resulting in a much higher percentage rate of "interest" than the rate of interest itself?

Our estimate shows that a household, on an average, spends more than 7% of its income as interest payments. When "other costs" associated with debts are added to our estimate, interest payment amounts to about 8.5% of their income. We can conclude then that indebted households in mid-sized cities pay at least 8.5% of their incomes as interest payments.

## E. BALLET OF BILLS

Our walk with Jay (described in the Chapter One) demonstrated how bills devastate a household. It will be interesting to know how and under what circumstances these bills originate. Here is an example of how it happens. The head of a household falls sick and is rushed to a hospital. Several tests and a couple of days' stay in the hospital produce a bill of several thousand dollars. There are few hospitals and few neurosurgeons (or other specialists) in most cities. Under these circumstances, it is unrealistic to expect competitive prices for these services in these cities. A talk of less than an hour with an attorney, a couple of hours of work by a plumber or a utility company mechanic may produce bills of several hundred dollars. In a similar fashion, others who happen to sell goods and services on credit keep on sending bills (amounting to hundreds of dollars) to households. At any point in time, the household's typical creditors are hospitals, physicians, lawyers, bankers, car dealers, plumbers, stores, and utility companies.

The current economy of a householder in a mid-sized city forces him to remain in debtor's status most of his life. After all, in a world of business, it is the creditor who writes the bills. It so happens that these creditors are professional people who often live near the debtor and are his neighbors. In many places, households and their creditors share a common environment, church, synagogue, restaurants and other recreational centers.

### The Writing of Bills

Unfortunately, when these professionals wear their uniforms, render services to households, and in the process develop claims on them, strange things transpire in their minds, they no more appear to be neighborly. As creditors, they enjoy prerogatives in dictating terms. In the absence of competition, as may be the case for some goods and services, the creditor uses his monopoly power in pricing his services or products.

In reality, households in most mid-sized cities are served by those who, by virtue of owning wealth, resources, businesses, and special skill, acquire some kind of monopoly power in pricing their services and products. This forces households to accept prices which far exceed the fair price of the product and services they need in their everyday lives. A reasonable margin of profit is expected and acceptable. But, when the "greed element" enters into the pricing process, it hurts households badly. All creditors who write bills are motivated to extract as much as they can, showing little regard for the principles of fair price and profit.

We often hear that a piece of furniture priced at $1,000 in a furniture store, costs only $500 to the store owner. A car dealers' bill for the repair of a car, or a plumber's charge for fixing a plumbing problem can reach far beyond the limits of "fair" pricing (which includes reasonable profits). Moreover, more than $20 to $25 billion are spent annually by big corporations in promoting the sales of their products and they conveniently pass the burden of advertising costs to the households who buy these products. Corporations may incur excess expenditures in the form of traveling first class, exotic dining, wining, and partying and indulging in other extravagant luxuries. Such expenses are then reflected in pricing of their products resulting in price hikes.

Let us examine how the marking up of prices affects households. Assume a 10% profit is fair and acceptable to stay in the business of producing goods and services. A commodity priced at $100.00 should include two variables, costs and fair profit. A simple price equation of this will be of the following form:

$$P = C + E \quad (P = \text{price}; C = \text{cost}; E = \text{profit})$$
$$\$110 = \$100 + \$10$$

Householders would have no objections to this price. A reasonable price and profit is acceptable to them. Problems arise when profit is substituted by "the greed element" and the normal cost is exceeded by unnecessary company expenses.[1] The "greed element" and unnecessary company expenses result in marking up of prices of goods and services,

[1]Unnecessary company expenses include traveling 1st class, dining, and partying.

reaching at times and at some places, as high as 100% of the normal price. These inflated prices force households to prolong their period of services to creditors. An example below shows how this happens.

To continue with our price equation, a commodity that was priced at $100 has now been marked-up to $150 to cover "the greed element" and the excessive expenses of the company. The equations appears as follows:

$$P = C^{1} + E^{2} + Gr^{3}$$
$$\$150 = \$100 + \$10 + \$40$$

A householder who earns $5.00 an hour has to devote 22 hours of work to earn $110 which is the fair price of the commodity. But, to earn $150, he has to devote 30 hours of work, an additional 8 hours of his work time, to cover the "markup" portion of prices caused by "greed" and "unnecessary expense elements" of a company. The formula to determine additional work-hours forced on households to cover the inflated prices of goods and services, given the wages per hour, fair prices, and inflated prices of goods and services may be written as follows:

**Additional Work Hours Forced on Households to Cover the Markup and Inflated Prices.**

Additional work-hours needed to cover inflated prices of goods and services

$$r = \frac{P_{inf}^{\;4} - P_{f}^{\;5}}{W_{g}}$$

(given the wages)

$$= \frac{\$150 - \$110}{\$5} = 8 \text{ hours}$$

This shows that the additional work-hours forced on households to cover the inflated or "marked-up" portion of the price equals 8 hours. The

---

[1]C = fair cost

[2]E = (fair) profit

[3]Gr = The rising price due to greed and excess expense of a company.

[4] Pinf: inflated prices of goods and services

[5] Pf: Fair priced goods and services

earnings of these additional work hours (r x w = 8 x 5= $40) go to those who mark up prices and inflate bills.

The marked-up and inflated prices compel households to put in additional work hours. But, the earnings of additional work hours go to the producers. In the same way, high interest rates force indebted households to put in many additional hours of work in servicing their debts. A fair cost of debt is acceptable, but a fairly priced debt is not available to low and middle-income households. To cite an example: A house with a purchase price of $100,000, at 10% interest, for 30 years, yields interest payments alone of more than $200,000.

Households with poor credit ratings (as with low-income households) pay much higher rates and pay much more interest than others for the same amount of loans. In addition, closing costs, late fees, penalties and other incidental charges add to the cost of servicing the debt. This requires more years of additional work hours. All these examples point to the fact that inflated prices, bills and high interest rates encountered in everyday life by households in mid-sized cities impose on them many years of additional work, while increasing the real burden of debt and the period of service to their creditors.

# CHAPTER NINE
## DEBT SETTLEMENT BOARD AND NEW BANKS

### The Rationale for Debt Settlement Board

According to our survey, a large section of households in mid-sized cities are in debt for one reason or another. Of these indebted households, 70% experienced considerable anxiety and sacrifices in servicing their debt. The agonies and other economic woes that an indebted household undergoes have been detailed in Chapter One "The Economic Saga of Jay." It would not be an exaggeration to say that the interest costs that many of these households bear vary between 10% and 18%, although the effective costs of borrowing may go much higher when late fees, penalties, and other charges are added. The rates of interest from unorganized and independent sources of credit vary between 24% and 300%.

We have shown that the size of the debt of lower income groups often equals well over 100% of their income, implying the nature of the debt burden that households bear. Economic hardships are multiplied when creditors add late fees, penalties, compound interest, repossess homes, cars, and furniture; and keep debtors under constant threats of lawsuits by writing registered letters.

Millions of households, because of the loss of jobs, income, businesses, calamities in the family, and other genuine reasons fail to keep their accounts up-to-date and are under constant pressure to settle their debts. They desperately need help. Unfortunately, society has been callous and indifferent to their needs and there exists no agency that can come to their rescue. They become helpless victims of the laws and regulations of the nation and are often not well treated by their creditors. No organized institution exists to help them.

To give relief to these indebted households, we recommend the establishment of a Debt Settlement Board in each state, with offices located in mid-sized cities. The Board should be charged with the responsibility of looking into the problems of indebted households. Once it is ascertained that the households have failed to make payments on genuine grounds, the

Board can negotiate with the creditor for suitable terms and conditions for the settlement of the debt.

An important objective of the Board will be to make the arrangements to settle the debt in its entirety rather than relieving the debtor of his obligation by writing off the debt while keeping the debtor's credit in good standing. This way, the creditor gets his money back, and the debtor is relieved of the prospect of losing his property. The arrangement of the settlement of debt through negotiations by the Debt Settlement Board will extend an urgently needed relief to households and give them a chance to reorganize their businesses, continue their normal work and contribute to the society while living with dignity and respect in their communities.

The Board should have the following authority in settling the debt:

1. It should have the legal right to summon both creditor and debtor to its office.

2. The Board should be able to impose an easy payment arrangement: longer time, lower rates, and lower payments.

3. The Board should have the right to write off the entire debt of the household if the creditor does not respond to its requests.

4. The Board should be able to negotiate with specialized financial institutions to arrange monetary help for the debtor's family to overcome the immediate financial need of the family, particularly, to make his accounts up-to-date, and thus prevent court action or harassment by the creditor.

5. The Board should have the ability to contact different governmental and private agencies to help provide jobs to those indebted households who are currently unemployed.

The Board should work as an intermediary in arranging payments from debtor to creditors. It should do so with patience, kindness, and sympathy for all borrowers who have approached it for help. By following this procedure, we can visualize an era of loss-proof loans given to households and at the same time, the society can avoid accusations of being indifferent to the indebted residents.

In summary, the Debt Settlement Board could assist in averting bankruptcy, in recovering borrowed money, and in providing much needed relief to indebted households. As we have mentioned earlier, bankruptcy is not an ideal solution for the indebted household. The bankruptcy decree is costly, time consuming, and psychologically depressing. It destroys the debtor's prospect of getting credit for many years to come.

Board initiated settlement benefits both the debtors and creditors. Both parties should gladly contribute to sharing the operational cost of the Board. The operational costs of the Board may be financed by allocation from state budgets with a matching funds from the federal government. Alternatively, a one time small fee of 1/10 of 1% of the loan amount from the borrower and a matching amount from the suppliers of credit may be collected. This entire amount should be matched by the federal government to be used in meeting the operating costs of the Board.

## Composition of the Debt Settlement Board

Each state or mid-sized city should have one such board. It should be composed of a chairman appointed by the mayor or the governor. The chairman may be chosen from among retired judges, principals, college presidents, professors and other qualified professionals. About four or five members should be chosen from among the prominent members of the community to represent a cross section of the society as far as possible.

## The Rationale for a New Bank

A big business has easy access to money markets to raise funds for capital expenditures, business expansion and to increase its income in the process. But households in mid-sized cities of the U.S. struggle for credit to have access to the essentials of daily life.

Credit is a powerful instrument for achieving economic and personal goals. Unfortunately, in the present-day economy, credit is the exclusive privilege of the prosperous and the fortunate ones in this society. The poor are unable to offer security and are disqualified from acquiring credit. This raises questions regarding the working philosophy of the financial institutions, the environment and the culture that governs existing credit institutions. The following is the rationale for bringing in new banks to cater to the needs of low-income households:

1. Thirty-three percent of the households in small and mid-sized cities cannot afford to offer security for loans and are thus generally disqualified for credit. Without credit, householders make compromises with the bare essentials of life and lose opportunities to prepare themselves and their families for better jobs, careers, and income.

2. As noted earlier, the rates of interest from organized financial institutions vary from 9% to 24%, depending on the sources of credit. Often, a household, after having been refused credit from organized credit institutions and compelled by circumstances, may take loans from independent loan companies, finance companies, credit cards, and professional money lenders. The cost of credit from these sources is exorbitantly high, varying from 14% to 300%. Low-income groups do not regularly associate with high-income groups in business undertakings and have no easy access to organized money markets or capital markets to raise funds for their needs.

3. Many households are not well-informed and educated about their rights and privileges in relation to credit markets.

4. At times, a bank sets a minimum limit below which it will not grant any loan, but this minimum is often too high for many households. During the recession of the early 80's, hundreds of households were denied badly needed credit because they could not qualify for the minimum amounts.[1]

5. Households stigmatized in the past by credit bureaus for late payments rarely have any chance for loans for homes, cars, boats, credit cards, and other consumer goods.

In summary, the denial of credit, the high cost of credit, the harassment of debtors by creditors,[2] the sacrifices and loss of assets that households experience in servicing their debt raise questions such as:

1. Is the credit market climate congenial to obtaining needed credit by low and middle-income households in the present credit markets?

2. Are there specialized credit institutions to cater to the peculiar credit needs of the low and middle-income groups who have no security to offer against their loans?

3. Is there an agency that would extend credit to households that are presently earning a decent income, have paid off their outstanding

---

[1]As we mentioned earlier, the minimum amount of a loan one could apply for was $3,000 during the recession the of the eighties.

[2]We discussed this in Chapters Two and Three.

debt, but are currently bearing the stigma of bad credit caused by late payments that occurred several years earlier?

The answer to all these questions is an emphatic "No." The essence of our analysis is that the existing lending institutions are not philosophically, culturally and functionally geared to providing needed credit to low and middle-income households. We recommend that a new type of credit institution, with a philosophy of providing credit help to needy households, at a reasonable cost, be brought into existence. This will cater to the peculiar credit needs of millions of households in the U.S. economy. Federal and state laws may be enacted to achieve this goal.

### Functions, Objectives and Philosophy of the New Banks: (Supplementary Credit Institutions)

1. The bank should be accessible, generous, and able to serve the credit needs of low and middle-income households at low cost.

2. The interest rates should not exceed the discount rate of the Federal Reserve Bank by more than 1%.

3. A household having a steady income but no collateral should not be refused badly needed credit.

4. The integrity of a loan applicant and the personal confidence of the loan officer in the applicant's ability to repay the loan should be the important criterion - not the credit report, which should have minimum weight in the decision-making process.

5. A householder who fails to make payment due to the loss of a job or a source of income should not be penalized by late fees and other penalties. A new convenient payment schedule should be made after consultation with the debtor.

6. An indebted householder who has a job and is determined to settle his debt and commands the confidence of the loan officer may be given a loan, at a low interest rate, on request to update his account despite his being a "credit outcast" in the light of "negatives" of his credit report.

7. The credit rating of a sincere, honest, and hard-working householder should be kept in good standing, as long as he is determined to settle his account and cooperates with the creditor.

8. A householder may be given a loan for educational purposes, or job training for his children.

9. On the request of a borrower's heir, a loan can be passed onto them when a borrower passes away without paying off his debt.[1]

10. Kindness, leniency, and sympathy should dominate in dealing with the credit problems of low-income households.

11. Credit should not be equated with charity.

12. A credit institution should have multiple roles as a creditor, guide and partner in leading the borrowers to success.

The philosophy and guidelines of present credit institutions permit only limited accommodation of low-income households in meeting their credit needs. As enterprises, these institutions are motivated to earning profit. "Leniency," "kindness," "consideration," and "sympathy" are elements that do not resonate in the book of business, particularly not in money-lending institutions. These elements should be the important prerequisites in any institution that works with low and middle-income households anywhere in the world.

Flexibility in costs, rates of interest and payment schedules are a must for these households whose economies are notoriously vulnerable (due to no fault of their own). Credit institutions look forward to soliciting the business of those people who have substantial incomes and assets. Unfortunately, the households with which we are concerned are not the ones in which the banks are interested. These households are made up of honest, sincere, responsible, hardworking people with vulnerable economies and meager assets. As regards their jobs and income, they are hired and fired by their employers according to fluctuating business cycles. They live from hand to mouth.

Guidelines for financial institutions are so designed that households with low income, poor credit reports, and no collateral, are destined to be denied credit. Exceptions are rare, for these households are the victims of a credit culture that evolved from laws and traditions that govern the credit market in this society. For many decades, this culture has left thousands of households helpless, defeated and at the mercy of economic perils. The denial of credit to the less fortunate people has also a harmful social effect.

---

[1]This system is prevalent in some countries.

Social values, traditions, and unfair distribution systems account for inadvertently created poverty in other countries as well as in the U.S. When we realize this and accept our mistakes, measures can be taken to correct this problem. We collectively owe obligations to the poverty-stricken population to improve their economic condition. The universal declaration of human rights is worth mentioning in this context. To ensure that the poor are credit-worthy and useful to their families and society, it is our duty to find ways that will contribute to a just distribution of wealth.

Our society should be in accord with the Universal Declaration of Human Rights, which states: "Everyone has the right to a standard of living adequate for the health and well-being of himself and his family, including food, clothing, housing, medical care, necessary social services, and the right to security in the event of unemployment, sickness, disability, widowhood, old age or other lack of a livelihood in circumstances beyond his control. The state is obligated under human rights to create conditions under which citizens can fulfill the needs expressed in the human rights system including the right to work, to food, to education, to shelter, to health, and so on."

The denial of credit very nearly amounts to a violation of human rights. The distribution system of many countries gives rise to gross inequality of income and compel a section of society to supplement its incomes by borrowing. Credit is therefore a must for them. Indebted households also need credit to supplement their inadequate income, meet bare essentials of life and to catch up with missed payments. They are also constantly haunted by fears of receiving certified letters from the creditors' attorneys threatening to sue them. The availability of credit at this critical hour relieves them of the anxieties they suffer and offers them a new lease on life. With credit, they can update their accounts, and keep creditors off their premises and feel reinvigorated to fight against the odds.

Briefly stated, with credit, a needy household is psychologically cheered up, rises out of depression, and starts making immediate plans for increasing its income by finding a new or additional job or by undertaking a business enterprise. Without credit, the household is completely immobilized. Has society provided fair and reasonable opportunities for education, training, and jobs to all citizens? No one seems to be able to answer this question in the affirmative. If the response is no, households that have low income, low credit worthiness, and are languishing in poverty may not be accountable for their miseries and the disqualification that prevents them from getting credit. In the U.S., more than 18% of the total population, involving millions of households, belong to this group. Their prospect of getting credit is bleak. In order for households to get a fair chance to improve their material well-being, their right to credit must be established and assured.

As the existing financial institutions are unwilling for one reason or another to accommodate low-income households with credit, it is the obligation of the state and the world community to provide alternative financial institutions which will guarantee the fundamental human rights of these households all over the world. In a fair distribution system, and with an easy access to credit, we may find the key to the economic emancipation of households who have been living below the poverty level and have been struggling under burdensome debt. "Credit" should and must be available to the needy households irrespective of their credit standings and income levels.

The present credit institutions with their philosophy and credit culture are simply unable to meet the peculiar credit needs of low-income households. Above all, the cost of credit from the existing credit institutions has been unusually burdensome. As we said earlier, indebted households with poor credit should also have access to credit. After all, credit has the capacity of rescuing an indebted person from being drowned in an ocean of sufferings. Given the opportunity, an indebted person can turn out to be a natural and better fighter against his adversaries than the non-indebted person. This indebted person is concerned about his human dignity and also about his children's present and future economic status. Finally, credit should be recognized as a fundamental human right, and should not be the exclusive privilege of the prosperous and the affluent.

# CHAPTER TEN
## SUMMARY OF FINDINGS & RECOMMENDATIONS

Below is the summary of our findings and a recapitulation of our recommendation[1].

### The Trend of Average Household Income

| **Year** | 1985 | 1988 | 1990 | 1991 | 1992 | 1993 |
|---|---|---|---|---|---|---|
| **Avg. Income** | $26,019 | $25,323 | $30,082 | $29,107 | $28,342 | $30,532 |

Average household income for 1990 - 1993 was . . . . . . . . . . . . . . . . . $29,516
Per year per household average change in income for 1990 - 1993 was . . . . $60
Per capita change in income for 1990 - 1993 was . . . . . . . . . . . . . . . . . . . . $150

### Average Size of Income
### $0 - 5000

| **Year** | 1985 | 1988 | 1990 | 1991 | 1992 | 1993 |
|---|---|---|---|---|---|---|
| **Avg. Income** | $4,300 | $3,052 | $3,343 | $3,424 | $2,710 | $2,723 |

Average household income for 1990 - 1993 was . . . . . . . . . . . . . . . . . . . $3,050
Per year per household average change in income for 1990 - 1993 was . . . $207
Per capita change in income 1990 - 1993 was . . . . . . . . . . . . . . . . . . . . . . ($83)

### Average Size of Income
### $5,000 - 10,000

| **Year** | 1985 | 1988 | 1990 | 1991 | 1992 | 1993 |
|---|---|---|---|---|---|---|
| **Avg. Income** | $7,079 | $7,461 | $7,602 | $7,665 | $7,347 | $7,706 |

The average household income for 1990 - 1993 was . . . . . . . . . . . . . . . . $7,555
Per year per household average change in income for 1990 - 1993 was . . . . $35
The per capita change in income 1990 - 1993 was . . . . . . . . . . . . . . . . . . . $14

---

[1]For the convenience of readers, we have repeated some excerpts from important chapters of the book.

## Average Size of Income
## $10,000 - 15,000

| Year | 1985 | 1988 | 1990 | 1991 | 1992 | 1993 |
|---|---|---|---|---|---|---|
| Avg. Income | $12,231 | $12,767 | $12,152 | $12,232 | $12,113 | $12,390 |

The average household income for 1990 - 1993 was ............... $12,222
Per year per household average change in income for 1990 - 1993 ........ $79
The per capita change in income 1990 - 1993 was .................... $32

## Average Size of Income
## $15,000 - 20,000

| Year | 1985 | 1988 | 1990 | 1991 | 1992 | 1993 |
|---|---|---|---|---|---|---|
| Avg. Income | $17,381 | $18,756 | $17,190 | $17,285 | $17,446 | $17,464 |

The average household income for 1990 - 1993 was ............... $17,346
Per year per household average change in income for 1990 - 1993 was ... $91
The per capita change in income 1990 - 1993 was .................... $36

## Average Size of income
## 20,000 - 25,000

| Year | 1985 | 1988 | 1990 | 1991 | 1992 | 1993 |
|---|---|---|---|---|---|---|
| Avg. Income | $22,164 | $23,301 | $21,927 | $22,270 | $22,732 | $22,793 |

The average household income for 1990 - 1993 was ............... $22,431
Per year per household average change in income for 1990 - 1993 was .. $289
The per capita change in income for 1990 - 1993 was ................. $116

## Average Size of Income
## $25,000 - 30,000

| Year | 1985 | 1988 | 1990 | 1991 | 1992 | 1993 |
|---|---|---|---|---|---|---|
| Avg. Income | $27,522 | $27,892 | $26,951 | $28,080 | $27,273 | $27,475 |

The average household income for 1990 - 1993 was ............... $27,445
Per year per household average change in income for 1990-1993 was ... $175
The per capita change in income 1990 - 1993 was .................... $70

### Average Size of Income
### 30,000 - 35,000

| Year | 1985 | 1988 | 1990 | 1991 | 1992 | 1993 |
|---|---|---|---|---|---|---|
| Avg. Income | $32,617 | $31,706 | $32,752 | $32,511 | $32,326 | $32,680 |

The average household income for 1990 - 1993 was . . . . . . . . . . . . . . . $32,567
Per year per household average change in income for 1990-1993 was . . . ($24)
The per capita change in income 1990 - 1993 was . . . . . . . . . . . . . . . . . . ($10)

### Average Size of Income
### $35,000 - 40,000

| Year | 1985 | 1988 | 1990 | 1991 | 1992 | 1993 |
|---|---|---|---|---|---|---|
| Avg. Income | $38,617 | $39,048 | $37,604 | $37,397 | $37,200 | $37,052 |

The average household income for 1990 - 1993 was . . . . . . . . . . . . . . . $37,313
Per year per household average change in income for 1990-1993 was . ($184)
The per capita change in income 1990 - 1993 was . . . . . . . . . . . . . . . . . . ($70)

### Average Size of Income
### $40,000 - 45,000

| Year | 1985 | 1988 | 1990 | 1991 | 1992 | 1993 |
|---|---|---|---|---|---|---|
| Avg. Income | $42,843 | $42,474 | $43,006 | $42,282 | $42,317 | $42,214 |

The average household income for 1990 - 1993 was . . . . . . . . . . . . . . . $42,455
Per year per household average change in income for 1990-1993 was . ($264)
The per capita change in income 1990 - 1993 was . . . . . . . . . . . . . . . . . .($106)

### Average Size of Income
### $45,000 - 50,000

| Year | 1985 | 1988 | 1990 | 1991 | 1992 | 1993 |
|---|---|---|---|---|---|---|
| Avg. Income | $47,994 | $46,526 | $47,071 | $47,697 | $47,993 | $47,660 |

The average household income for 1990 - 1993 was . . . . . . . . . . . . . . . $47,605
Per year per household average change in income for 1990-1993 was . ($196)
The per capita change in income 1990 - 1993 was . . . . . . . . . . . . . . . . . . ($78)

### Average Size of Income
### $50,000 - 55,000

| Year | 1985 | 1988 | 1990 | 1991 | 1992 | 1993 |
|---|---|---|---|---|---|---|
| **Avg. Income** | $51,847 | $52,671 | $52,682 | $52,159 | $52,343 | $52,802 |

The average household income for 1990 - 1993 was . . . . . . . . . . . . . . . $52,497
Per year per household average change in income for 1990-1993 was . . . . . $40
The per capita change in income 1990 - 1993 was . . . . . . . . . . . . . . . . . . . . $16

### Average Size of Income
### $55,000 - 60,000

| Year | 1985 | 1988 | 1990 | 1991 | 1992 | 1993 |
|---|---|---|---|---|---|---|
| **Avg. Income** | $56,898 | $55,676 | $57,758 | $57,142 | $57,491 | $57,463 |

The average household income for 1990 - 1993 was . . . . . . . . . . . . . . . .$57,464
Per year per household average change in income for 1990 - 1993 was . . . . $98
The per capita change in income 1990 - 1993 was . . . . . . . . . . . . . . . . . . . . $39

### Average Size of Income
### $60,000 +

| Year | 1985 | 1988 | 1990 | 1991 | 1992 | 1993 |
|---|---|---|---|---|---|---|
| **Avg. Income** | $60,176 | $65,711 | $71,310 | $67,811 | $70,126 | $71,435 |

The average household income for 1990 - 1993 was . . . . . . . . . . . . . . . $70,171
Per year per household average change in income for 1990-1993 was . . . . $42
The per capita change in income 1990 - 1993 was . . . . . . . . . . . . . . . . . . . . $17

**Household Income Below Poverty Level**
(Income in Thousands)

| Income | 1985 | 1988 | 1990 | 1991 | 1992 | 1993 |
|---|---|---|---|---|---|---|
| **$0-5,000**<br>**Percent of Sample** | $4,300<br>(1%) | $3,052<br>(1%) | $3,343<br>(2%) | $3,424<br>(6%) | $2,710<br>(6%) | $2,723<br>(7%) |
| **$5,000-10,000**<br>**Percent of Sample** | $7,079<br>(12%) | $7,461<br>(11%) | $7,602<br>(13%) | $7,665<br>(11%) | $7,247<br>(10%) | $7,706<br>(9%) |
| **$10,000-15,000**<br>**Percent of Sample** | $12,231<br>(11%) | $12,787<br>(18%) | $12,152<br>(11%) | $12,232<br>(14%) | $12,113<br>(11%) | $12,390<br>(12%) |
| **$15,000-20,000**<br>**Percent of Sample** | $17,361<br>(13%) | $18,756<br>(13%) | $17,190<br>(13%) | $17,285<br>(12%) | $17,446<br>(13%) | $17,464<br>(12%) |
| **$20,000-25,000**<br>**Percent of Sample** | $22,164<br>(12%) | $23,301<br>(10%) | $21,927<br>(10%) | $22,270<br>(8%) | $22,732<br>(9%) | $22,793<br>(8%) |

**Per Capita Income of Households Below Poverty Level**

| Income (In Thousands) | 1985 | 1988 | 1990 | 1991 | 1992 | 1993 |
|---|---|---|---|---|---|---|
| **$0 - 5,000** | $1,720 | $1,221 | $1,337 | $1,370 | $1,084 | $1,089 |
| **$5,000 - 10,000** | $2,832 | $2,984 | $3,041 | $3,066 | $2,899 | $3, 082 |
| **$10,000 - 15,000** | $4,892 | $5,115 | $4,861 | $4,893 | $4,845 | $4,956 |

About 25% of households in our survey have been living below poverty level. The average income of these households varied between $2,710 and $12,787. The per capita income of these households varied between $1,084 and $5,115. Twenty-four to thirty percent of the households in our survey area earned less than $15,000 per year. In our survey, 13% to 17% of households reported having income below $10,000 yearly. The average income of these groups varied between $2,710 and $7,706. The per capita income for these groups varied between $1,084 and $3,082 during the years of our survey.

**The Trend of Average Size of Household Debt**

| | 1985 | 1988 | 1990 | 1991 | 1992 | 1993 |
|---|---|---|---|---|---|---|
| Sample Average Debt | $16,300 | $14,050 | $15,430 | $15,280 | $11,340 | $12,210 |
| Average Debt of Indebted Household | $16,780 | $22,820 | $33,320 | $31,880 | $31,180 | $33,590 |
| Sample's average of last four years' (1990-1993) household debt: | | | | | | $13,565 |
| Sample average per year average decrease in debt for 1990-1993: | | | | | | ($1,073) |
| The average of indebted households' debt for 1990-1993: | | | | | | $32,493 |
| Per year per household average increase in indebted households debt: | | | | | | $90 |

**Sample Average Size of Debt**
(item wise)

| | |
|---|---|
| The sample average home loan for 1990-1993 was | $9,171 |
| The sample average car loan for 1990-1993 was | $2,691 |
| The sample average personal and business loan for 1990-1993 was | $1,027 |
| The sample average credit card loan for 1990-1993 was | $1,658 |
| The sample average household income for 1990-1993 was | $29,516 |

**Frequencies and Debt Average (Of Indebted Households)**

| | 1985 | 1988 | 1990 | 1991 | 1992 | 1993 |
|---|---|---|---|---|---|---|
| Averages of Indebted Households | $16,780 | $22,820 | $33,320 | $31,880 | $31,180 | $33,590 |
| Frequencies of Indebted Households | 97% | 62% | 46% | 48% | 33% | 32% |

**Average Size of Debt and Frequencies of Indebted Households**[1] (Item Wise)

| Average Size of Debt for Indebted Households | 1985 | 1988 | 1990 | 1991 | 1992 | 1993 |
|---|---|---|---|---|---|---|
| **Home Loan** | $16,628 (64%) | $21,719 (39%) | $27,227 (39%) | $27,281 (35%) | $23,942 (32%) | $26,731 (33%) |
| **Car Loan** | $4,850 (28%) | $6,929 (9%) | $16,132 (13%) | $15,789 (23%) | $11,260 (8%) | $10,000 (15%) |
| **Personal and Business Loans** | $6,553 (51%) | $9,233 (48%) | $11,394 | $8,855 | $8,500* | $9,160* |
| **Credit Car Loan** | $844 (84%) | $1,684 (19%) | $7,430 (31%) | $5,140 (25%) | $4,400 (13%) | $4,220 (20%) |
| The average size of home loan for 1990-1993 was | | | | | | $26,295 |
| The average size of car loans for 1990-1993 was | | | | | | $13,295 |
| The average size of personal and business loans for 1990-1993 was | | | | | | $9,477 |
| The average size of credit card loans for 1990-1993 was | | | | | | $5,298 |

**Estimated Figures*

***Numbers in ( ) Denote Frequencies*

[1]Not many households maintained accurate data regarding interest payments on car loans and personal and business loans after these items were declared non-deductible item for tax purposes.

**Household Debt and Other Debts**[1]

| | |
|---|---|
| Average size of household debt for 1990-1993 | $32,493 |
| Average size of corporate debt for 1990-1993 | $40,305 |
| Average size of federal debt for 1990-1993 | $39,646 |
| Average size of household income for 1990-1993 | $61,758 |
| Average size of state debt for 1990-1993 | $3,989 |
| Average increase of per household income per year for 1990-1993 | $2,447 |
| Average increase of per household corporate debt/year for 1990-1993 | $3,510 |
| Average increase of per household federal debt per year for 1990-1993 | $3,938 |
| Average increase of per household state debt per year for 1990-1993 | $361 |
| Average increase of per household debt per year for 1990-1993 | $90 |

**Per Capita Debt**

| | |
|---|---|
| Average of per capita household debt for the 1990-1993 period (in survey area) was | $12,571 |
| Average of per capita federal debt for the 1990-1993 period was | $14,862 |
| Average of per capita corporate debt for the 1990-1993 period was | $15,109 |
| Averages of per capita state debt for the 1990-1993 period was | $1,495 |
| Average of per capita household GNP for the 1990-1993 period was | $23,153 |
| Average of per capita interest paid debt for the 1990-1993 period was | $1,121 |

[1]All averages have been estimated by taking into account the amounts of debt outstanding and the numbers of households for the years with which we are concerned.

## Interest Paid by Different Groups

### The Trend of General Interest Payment

**$10,000 - 15,000**

The average interest paid for 1990 - 1993 was .................... $1,570
The average increase in interest paid for this group during 1990 - 1993 was $111

**$15,000 - 20,000**

The average interest paid for 1990 - 1993 was .................... $2,263
The average increase in interest paid for this group during 1990 - 1993 was $253

**$20,000 - 25,000**

The average interest paid for 1990-1993 was ...................... $1,700
The average increase in interest paid for this group during 1990-1993 was ... $0

**$25,000 - 30,000**

The average interest paid for 1990-1993 was ...................... $2,274
The average increase in interest paid for this group during 1990-1993 was .. $44

**$30,000 - 35,000**

The average interest paid for 1990 - 1993 was .................... $2,367
The average decrease in interest paid for this group during 1990-1993 was ($286)

**$35,000 - 40,000**

The average interest paid for 1990 - 1993 was .................... $2,765
The average decrease in interest paid for this group during 1990-1993 was .. ($4)

**$40,000 - 45,000**

The average interest paid for 1990-1993 was ...................... $2,734
The average decrease in interest paid for this group during 1990-1993 was ($670)

**$45,000 - 50,000**

The average interest paid for 1990-1993 was ...................... $3,300
The average decrease in interest paid for this group during 1990-1993 was ($426)

**$50,000 - 55,000**

The average interest paid for 1990-1993 was ...................... $4,243
The average decrease in interest paid for this group during 1990-1993 was ($1,100)

**$55,000 - 60,000**

The average interest for 1990-1993 was ........................ $3,483

The average decrease in interest paid for this group during 1990-1993 was ($324)

**$60,000 - 102,000**

The average interest paid for 1990-1993 was ...................... $4,419

The average decrease in interest paid for this group during 1990-1993 was ($541)

## Other Interest Payments, Interest Earnings and Regression Data

### The Trend of Interest Paid (Sample Average)

| 1985 | 1988 | 1990 | 1991 | 1992 | 1993 |
|---|---|---|---|---|---|
| $1,630 | $1,405 | $1,543 | $1,528 | $1,135 | $1,221 |

### The Average Amount of Interest Paid by Indebted Households

| 1985 | 1988 | 1990 | 1991 | 1992 | 1993 |
|---|---|---|---|---|---|
| $1,678 | $2,282 | $3,332 | $3,188 | $3,118 | $3,359 |
| Average interest payment for 1990-1993 | | | | | $25,916 |
| Per year decrease in sample average interest payment 1990-1993 | | | | | ($107) |
| Average interest paid by indebted households 1990-1993 | | | | | $3,249 |
| Per year changes in averages of household debt 1990-1993 | | | | | $9 |

**The Average Amount of Interest Paid (By Item) by Households**

| | |
|---|---|
| Average amount of interest paid on home loans 1990 - 1993 | $917 |
| Average amount of interest paid on car loans 1990 - 1993 | $269 |
| Average amount of interest paid on personal & business (P&B) loans | $364 |
| Average amount of interest paid on credit card (CC) loans 1990 - 1993 | $166 |
| Average change in interest payment per year for home loans 1990-1993 | ($56) |
| Average change in interest payment per year for car loans 1990 - 1993 | ($21) |
| Average change in interest payment per year for P&B loans 1990-1993 | ($89) |

**Average Size of Interest Paid by Indebted Household (Item Wise) by Households**

| | |
|---|---|
| Average interest paid on home loan for 1990 - 1993 was | $2,612 |
| Average interest paid on car loan for 1990 - 1993 was | $1,330 |
| Average interest paid on P&B loans for 1990 - 1993 was | $948 |
| Average interest paid on credit card loans for 1990 - 1993 was | $530 |

**Interest Paid on Home Loan and Car Loan (Together)**

| | |
|---|---|
| Average interest payment for both home & car loans for 1990-1993: | $4,324 |
| Average percent of income paid as interest on home & car loan together for 1990 - 1993: | 8.62% |

**Interest Paid on Household Debt and Other Debt**

| | |
|---|---|
| Average size of interest paid by indebted households for 1990-1993 | $3,249 |
| Average size of interest paid on federal debt (per household) for 1990-1993 | $2,990 |

**Total Interest Paid as % of Income (Indebted Households)**

Total interest paid by indebted households as a percent of income was . . . 7.8%
Total interest paid on home loans as a percent of average income was . . . . 7.2%
Total interest paid on car loans as a percent of average income was . . . . . . 3.8%
Total interest paid on personal and business loans as a % income was . . . . 3.3%
Total interest paid on credit card loans as a percent income was . . . . . . . . . 1.3%

**Interest Earned**
(Sample Average)

| 1988 | 1990 | 1991 | 1992 | 1993 |
|---|---|---|---|---|
| $1,435 | $1,911 | $2,006 | $974 | $936 |

**Average Earned by Interest Earning Households**

| 1988 | 1990 | 1991 | 1992 | 1993 |
|---|---|---|---|---|
| $2,128 | $2,513 | $2,712 | $1,590 | $1,639 |

| | |
|---|---|
| Average interest earned by all households in our sample during 1990 - 1993 was | $1,457 |
| Per year per household average decrease in interest earned during 1990 - 1993 was | ($325) |
| Average interest earned by interest earning households during 1990 - 1993 was | ($2,114) |
| Per household per year average decrease in interest earnings during 1990 - 1993 was | ($291) |

The sample average interest earned by households varied between $936 and $2,000 during the 1990 - 1993 period, yielding a decrease in interest earnings of $326/year.

**Interest Earned by Different Income Groups**

**$0 - 5,000**

| | |
|---|---|
| The average interest earned for 1990 - 1993 was | $1,318 |
| Per household per year average increase in interest earned for 1990-1993 was | $83 |

**$5,000 - 10,000**

| | |
|---|---|
| The average interest earned for 1990 - 1993 was | $1,606 |
| Per household per year average increase in interest earned for 1990 - 1993 was | $143 |

**$10,000 - 15,000**

| | |
|---|---|
| The average interest earned for 1990 - 1993 was | $2,047 |
| Per household per year average decrease in interest earned for 1990 - 1993 was | ($642) |

**$15,000 - 20,000**

| | |
|---|---|
| The average interest earned for 1990 - 1993 was | $2,113 |
| Per household per year average decrease in interest earned for 1990 - 1993 was | ($237) |

**$20,000 - 25,000**

| | |
|---|---|
| The average interest earned for 1990 - 1993 was | $1,875 |
| Per household per year average decrease in interest earned for 1990 - 1993 was | ($515) |

**$25,000 - 30,000**

| | |
|---|---|
| The average interest earned for 1990 - 1993 was | $1,709 |
| Per household per year average decrease in interest earned for 1990 - 1993 was | ($605) |

**$30,000 - 35,000**

| | |
|---|---|
| The average interest earned for 1990 - 1993 was | $2,738 |
| Per household per year average increase in interest earned for 1990 - 1993 was | $624 |

**$35,000 - 40,000**

| | |
|---|---|
| The average interest earned for 1990 - 1993 was | $1,130 |
| Per household per year average increase in interest earned for 1990 - 1993 was | $170 |

**$40,000 - 45,000**

| | |
|---|---|
| The average interest earned for 1990 - 1993 was | $1,656 |
| Per household per year average decrease in interest earned for 1990 - 1993 was | ($504) |

**$45,000 - 50,000**

| | |
|---|---|
| The average interest earned for 1990 - 1993 was | $2,446 |
| Per household per year average decrease in interest earned for 1990 - 1993 was | ($333) |

**$50,000 - 55,000**

| | |
|---|---|
| The average interest earned for 1990 - 1993 was | $2,272 |
| Per household per year average decrease in interest earned for 1990 - 1993 was | ($1,609) |

**$55,000 - 60,000**

| | |
|---|---|
| The average interest earned for 1990 - 1993 was | $1,826 |
| Per household per year average increase in interest earned for 1990 - 1993 was | $264 |

**$60,000 - 65,000**

| | |
|---|---|
| The average interest earned for 1990 - 1993 was | $1,480 |
| Per household per year average increase in interest earned for 1990 - 1993 was | $513 |

**Interest Paying Households' Income and Interest Earnings Summary**

| | Average Income of Interest-Paying Households | Average Interest Paid by Interest-Earning Households | Average Interest Earned by Interest-Paying Households | Average Interest Paid as % of Average Income | Average Interest Earned as % of Average Income |
|---|---|---|---|---|---|
| 1988 | $29,463 | $2,267 | $880 | 8% | 3% |
| 1990 | $39,360 | $3,332 | $1,448 | 8% | 4% |
| 1991 | $39,918 | $3,188 | $1,193 | 8% | 3% |
| 1992 | $42,437 | $2,429 | $1,087 | 6% | 3% |
| 1993 | $46,369 | $2,864 | $555 | 6% | 1% |

**Interest Paid and Interest Earned Relationship**

| | |
|---|---|
| Average size of interest earned in 1990 - 1993 | $2,114 |
| Average size of interest paid for 1990 - 1993 | $2,951 |
| Per one dollar debt average interest earned for 1990 - 1993 | $.08 |
| Per one dollar debt average interest paid for 1990 - 1993 | $.10 |

## Interest Earned and Paid by Interest Paying Households

| | 1988 | 1990 | 1991 | 1992 | 1993 |
|---|---|---|---|---|---|
| The average income of interest-paying households | $29,463 | $39,360 | $39,918 | $42,437 | $46,369 |
| The average interest paid by interest-earning households | $ 2,276 | $ 3,332 | $ 3,188 | $ 2,429 | $ 2,864 |
| The average interest earned by interest-paying households | $ 880 | $ 1,448 | $ 1,193 | $ 1,087 | $ 555 |

Average interest paid by interest-paying households for all six years of the survey amounted to .......... 7% of income

Average interest earned by interest-paying households for all six years of the survey amounted to .......... 3% of income

## Regression Summary
## Interest Paid on Home Loan

1988: $IPH = 10.64 + .034_Y$
$(13.65) \quad (.01)$

1990: $IPH = -248.7 + .043_Y$
$(1532.9) \quad (.004)$

1991: $IPH = -214.7 + .040_Y$

1992: $IPH = -245.35 + .035_Y$

1993: $IPH = -177.71 + .0348_Y$

As expected, a positive relationship exists between household income and the interest paid on home loans. Each additional dollar increase in household income yielded an interest payment of 3.4 cents in 1988, 4.3 cents in 1990, 4.0 cents in 1991 and 3.5 cents in 1992 and 1993. For each dollar increase in income, interest payments on home loans, on average, for the six years of the survey amounted to 4 cents.

## Interest Paid on Car Loan

1985: $I = 57.3 + .0031Y$

1988: $I = 14.0 + .0200Y$ IPC: Interest paid on a car loan

1990: $IPC = -107.7 + .1000Y$

1991: $IPC = -198.7 + .0190Y$

The equation shows that for each $1 increase in income interest payments on car loans on average amounted to one cent.

**Interest Paid on Credit Cards**

1990 IPCC = -51.74 + .009y

1991 IPCC = -69.13 + .0069y

On average, interest paid on credit cards for each $1 increase in income was about one cent.

**Total Interest Paid**

1985 TIP = 655.6 + .038y

1988 TIP = 57.6 + .05y

1990 TIP = 412.3 + .065

1991 TIP = 491.4 + .069

1992 TIP = -438.88 + .065

TIP = Total Interest Paid

Y = Income of the Household

The equation shows that for each $1 increase in income, households paid on average (during 1990 - 1993) seven cents as interest and in 1985, four cents.

**Total Interest Paid**

A regression model of total interest payments was constructed taking household income and interest earned as explanatory variables.

1988 IP: = 78.6 - .11 IE + .064y

IP: = Interest Paid

IE: = Interest Earned

y: = Income of Households

1990 IP: = -298.5 - .097 IE + .067y

IP: = Interest Paid

IE: = Interest Earned

1991 IP: = -436.4 - .059 IE + .071y

IP: = Interest Paid

IE: = Interest Earned

The coefficient of income clearly supports the hypothesis that the higher the level of income, the higher the size of interest payments. Each additional dollar increase in income yielded an interest payment of 6.4 cents in 1988, 6.7 cents in 1990, and 7.1 cents in 1991.

**Interest Earned**

$$405.84 + .0174y$$

The equation shows that the households in the survey area earned an average interest of less than two cents for each dollar increase in income.

**Prime Rate of New York Banks Regressed on Discount Rate**

Time Series Data (1960 - 1990)

1. Prime Rate (PR) = 0.261 + 1.2021 DR (discount rate)
   (1.569) (0.1144)
   $R^2 = 0.83$ $N = 29$
2. Change in prime rate = -0.113 + 0.8917 Change in discount rate
   (1.72) (.230)

The equation shows that for every one percent increase in the discount rate there is a 1.40 percent increase in the prime rate. The second equation shows that if the current annual difference in the discount rate deviates from the mean level by one percent, the annual change in the prime rate would deviate from the mean by 0.89 percent.

**The Frequency of the Prime Rate Changes**

Prime = 0.476 + 0.7760 DR + 0.0813f[1]
(1.25) (0.214) (0.028)

$R^2 = 0.59$

Number of Observations = 20

As the frequency of the discount rate increases, the estimated coefficient of the prime rate decreases. This demonstrates that the higher the frequency

[1] f = frequency.

of the discount rate change, the lower the size of the prime rate change. It may be noted that every one percent increase in the frequency yields a reduction in the annual change of the prime rate from its mean difference. The estimated coefficients are significant at the 5% level.

### Regional Rate

RR = 3.83 + .76PR

The regression of regional rate shows that for each 1% increase in the prime rate, there has been, on an average a 0.76% increase in the regional rate.

### Arkansas Consumer Rate

Ark CR = 6.18 + 0.8704 DR

This equation shows that for one percent increase in discount rate there has been, on an average, a 0.87 percent increase in the Arkansas consumer rate. It may be mentioned here that in Arkansas the consumer rate of interest stays approximately 5% above the discount rate.

Ark CR = 1.98 + 1.141 PR

This equation shows that for each 1% increase in the prime rate of the New York banks there has been, on an average, a 1.14% increase in Arkansas consumer rate.

### Prime Rate of New York Banks

**Summary:**

- Number of years the prime rate of the New York banks remained higher than the discount rate of the Federal Reserve Bank .................... **21**
- Number of times the prime rate of the New York banks was at a higher level than the discount rate of the Federal Reserve Bank ................ **55**
- The percentage at which the New York prime rate exceeded the discount rate of the Federal Reserve Bank varied from a low of ............... **1.25** to a high of ............................................ **5.02**
- The average percentage point at which the prime rate of the New York banks was greater than the discount rate of the Federal Reserve Bank for the last 25 years was ....................................... **2.96%**

- The prime rate of the New York banks during the period of 1929 to 1996 varied between . . . . . . . . . . . . . . . . . . . . . . . . . . . . . . **1.5% and 21.5%**

## Discount Rate

The number of times the discount rate of the Federal Reserve Bank changed since 1934 . . . . . . . . . . . . . . . . . . . . . . . . . . . . . . . . . . . . . . . . . . . . . . . . **114**

The average rate of upward change in the discount rate of the Federal Reserve Bank since 1960 . . . . . . . . . . . . . . . . . . . . . . . . . . . . . . . . . . . . . . . . **6%**

The average rate of downward change in the discount rate in the Federal Reserve Bank since 1960 . . . . . . . . . . . . . . . . . . . . . . . . . . . . . . . . . . . . . . . **51%**

The range of variation in the discount rate of the Federal Reserve Bank since 1970 . . . . . . . . . . . . . . . . . . . . . . . . . . . . . . . . . . . . . . . . . . . . . . . **3% to 14%**

The average number of times per year changes were made in the Federal Reserve Bank rate since 1970 . . . . . . . . . . . . . . . . . . . . . . . . . . . . . . . . . . . . . **2.29**

## Regional Rate (Arkansas)

The number of years the Arkansas consumer rate remained higher than the discount rate of the Federal Reserve Bank for 1975-1996 . . . . . . . . . . . . . . . . . . . . . . **22**

The number of years the Arkansas consumer rate remained higher than that of the New York prime rate for 1975 - 1996 was . . . . . . . . . . . . . . . . . . . . . . . . . . **21**

The range of variation that Arkansas consumer rate exceeding the discount rate of the Federal Reserve Bank for 1975 - 1990 period was . . . . . . . **2.97% - 7.64%**

The average percentage that the Arkansas consumer rate exceeded the New York prime rate for the 1975-1990 period was . . . . . . . . . . . . . . . . . . . . **41% - 6.27%**

The average percentage that the Arkansas consumer rate was greater than the discount rate of the Federal Reserve Bank for the 1975-1996 period was. . **5.27%**

The average percentage that Arkansas consumer rate was greater than the New York prime rate for the 1975-1990 period was . . . . . . . . . . . . . . . . . . . . **2.45%**

## Regional Rate (Michigan)

The number of years the Michigan consumer rate remained higher than the New York prime rate for the 1975-1996 period was . . . . . . . . . . . . . . . . . . . . . . . **10**

The number of years the Michigan consumer rate remained higher than the discount rate of the Federal Reserve Bank for the 1975-1996 period .............. **10**

The range of variation by which the Michigan consumer rate exceeded the New York prime rate for the 1975-1996 period was ................ **73% - 5.5%**

The range in variation by which the Michigan consumer rate was greater than the New York prime rate for the 1975-1996 period was ................ **3.35%**

The range of variation by which the Michigan consumer rate exceeded the discount rate of the Federal Reserve Bank for the 1975-1996 period was ....... **6.90%**

## **Regional Rate** (Mortgage)

The number of years the mortgage rate remained higher than the discount rate of the Federal Reserve Bank for the 1975 - 1996 period was ............... **22**

The number of years the mortgage rate remained higher than the New York prime rate for the 1975 - 1996 period was ................................ **15**

The range of variation by which the mortgage rate exceeded the discount rate of the Federal Reserve Bank for the 1975 - 1996 period was ......... **31% - 6.08%**

The range of variation by which the mortgage rate exceeded the New York prime rate for the 1975 - 1996 period was ........................ **13% - 2.48%**

The average percentage by which the mortgage rate was greater than the discount rate of the Federal Reserve Bank for the 1975 - 1996 period was ...... **3.67%**

The average percentage by which the mortgage rate was greater than the New York prime rate for the 1975 - 1996 period .......................... **1.55%**

# CHAPTER ELEVEN

## CONCLUSION:
## AUTHOR'S COMMENTS AND RECOMMENDATIONS

### The Prime Rate of New York Banks

Over the last two decades, regional rates have remained greater than the discount rate and the prime rate of the New York banks. In the absence of announced changes in the prime rate of the New York banks, the regional rate would have settled at a much lower rate than it did in the past. This resulted in households paying much higher interest rates. Our regression results show that for each 1% or more increase in the discount rate, there has been an average of 1% increase in the consumer and other regional rates.

The prevalence of the "prime rate tradition"[1] has divided the loan market into two sectors: consumer loans and business loans. The rate of interest of the former is influenced by the discount rate of the Federal Reserve Bank while that of the latter is influenced by the prime rate of the large banks of New York. This division of authority over loan markets limits the effectiveness of manipulation of the instruments of credit control used by the Federal Reserve Bank. In order to achieve the objectives of a sound monetary policy, all areas of the loan market should be directly influenced by changes in the discount rate of the Federal Reserve Bank. However, this is not the case because of the coexistence of another rate, the prime rate of the New York banks.

When the prime rate of a New York bank is raised, the regional banks raise their rates by a percentage point or more. This "tradition" has been built over the years. The fact remains that the big banks raise their rates in view of their own interests. However, other banks do not participate in the big banks' decision-making process. Because of this tradition (the following of New York banks' rate by regional banks), householders and

---

[1]The tradition that makes the regional banks increase their rates when the New York banks raise their prime rates.

businesses have been paying much more interest than they should have paid. Had there been no "prime rate tradition," the interest rate at the local level, as stated earlier, would have been influenced by the discount rate of the Federal Reserve Bank and the supply and demand forces for loans. But, this "tradition" has forced the regional banks to consider the rate of New York banks as an important determinant of their own rates.

The tradition of announcing the changes in the prime rate of New York banks combined with the tradition of following the rate by the regional banks increases the cost of credit to households and businesses by billions of dollars each year. We believe that this announcement of the changes in the rate of the New York banks is unwarranted under changed socioeconomic conditions. It has outlived its utility and importance. The "prime rate tradition"with its apparently innocent facade has been burdening the nation with an unwarranted and undesirable higher cost of credit. We recommend, in the interest of the economy and of the millions of households in small and mid-sized cities in the U.S., the silent burial of this tradition of announced changes in the rate of the New York banks.

### The Establishment of New Banks

About 33% of the households in the cities we studied cannot offer loan security and are generally disqualified for credit. Without credit, households are forced to make compromises with the essentials of life and lose opportunities to prepare themselves for better jobs, careers and incomes. As noted earlier, the rates of interest charged by organized financial institutions vary from 9% to 24%, depending on the sources of credit. The rates of unorganized sources of credit, such as small loan companies, finance companies, pawnshops and professional money lenders, vary from 14% to 300%. Often, a householder after being refused credit from an organized credit institution and compelled by circumstance, takes loans from small loan companies, finance companies, credit card companies, and professional money lenders. The cost of credit from these sources is exorbitantly high.

Households stigmatized in the past for late payments rarely have any chance for loans, at a fair cost, from existing organized credit institutions to buy homes, cars, boats, or to pay off credit card loans. Unfortunately, in the present-day economy, credit has become the exclusive privilege of prosperous and solvent individuals. The poor are unable to offer security and are disqualified from acquiring required credit. This raises questions regarding the working philosophy of the financial institutions and of the environment and culture that govern existing credit institutions. The operating guidelines of financial institutions are such that households with low income, poor credit reports and no collateral are destined to be denied credit.

When a big bank buys a small bank located in a mid-sized city, it shows little interest in the credit needs or the credit problems of the local residents. The big city orientation of the big banks leads to policies that contrast with the previous experiences of the householders who are the bank's loan customers. After the merger, local officers are frequently left with little authority to grant loans to marginal credit risks or to extend the repayment periods of loans. Such decisions are made in the big bank's regional office located somewhere in St. Louis, Atlanta, New York, or Dallas -- hundreds of miles away from the small local banks and world away from the needs of the bank's customers in the rural areas and smaller cities of America. At times, after a merger, these banks will even alter the existing loan arrangements of the small bank's customers to force the borrowers to make larger payments to pay back the debt in a shorter period of time. When this happens, the merger exacerbates the pains associated with the credit problems of householders in small and mid-sized cities.

Finally, in view of the high cost of debt, the harassment of debtors by creditors, and the denial of credit to thousands of households for one reason or another, we recommend that a new type of credit institution be brought into existence to cater to the peculiar credit needs of millions of households in the U.S. economy. These specialized credit institutions should function more as supplementary credit institutions than as substitutions for the existing ones.

### Household Debts

There is a general notion that household debt does not pose a problem because the earnings from the assets acquired by borrowed funds far exceed the interest payments and other costs of debt. Our findings show that this statement does not hold true for low and middle-income households, particularly for those who are living in small and mid-sized cities in the U.S. Households being turned down for credit by organized institutions for one reason or another are forced to turn to loan sources that charge exorbitant interest rates which vary from 12% to 30% depending on the sources of credit.

We have shown that the average interest payment of households in small and mid-sized cities equals more than 8% of their income. For those who own homes and cars, the interest payments per year vary from 8% to 12% of their income, evidencing that interest payments take their toll on the meager income of these households. Besides, the real burden of debt often takes the form of receiving frequent calls and registered letters from creditors threatening to sue, the repossession of the debtor's home or car, the forced disinvestment of assets, and the pawning of household assets, guns, cars, family jewelry and other personal assets. In addition, indebted households have very limited opportunity to improve their situation in life. All the deprivation, denial, sacrifice, woes, and anxiety that indebted households undergo represent the real burden of debt.

### Cost of Credit

Both the monetary and real burden of debt have kept many debtors in a lifelong struggle to service their debts. The average size of the debt of indebted households for the 1990-1993 period was $32,493, equaling almost 100% of these households' income. Our estimate of per capita household debt for 1990-1993 amounts to $12,571. Debt of this magnitude, combined with a temporary job and low income, can be depressing and produce overwhelming psychological conditions.

It is noteworthy that the per capita household income in our survey area of $12,212 is only slightly lower than the per capita household debt. This illustrates the depressing situation of households relative to their income. The average amount of interest payments by indebted households for the 1990 -1993 period was $3,249, representing 7% of their income. This means that from each dollar increase in income, a household has to set aside seven cents for interest payments. When other debt-related costs are included, interest payments equal about nine cents per dollar increase in income. Some households' interest payments exceed 15% of their income. This high interest cost has been a source of significant erosion of household income. We observed the anxiety of the typical indebted households in our walk with Jay and his struggles with bill payments while trying to find a strategy to keep his creditors at bay.

Household interest earnings, on the other hand, amount to less than two cents for every dollar increase in income. The interest payments of interest-paying households far exceed the amount of interest earned.

We also noted that interest-earning and interest-paying households are two different groups of households. Inadequate income forces most households to borrow to supplement their meager incomes. But, in the credit world, there is a third party, the credit bureau, whose report is a principal determinant in deciding who gets credit, even though these reports are rarely "up-to-date."

## Credit Bureaus and Credit Institutions

Low-income borrowers generally work in unstable jobs and businesses. The loss of their jobs and sources of income result in defaults in payments which are reflected in the credit report as "late payments, past dues, and delinquencies." These attributes are known as the "negatives" of the account. They are sticky and hard to erase. After many years these negatives may disappear from the report but never from the minds of the officials of some credit-giving institutions who continue to punish these account holders by denying credit or charging higher rates of interest. In doing this, the credit bureau's response is that they are only following the regulations.

On the other hand, credit institutions use an adverse credit report as an excuse for the denial of credit, and also say that they simply followed the regulations. Both the credit bureaus and the credit institutions may be correct. We are not seeking to find faults with either the credit bureaus or the credit institutions. However, the fact remains that the credit report has radically changed the credit culture of this country.

Today, credit institutions have become completely dependent upon the credit report in approving and rejecting loans, and in changing rates of interest on loans. "Negatives" in the credit report result in the denial of credit. Nothing has done so much harm as the credit report in depriving millions of households of credit and opportunities of life.

The present form of credit reporting is harmful and against the interest of households. It is stunning and even shocking to see how many millions of households are systematically deprived of credit on the basis of past inaccurate "negatives" reported by credit bureau. The ability to pay debt, honesty, sincerity, and a willingness to cooperate with credit institutions should be taken into account in judging one's credit standing not only "past delays" and "delinquencies" which may have occurred several years ago.

The punishing of households based on the past negatives long after the debt has been paid is revengeful, unproductive, and unjust. We recommend that a National Credit Commission look into the social cost of the problem of low-income households who never obtain cheap credit[1] (even when official market rates are very low) because of the "negatives" and often inaccurate reports contained in credit reports.

---

[1]In the recent past, the interest rate was as low as 6%, but this low rate was never meant for low-income households. Their credit reports deprived them of loans or forced them to pay interest rates which were as high as 10% to 12%.

The credit bureau's sloppiness in correcting inaccurate information is irksome. At times, the bureau continues reporting the existence of a lien against an account holder although the account has been settled as long as five years ago. A letter of release of the lien from the court is of no value when the credit institution gives more importance to what the credit report states. Often it takes several months for the bureau, after it has received the notice of lien release, to report that the account is paid. In the meantime, credit institutions continue to refuse credit to these households until their record no longer shows the lien.

The commission may also look into why credit reports focus more on the "negatives" than on the "positives" of the accounts, examine the codes of credit reporting, the pedagogy of reporting, and how the credit report is interpreted. Finally, the commission may suggest measures to modify or replace the present credit-reporting system with a new method of credit reporting which may address "negatives" of accounts that were paid up several years ago. The credit commission would do a tremendous service to the nation by assessing the impact of denial of credit on low-income households based on credit reports, and by bringing about changes in the credit reporting system.

The large New York banks assume themselves to be lead banks and adopt interest rate policies in their own self interest. The regional banks instinctively follow the interest rate changes of the New York banks, ignoring the impact on cost of credit at the local level.

Our findings also show that interest payments constitute 7% to 10% of household income (depending on circumstances) in small and mid-sized cities of the U.S. This means that for a one dollar increase in income, households have to set aside seven to ten cents for interest payments. This makes interest payments an important item in the household budget and also a source of income erosion. This fact should have important bearing on all interest rate policies initiated by the Federal Reserve Banks and by lead banks, as well as on the policies of governments and employers in determining wages of their employees. This issue has hardly been an item for public discussion so far.

Credit institutions (pawnshops and other local sources) arbitrarily charge exorbitant rates ranging from 20 % to 300%. These rates magnify the size of the debt and render it more burdensome and unbearable. In addition, the greed element motivates creditors to inflate bills, thus prolonging the obligation debtors owe to their creditors.

Costs other than interest charges in servicing debts, such as late fees, fines and penalties for late payments on homes, cars, business loans, credit cards, unpaid taxes (property and personal income taxes) and on returned checks, total to a substantial amount each month. Assuming that an indebted household fails 33% of the time to make timely payments, the fines and penalties will amount to more than $450 a year. This increases the size of the debt–raising the effective rate of interest much higher (to probably double the rate) than the original contract rate.

### Federal Reserve Bank

The Fed's contribution, as we said earlier, is unique in the growth process of the vast U.S. economy. The Fed is the unsung hero of this nation, but the benefit of the Fed's policies did not trickle down to a large section of the American Society.

At times, the Fed has been less than prompt in taking action to correct the problem of rising interest rates. This we noticed when the federal discount rate rose to 12%, the prime rate of New York banks rose to 21%, and the regional rates rose to 23%.

According to our findings, interest payments in, general, constitute 7% to 10% of households income. Indebted households interest payments make up 10% to 14% of their incomes. This means that out of each dollar of income a householder has to set aside seven to fourteen cents to pay interest, depending upon his income and the size of the debt with which he is encumbered. The Federal Reserve Bank must pay heed to this fact when raising its discount rate because a higher discount rate spells higher interest rates and a higher erosion of the householders' income in small and mid-sized U.S. cities.

When the Fed decides raise its rate to control inflation, it invariably raises the cost of credit, driving out thousands of low income households out of the credit market. Unfortunately, in the Fed's policy, there is no provision for the accommodation of this low income group in the credit market. If the inflation is controlled at the expense of millions of low income households, the job is not done well.

Finally, we repeat, the Federal Reserve Bank must wrestle to free itself from the inflation phobia from which it apparently suffers: the raising of the discount rate should not take the form of a ritual. The Fed is overly concerned about its "inflation enemy." It battles this foe -often long before it invades the economy -with its only weapon, Discount Rate changes which bring mixed blessings. High interest rates contain inflation but devastate the economies of millions of households in small and mid-sized U.S. cities. The Fed hardly assesses the damages caused by high rates on these households. Besides, the frequent changes in the discount rate of the

Federal Reserve Bank (which happened eight times in one year in the past) cause uncertainties about the future and are, generally, not welcomed by the business community. Japan's central bank held its rates at 5% for the years 1983, 1984 and 1985 at 2.5% for 1987 and 1988. Japan's central bank tends to maintain low and stable rates whereas the Fed is prone to higher and frequent changes of its rate. The frequent Discount Rate changes also indicate the inability of the Fed to have a long term vision of the economy.

## Jay's Last Wishes: To Discover Rich America and the American Dream

The Gross National Product of the U.S. has surpassed the eight trillion dollar mark in recent years, yielding a per capita income of well over $28,000. This vast land with all its natural resources provides food, clothing, and shelter for more than 250 million people and is capable of supporting a population five to ten times this size and for many years to come. But the real strength and potentiality of the U.S. economy is far greater than these indices suggest.

The U.S. economy has reached a stage where any estimated dollar value will likely be an underestimation of the economy. Because of the uniqueness of the U.S. economy among economies of the world, it is appropriate to discuss briefly some important variables, both economic and non-economic, that have directly and indirectly contributed to the rapid and impressive growth of this economy over the last several decades. The country's vast open space of more than three million square miles with a huge, well-built infrastructure and a large number of skilled workers are the bases of the economic edifice of this country.

In "ingenuity" and "innovation," the United States economy is better than any other. Very few countries possess such an efficient and functional infrastructure as we have in the United States. The network of U.S. super highways has no parallel elsewhere. Universities, schools, training centers and other educational institutions are well equipped to prepare the work force, the researchers, and the future political, economic, business and community leaders of this country and of other countries.

In this connection, the contribution of American professors and trainers must be recognized with gratitude and appreciation. They have trained the largest number of foreign professionals who now work as teachers, technicians, politicians and community leaders in their own countries and who are eager to have economic and commercial ties with the U.S. Such beneficiary nations would gladly provide supplementary resources to meet the needs of the U.S. economy in emergencies.

The U.S. economy with its own inherent strength and the potential for obtaining supplementary resources from other countries in emergencies has become practically the only crisis-proof economy of the world. Its financial institutions are very experienced and have established a commendable discipline in the monetary arena. Its central bank, the Federal Reserve Bank, is the most respected central bank among nations, having been instrumental in making the U.S. currency the "most wanted currency in the world." It has also shown a remarkable dexterity in developing an efficient financial market in the nation. These financial institutions have played important roles in mobilizing and diverting savings for the vast capital accumulation this country enjoys.

Politically, American's doctrine of democracy has been defined, practiced and nurtured, even in the remotest parts of the country in a fashion that is almost unique. The effectiveness of this practice is immeasurable in the sense that even an ordinary man in the street, away from the center of federal and provincial governments, feels that he is a part of the day-to-day administration of the country[1].

The ideals of democracy make as strong an appeal to Americans as scriptures do to religious adherents. This profound belief and conviction in democracy have given rise to political institutions and traditions that play an important role in the regular decision-making process and shape the material destiny of the American people. Along with this conviction, Americans continually affirm their faith in the market mechanism to allocate resources and determine the prices of goods and services.

The pursuit of the nation's political and economic philosophies has given birth to various socioeconomic institutions, which in turn have significantly accelerated the spectacular growth of the U.S. economy. Amidst an unstable socioeconomic climate, an economic progress of this magnitude would have been impossible. In these institutions governing the day to day life of Americans, one can discover the real blueprint of America. This blueprint is invisible and indestructible, representing America and American life. In a disaster of high magnitude, the physical destruction of America could take place, but the nation would quickly revive in its full physical and functional form because of this blueprint.

We must salute those American leaders who helped build this indestructible blueprint. Fortunately, to protect the socioeconomic climate,

---

[1] This is what is not happening in developing nations and it accounts for much of the political unrest in those countries.

a forceful, effective, and alert unarmed army of journalists is diligently guarding the events and actions of policy-makers, business executives and community leaders. If any laxity or impropriety is detected anywhere, it is immediately brought to public notice for correction.

Against the backdrop of these bright and shining elements of the U.S. socio-economic arena, less glittering elements have shadowed and diminished the economy's accomplishments. In the small and mid-sized cities of the U.S., a large section of the population feels that it does not receive a legitimate share of the vast wealth of the U.S. economy for contributions they make to create it. Often these groups are forced to supplement their inadequate incomes by borrowing from costly sources and by bearing heavy debt burdens which often far exceed their incomes.

Inherent in the traditional distribution system lie forces that tend to widen disparities in income and help concentrate wealth in the hands of few. In the absence of the economic betterment of low and middle-income households, the richness of this nation may be misread as the prosperity of the few. In the days of mercantilism, physiocracy and Adam Smith, the predominant concern was how to increase the wealth of a nation. The U.S. economy, in its present phase, can be said to have achieved those goals. With its current accumulation of capital, resources and vast infrastructure, it is the most powerful economy in the world. Against this richness of the economy, the financial woes of millions of households in small and mid-sized cities stand out like a sore thumb.

Our findings demonstrate that the economies of low income households are characterized by their incurring of debt that exceeds their income (debt exceeds 100% of income) and that the interest paid by these households constitutes 14% of their income. This means that they have to set aside 14 cents out of each $1 of their earnings to pay interest.

High debt-income ratios, low incomes, the inability to service debt, the agonies of living and dying in debt have become, over the years, a part of life for these poverty stricken households. This scenario contrasts with the abundant wealth and prosperity of the economy in which they live. This has been continuing for decades unnoticed and neglected. The time is ripe to address this issue once and for all. The woes, anxieties, pains and anguish originating from low income, burdensome debt and the man-made obstacles they confront in everyday life are sorry spectacles. Traditional unfair distribution principles, abuses in credit markets and the callousness of society are at the root of their problems.

We can salvage these households by being fair, by putting guidelines in place to assure them their fair share for their contributions in the national wealth. Their rightful share in the credit market and fair opportunities for improving their economies should be assured. The measures to accomplish these goals have been enunciated in the earlier pages of the concluding chapter.

Economic principles and policies should deliver what is expected of them: fair opportunities for all people to pursue happiness and obtain a decent standard of living. Continuous compromise with sufferings stemming from pitifully low incomes results in frustration with the policies and principles of economic order. To repeat: the grim facts for the poverty stricken households are as follows:

| | |
|---|---|
| **Number of households living below poverty:** | **Varied between 25% & 31% (1985 - 1992)** |
| **Average income of households living below poverty level:** | **$2,710 to $12,787** |
| **Per capita income:** | **Varied between $1,084 & $4,956** |
| **The average size of debt for the income group ($10,000 to $15,000) runs around:** | **$15,700** |
| **The average amount of interest paid by this group:** | **$1,570** |
| **Interest paid as percentage of income (for this group) amounts to:** | **14%** |

To correct this imbalance in the economy caused by current principles of distribution, a deliberate and determined attempt must be made at the national level. This could be achieved by making it a constitutional obligation of the federal government to enact laws and take measures that keep the level of disparity in income within acceptable limits. This particular obligation would make the government accountable at the national level if the income gaps continue to grow or for not taking action to prevent this from happening. These measures may entail amending the Constitution.

The wages of most households in small and mid-sized cities are at unacceptably low levels relative to the hard work expended and the size of the country's Gross Domestic Product (GDP) they helped create. Fair wages and compensation in exchange for works and services in any democratic society is desirable. The objective of the government should be to narrow the income gap by allowing a fair share of wealth among those who create it. A commission for fair pay and wages could recommend appropriate changes in the pay scales of those employees who have been receiving wages that are not fair relative to their hard work and their share of contribution to national wealth.

The commission should also recommend measures for a "better" tenure system in all jobs–both private and public. Some provision to share with their employees a part of the profit (however small in size it may be) by corporations and business enterprises will go far toward keeping dissatisfaction of employees at a minimum level. This may also provide incentive to employees to be more productive in their work. The maintenance of full employment and stability of prices in the economy helps considerably in warding off frequent loss of jobs and erosion in income that constantly confront low-income households.

Unless strong and effective measures are taken, the disparity in income will continue increasing and emerge, over time, as a dangerous social, political, and economic issue. Unscrupulous demagogues could exploit this situation to destabilize the once viable social, political and economic institutions upon which the progress of the U.S. economy was based. These institutions are invaluable, immeasurable in monetary terms, and must be preserved. Society's lack of interest and its indifference to resolve these concerns of households amounts to walking away from its social and moral obligations. It is tantamount to our being callous toward fellow citizens and fellow human beings at large.

An unstable society invites chaos in the form of strikes, demonstrations in the street, disobedience to law and order, and gross undiscipline in factories, industries, offices, schools, colleges, and all work places. The off shoot of this environment is the birth of a corrupt, unstable and inefficient society, something we do not want in this country. We can prevent this by being kind, generous, and fair toward those who are in the lower strata of society. The economy is strong enough to bear the burden of improving their economic status. All that is needed is a change of heart and of outlook accompanied by a determined effort by the society toward uplifting the economy of those at the margin of existence.

We must ask ourselves many questions. Do our callousness, inaction and inappropriate economic policy account for the economic woes of low and middle-income households? What is the cause of the gross disparity in income existing between different professions and regions? Who is responsible for the heavy debt burden that these households have been bearing for decades? Should we let time-honored "tradition" dictate the share in our nation's wealth that low-income households are able to command? Is the present disparity in income between professions and regions to continue or should we enact laws to correct unfair distribution principles so that millions of households can be better off?

Policy makers will earn the heartfelt gratitude of the nation as well as salutes from our posterity if they enact laws that make it a constitutional obligation of the national government to reduce the current level of disparity in income, increase the income of low-income households, prevent the disparity of income from being widened and provide succor to debt burdened households. These measures will rescue those trapped in a stagnant economy and vicious cycle of poverty, facilitate a fair distribution of wealth, and eradicate reasons for discontent and restlessness in society.

Fair distribution principles will also usher in a new era of contentment among all citizens of the U.S., preserve the socioeconomic institutions of this country and the doctrine of economic freedom. In the absence of these measures, the income gap may continue to widen and households in small and mid-sized cities may continue to suffer from low income and burdensome debts. This will pose a threat to the stability of existing socioeconomic institutions.

The agonies and economic woes of Jay, described at the beginning of our book, well illustrate the impact on low-income households of our flawed distribution principles. In conclusion, we reflect on Jay's disillusionment in his pursuit of a decent living, the concerns that haunted him throughout his youth until old age, his failed dreams, and finally his queries about where rich America is?

Jay is old and now looks back upon his ever-struggling and precarious existence in the U.S. economy. He is bitter in recollecting that he has not tasted a life that was ever free from debt or shortages of life's bare essentials. Each and every day, his mind had been preoccupied with the concerns of meeting his obligations to his creditors and making compromises with the basic wants of life. "Cut-off" and "shut-off" notices, job terminations, notices of threats to sue him, and the worries and anxieties associated with these situations have worn him out.

The most productive years of his life have been spent serving his creditors and living in constant fear of losing his job and his sources of income. His physical and mental strength have started to wane. The unkind and uncharitable treatment by his employers, creditors, and society have left scores of psychological wounds and scars which have yet to heal. Jay dreads the thought of retired life. His lifelong earnings were inadequate to permit him to plan a worry-free retirement. The agonies arising out of low income continue to be his lifelong companions.

During his work-years, Jay's cousin, who earned a substantial income, was able to set aside for investment a part of his income and now enjoys a carefree retirement. By contrast, Jay's low income did not permit him to invest in even a moderate retirement plan. Jay's hand-to-mouth economic existence extends beyond his work-years to the day he breathes his last.

"Money begets money" is a proverb that does not apply to Jay and his family. This bothers Jay considerably. He is convinced that the root causes of his income group's plight primarily lie with ill-conceived economic policies. To this one can add outdated socioeconomic traditions, greed among a section of society and, above all, society's callousness and lack of compassion for the plight of low-income households. While society refuses to bring changes to Jay's income group, their long-cherished dream of freedom from debt and the basic needs of life remains unfulfilled.

Before Jay and his woeful economic tale is lost to oblivion, he leaves behind not only the legacy of hard work and struggle for a decent life, but also some questions that have agitated his mind all these years and which remain unanswered up to now: Why does the U.S. economy, in spite of being the world's richest, fail to provide stable and decent income to people like Jay and his kind so that they can have freedom from basic wants and burdensome debts? Do we, as human beings, live only to preserve some given economic systems and principles? Should not a good economic system treat its people fairly? Where is the rich America?

"How can we discover the rich America?" cries Jay from the innermost depths of his heart. In tune with this heartfelt cry of Jay are the voices of millions. In order to prevent questions like these from being raised in the future, some changes in the distribution system are required. The economic order should be geared to facilitate distribution of wealth fairly, equitably, and justly among those who create it and should also provide low-cost credit to those who need it. This change will help rescue thousands of households trapped in debt, poverty and oppressive economic conditions. In the process, it will restore the decency, dignity, and joy of living which Jay and his family have pursued for many decades, but have never attained.

Most households – millions in number – in mid-sized cities struggle day in and day out to meet their basic needs of life. Thousands of them fail to provide a decent life for their families or support the higher education of their children. They live in debt and die in debt. This situation makes them feel that they live less than a full life.

Given the present economic opportunities, credit climate, and distribution principles, it is an uphill task for most households in mid-sized cities to live a full life which is attainable in view of the richness of the economy but which has remained beyond their reach up to now due to the lack of appropriate economic policy and cooperation of society. A less than full life gives the feeling of being a less than a whole person. Such a feeling diminishes one's enthusiasm and willingness to put in one's best at the work place and makes it impossible to enjoy life as a full productive citizen.

Often beautiful days dawn on the cities which form the basis of our study. The brightness of the sun, the openness of the surroundings and hopeful faces of householders hide their secret anxieties arising out of their inability to meet creditors' demands and to satisfy the needs of their family. These concerns occupy their minds with the break of each bright day and stay deep in their thoughts until they retire at night.

The tall buildings, newly built shopping malls, posh residential areas, crowded streets and parking lots misrepresent the true economic tale of low and middle income households in mid-sized cities of America. Buried and inaudible remain the householders' cries for help amidst the city's hustle and bustle, the noise of the market, and the lip service paid by society to the plight of these households.

We see a robust growth in this U.S. economy now and in the future. Nevertheless, we do not want to see the economic woes and agonies of low-income households continue to go unnoticed and neglected. The economic estrangement of this group from the rich life America offers demonstrates an inherent weakness in the current system of distribution. This needs to be addressed and remedied.

Throughout this book, we have demonstrated the economic problems facing households in the small and mid-sized cities of the United States. These problems are rooted more in social and economic institutions and culture than in the personal inadequacies of these people. The people who are the subject of this study are mired down in the predicament caused by low income, frequent job losses due to whims of the employers or down turns in the economy, the high costs of available credit, the inflated price of goods and services, the inflation phobia of the Federal Reserve, and the prime rate tradition of New York banks (the tradition of changing regional rates as New York banks do). Another significant factor which has contributed to their hapless plight is the inequity in our society which sets conventional and traditional limits to the income of some professional groups (such as secretaries, clerical workers, teachers, manual laborers and the like), while providing exorbitant amounts of wealth to CEO's, sports celebrities, show business people, attorneys and physicians. Combined with the pressing necessities of daily life and social pressures to buy (so evident in all areas of our consumer economy) are systematic contributing factors that shape the above-mentioned predicament of a large section of our nations' population.

These households are caught in a situation of economic servitude where the most obvious escape routes are blocked by institutional forces. Acquiring skills or higher education could be the key that opens the way to real opportunity, but higher education is expensive and beyond the reach of most of the households in these cities. These households have no opportunity to excel and find themselves passed over for the positions they had hoped for. This is the nature of the plight of the working class families in the small and mid-sized cities of our nation. It is our hope that this book will bring the predicament of households in small and mid-sized cities to the notice of our policy makers so that steps may be taken to level the playing field so that fair opportunity is extended to all of the citizens of our great nation.

As we stated earlier, if no measures are taken to improve the material destiny of these households who are being denied simple comforts of life, unscrupulous demagogues may be able to harness frustrations, failures, and alienation to destabilize the socioeconomic institutions built over many decades.

The queries and the cries of Jay will remain unanswered and will continue to reverberate in the air of the United States. Millions will echo Jay when he says that he has before him a long, unending, barrier-strewn road to travel to discover the rich America about which he reads and hears so much, but which will remain forever unattainable to him.

# INDEX


Average debt . . . . 39, 139, 204
Bankers . . . . 149, 153, 187
Banking system . . . . 162
Banks . . . . xii, 2, 36, 69, 103, 110-116, 118, 120, 124, 125, 141-151, 155-158, 163-166, 168, 171-177, 180, 185, 191, 193, 195, 196, 216-218, 221-223, 226, 227, 235
Bills . . 1-4, 6, 8, 47, 68, 121, 123-125, 143, 147, 148, 151, 175, 177, 179, 187, 188, 190, 226
Business failures . . . . 142
Car loans . . . . 37, 43, 44, 61, 75, 90, 96, 98, 105, 186, 205, 209, 210, 214
Commercial banks . . . . 143, 148, 151, 157, 173, 177
Compensation . . . . 34-36, 231
Consumer rates . . . . 114, 115, 170, 171
Credit bureau . . . . 2, 178, 180, 183, 185, 224, 225
Credit bureaus . . . . 177-179, 182, 194, 225
Credit cards . . . . 4, 44, 76, 92, 106, 123, 179, 186, 194, 215, 227
Credit report . . . . 178-184, 195, 225, 226
Debt . i, iii, iv, xi-xiii, 5-8, 10, 11, 35, 37-39, 41-49, 66-70, 77, 97-99, 103, 117, 120, 122-127, 130, 139, 141, 163, 177-180, 182, 185, 186, 190-196, 198, 204-206, 208, 209, 213, 223-227, 230-234
Debt Settlement Board . . . . 191-193
Depression . . . . 1, 6-8, 116, 124, 142, 143, 149, 197
Discount rate . . . . xii, xiii, 69, 103, 110-116, 123, 145-156, 158, 159, 163-166, 168, 170-176, 195, 216-219, 221, 222, 227, 228
Disparity . . . . xii-13, 29, 31, 34-36, 231-233
Employment . . . . 5, 151, 156, 163, 232
Fed . . . . 115, 150, 163, 164, 227, 228
Federal Reserve . . xii, xiii, 69, 103, 110-116, 125, 145-152, 154-159, 163-166, 168, 170-176, 195, 217-219, 221, 222, 226-229, 235
Federal Reserve Bank xii, xiii, 69, 103, 110-116, 125, 145-152, 154-159, 163-166, 168, 170-176, 195, 217-219, 221, 222, 227-229
GNP . . . . xii, 29, 31, 33, 35, 44-46, 48, 97, 151, 206
Gold standard . . . . 155
Home loans . . . . 42-44, 49-59, 73, 75, 89, 96, 98, 104, 105, 154, 209, 210, 214

Household debt 37-39, 41, 44-48, 68-70, 97, 98, 185, 204, 206, 208, 209, 223, 224

Household income . xi, 13, 15, 19, 21, 22, 24, 29, 30, 33, 35, 36, 41, 42, 45, 48-59, 69, 70, 97, 98, 103, 104, 107, 109, 117, 138, 199-204, 206, 214, 215, 224, 226

Income groups . . . xii, 15, 17, 26, 28, 30, 37, 49, 61, 63, 66, 70, 76, 77, 89, 92, 94, 106, 129, 130, 164, 191, 194, 211

Indebted households . . . xi, xv, 38, 39, 42, 43, 47, 49-59, 61, 63, 65, 67, 70, 72, 75, 89, 90, 92, 94, 98, 99, 117, 126, 127, 139, 187, 190-192, 197, 198, 204, 205, 208-210, 224, 227

Inflation . . . . . . . . . . . . . . . . . . . . . xiii, 149, 151, 155, 159, 163, 164, 227, 235

Interest earned . . . . . . . . . . . . . . . xi, xii, 108-110, 127, 129-139, 210-216, 224

Interest paid . xi, xii, 48, 72, 73, 75, 77-87, 89, 90, 92, 94, 96-99, 104-109, 127, 138, 139, 206-210, 213-215, 230, 231

Interest payments xi, 5, 7, 42, 43, 49, 69, 70, 72, 73, 75-87, 89, 90, 96-98, 103-106, 110, 125, 130, 138, 177, 187, 190, 205, 208, 214-216, 223, 224, 226, 227

Interest rates . . . . xii, 69, 110, 119, 123-126, 143, 144, 149-151, 154, 156, 157, 163-165, 168, 171, 173, 175, 186, 190, 195, 221, 223, 225, 227

Investments . . . . . . . . . . . . . . . . . . . . . . . . . . . . . . . . . . . . . . . . . . . 127

Lending rates . . . . . . . . . . . . . . . . . . . . . . . . . . . . . . 148-150, 156, 157, 162

Loan shark . . . . . . . . . . . . . . . . . . . . . . . . . . . . . . . . . . . . . . . . . . . 122

Mergers . . . . . . . . . . . . . . . . . . . . . . . . . . . . . . . . . . . . . . . . . . . xi, 142

Money . xi, xii, 4, 9, 69, 103, 118-124, 127, 141, 143, 144, 151, 162, 163, 173, 174, 186, 192-194, 196, 222, 234

Money market . . . . . . . . . . . . . . . . . . . . . . . . . . . . . . . . . xii, 103, 141, 144

Monthly payments . . . . . . . . . . . . . . . . . . . . . . . . . . . . . . . . . . . . 3, 4, 120

Mortgage rates . . . . . . . . . . . . . . . . . . . . . . . . . . . . . . . . . . . . . . . . 172

National debt . . . . . . . . . . . . . . . . . . . . . . . . . . . . . . . . . . . . . . . . . . 47

New Bank . . . . . . . . . . . . . . . . . . . . . . . . . . . . . . . . . . . . . . . . . . . . 193

New York banks . . xii, 36, 69, 103, 110-116, 141-151, 156, 163-165, 168, 171, 172, 174-176, 216-218, 221, 222, 226, 227, 235

Pawnbroker . . . . . . . . . . . . . . . . . . . . . . . . . . . . . . . . . . . . . . . . 122, 185

Pawning . . . . . . . . . . . . . . . . . . . . . . . . . . . . . . . . . . 117, 119, 185, 224

Pawnshops . . . . . . . . . . . . . . . . . . . . . . . . . . . . . . . . 185, 186, 222, 226

Per capita debt . . . . . . . . . . . . . . . . . . . . . . . . . . . . . . . . . . . . 44, 48, 206

Per capita income . . . . . . . . . . . . . . 5, 20, 22-24, 26, 30, 31, 151, 203, 228, 231

Poverty . . . . . xii, 5, 10, 11, 13, 17, 29-31, 67, 99, 184, 197, 198, 203, 230, 231, 233, 234

Prime rate . . . . xii, 36, 69, 103, 110-116, 141-151, 156, 163-166, 168, 170-172, 174-177, 216-219, 221, 222, 227, 235

Prime rate tradition . . . . . . . . . . 116, 141-144, 148-150, 174, 177, 221, 222, 235

Recession . . . . . . . . . . . . . . . . . . . . . . . . . xi, 117, 141-143, 156, 163, 174, 194

Regional rates . . xii, 69, 110, 112, 113, 116, 142, 143, 145, 146, 149, 156, 163, 165, 166, 168, 172, 174-177, 221, 227, 235
Regression . . . . . . . . 70, 103-116, 147, 148, 174, 176, 208, 214, 215, 217, 221
Repayment . . . . . . . . 47, 223
Retirement . . . . . . . . 234
Salary . . . . . . . . 7, 180
Savings . . . . . . . . 120, 127, 138, 151, 229
Security . . . . . . . . 164, 193, 194, 197, 222
Small loan companies . . . . . . . . 185, 222
Trend of GNP . . . . . . . . 31
Unemployment . . . . . . . . 8, 142, 143, 149, 151, 154, 163, 172, 173, 197
Wages . . . . . . . . 34-36, 179, 189, 226, 231, 232